Democracy
and the
Challenge
of
Power

Democracy
and the
Challenge
of
Power

By DAVID SPITZ

Columbia University Press

NEW YORK   1958

For Ruth
who in this, as in all things, is
the heart of the enterprise

Foreword

No democrat is surprised, though his sense of humanity may protest, when abuses of power occur in oligarchical states; for what else can be expected in states where power is derived not from the freely recorded and continuing consent of the people but from the arbitrary use of force in its various forms? To be sure, oligarchs, like shepherds, protect their sheep and display at times a real interest in their well-being—a guardianship and concern that are strikingly apparent whenever other wolves appear. But the interests of the rulers being normally opposed to those of their subjects, and their power being effectually divorced from any responsibility to the rest of the population, it follows that the sacrifice of the herd is a regular concomitant of oligarchical rule.

Two considerations only can check the despotic practices to which oligarchical governments are prone: a fear of revolution and a compassionate heart. But tyrants aware of the apathy and timidity that suffocate even discontented men—especially men who are themselves rent into factions by divisive group and ideological allegiances—have rarely been hindered by a fear of general rebellion; and as the history of authoritarian regimes only too well attests, tyranny and tenderness go ill together. Self-restraint alone is no sufficient brake on power.

For these and other reasons, oligarchical governments are clearly incapable of preventing or controlling abuses of power; what they do instead is to institutionalize them.

What is disconcerting, however, is that democratic states may also act oppressively, may also abrogate the basic rights of citizens. In part, this may be explained by the general tendency of power, in democratic as in nondemocratic systems, to corrupt. In part, it may be because power tends to attract those who seek to be, or who already are, corrupted. And in part, it may be the inevitable consequence of that propensity in man, when in power as well as when seeking it, to indulge his own interests and passions with no due regard for the rights and welfare of other men. Whatever the reasons, this much at least is clear: that while democracy is, in principle, a way of controlling abuses of power, such abuses nevertheless persist in the practices of democratic states. And it is this persistence of oppressive power in a democracy that constitutes what I here call the challenge of power.

At one time, it is true, convinced democrats might have contested the very meaning of such a formulation, for it was characteristically believed that every extension of democratic institutions would enlarge the area of freedom, or at least progressively reduce the area of tyranny. Today, however, partly as a result of the tragic experiences of democratic states in the last generation—not least with respect to race relations and civil liberties—it is impossible to cling to so unsophisticated a view. We realize, or at the very least suspect, that no institutional arrangements, no forms of government, can by themselves offer any guarantee that power will not be abused.

In this book I have sought to indicate various areas of American life where one can justifiably speak of abuses of power (in the sense in which I later define this term), to discuss the reasons why such manifestations of oppressive rule have defied the general extensions of political democracy, and to consider some of the principal solutions offered. I would emphasize that this book is not a treatise but an essay, and as such it is put forward more as a stimulus to thoughtful discussion and reconsideration of the problems than as an exhaustive treatment of the subject.

It ought, perhaps, to be added that this book is in no way intended to convey the impression that democracy is bound to be a façade for its opposite, oligarchy. On the contrary, the mere title of this essay implies, as it should, that I recognize the reality of the democratic framework. I might add, for reasons suggested in the text as well as in an earlier book on a related theme, that I also regard it as a morally and politically desirable system. All that I am concerned with here are departures from the democratic principle; and to the extent that my argument may have merit, I would like to believe that it does so as a whole rather than as a pastiche of unconnected parts.

If in the course of my remarks some harsh things are said and some grim conclusions are drawn, I can only hope that these are dictated less by personal perversity than by the nature of the evidence itself.

DAVID SPITZ

The Ohio State University
Columbus, Ohio
January, 1958

Acknowledgments

For so slender a volume, my obligations are many. I am much indebted to my friends Marvin Fox, Morton A. Kaplan, David Kettler, and Howard Rosen, who subjected a portion or the whole of the manuscript to their customary irreverent criticisms. To R. M. MacIver I owe a continuing obligation, both for his encouragement and for his perceptive observations on a draft of this book. Above all, I am indebted to my friend Morris Watnick and to my wife Ruth Sachere Spitz—not alone for careful and critical readings of the manuscript in its several stages and for endless hours of provocative discussion, but, over many years, for a measure of devotion quite beyond my power of repayment.

I am grateful, too, to the Rockefeller Foundation for a fellowship which enabled me to devote the academic year 1955–56 to the writing of the first draft of this book; to the Fund for the Republic for a grant which released me from a teaching commitment in the summer of 1955; to the librarians of the Library of Congress for research facilities afforded me during my fellowship year; and to Mrs. Willard Plegge and Miss Ruth G. Martin for admirable assistance in the typing of two drafts. Chapters III, V, and X have previously appeared in the pages of the *Midwest Journal of Political Science* (November, 1957), *Political Science* (New Zealand, September, 1957), and the *American Political Science Review* (March, 1958), and I am grateful to the editors of these publications for leave to reprint.

It seems hardly necessary to add that none of the individuals, journals, or institutions mentioned here bears any responsibility for the views, or errors, of this book.

Contents

PART ONE

Democracy and the Abuses of Power

I

The Problem of
Power Stated

In one sense the title of this chapter is misleading, for there is no problem of power, there are only problems of power. In the traditional literature, however, the issue is generally treated as if it were a single problem; and though I must end by rejecting the traditional approach—and consequently the traditional solutions —I ought not, perhaps, begin by rejecting the teachings of that tradition out of hand.

From the traditional standpoint, then, the problem of power is the control of the abuse of power, the curbing of that tendency in men of high station to degrade and oppress other men as they (the powerful) uncritically indulge their prejudices and pursue their conceived interests. And since, in this view, it is government that is the primary instrument of such oppression, the quest for the control of power has traditionally been the quest for a principle or a set of institutions by which governments might be restrained.

In these terms, a Socrates could argue that because, in his view, most men are generally wrong in what they conceive their interests to be, reason is required if they (or at least some few among them) are to act wisely and not oppressively. For much the same cause, but without an equivalent faith in man's capacity to be guided by his unaided individual reason, an Aquinas or an Edmund Burke could insist, alternatively, that only when men submit to God's will or adhere to an established tradition can the problem of power be resolved. Men like Montesquieu and James Madison and democratic theorists generally, on the other hand, have looked rather to mechanistic devices to control the abuse of power. They sought to mitigate (even to remove) the excesses of arbitrary rule by fragmenting and distributing political power, and above all by rendering governments responsible to the people. Through some such single solution, then, both democratic and nondemocratic theorists alike have sought to control what they took to be the single problem of the abuse of power by government.

But this single-minded approach is surely much too simple to deal with the abuses of power in a complex society. For in such a society a variety of power groups, both in and out of government, exercise their powers individually or in concert in such a way as to oppress some of the citizenry in some things at some times, and not necessarily to oppress all men (or even the citizens generally) in all things at all times. If this is so, the exercise of governmental power may, by restraining an economic or religious or other nonpolitical power group, liberate an individual or group from the abuses to which he or they might otherwise be subjected. From the standpoint of the power that is restrained, to be sure, such an exercise of governmental power may appear to be (and subjectively is) an abuse; but this is not likely to be the judgment of the citizen who is thereby freed.

Hence, the problem of power is reduced, in the real world, to the control of specific acts of particular powers. It is not one problem but many problems; for there is no one abuse of power, there are only abuses, various in form and often markedly different in degree. Our quest, then, is the quest for solutions to the problems generated by the multiple abuses of power.

Now of such abuses a necessary distinction must be drawn between those abuses associated with the acquisition of power and those resulting from the way in which that power, once acquired, is exercised. In the first instance, the fundamental abuse is the usurpation of the legal authority itself, the acquisition of power by unconstitutional or wrongful means. This, for Rousseau as for the ancient Greeks, was so grievous a violation of right conduct as to constitute tyranny.[1] Consequently, one who derived his power not from the consent of the people—which was for Rousseau, as it is for all democratic theorists, the only proper principle of authority—but from force or fraud, was an illegitimate and therefore a tyrannical ruler. He might mean well, and have every intention to act wisely and benevolently. He might even, on occasion, succeed in doing so. But whatever judgment men might place on any or all of his deeds, the fact that he unlawfully seized power was in itself the sufficient mark of despotism.

In the second construction, power is abused not so much because it is acquired illegitimately but because a government acts unlawfully or oppressively, i.e., it acts contrary to justice and law. One who knows or who observes no restraints on his impulses and desires is of necessity an arbitrary ruler, for he tends always to go to the limit of his power, doing whatever his strength and his opportunities enable him to do. Indifferent to what other men might regard as the elementary dictates of human decency, he does not scruple to deprive his subjects of their rights even when there is no compelling reason for him to do so. And because he exercises so absolute and despotic a power over the entire community and every member therein, he embodies, as Aristotle insisted,[2] the basest qualities of the tyrant.

To speak of justice or of the unwarranted deprivation of rights, however, is to raise certain difficulties, for these are clearly matters of disputation, and they are likely to remain so. Rights, for example, have most commonly been held to be those claims assured to men by the political system under which they live or by the moral code to which they give or ought to give their allegiance. These two sources of rights are not necessarily connected. They may, in fact, be intrinsically opposed. Thus, Calvin's reading of Christian doctrine would not permit him to accept the democratic notion of political equality. Where discussion has failed satisfactorily to resolve a conflict among men as to what their rights are, resort has too often been had to trial by combat. But whatever we take the basis of right conduct to be—whether it be the principles of the legal order or the dictates of an ethical system—it remains clear that an action of the ruler which unjustifiably interferes with what are conceived to be the rights of men is in this construction vexatious and oppressive.

We have, then, two views of abusive power: one that looks to the way in which the ruler acquires his domination, the other to the way in which he exercises it. And it is to this twofold aspect of the abuse of power that writers on politics, with but rare exceptions prior to Tocqueville and John Stuart Mill, have generally addressed themselves. Thus, when men argued in favor of a particular form of state, say democracy, they did so on both of these grounds. They asserted, first, that it rests on a right principle of authority, that is, on the freely rendered consent of the governed; and secondly, that it provides a political mechanism which tends to prevent, or at least to mitigate, abuses of power by enabling the ruled to recall the ruler should he get out of hand.

But this does not exhaust the problem. Three questions, at least, remain open. One is whether the principle of consent is indeed a valid principle of authority. A second is whether democracy, even though based on consent, is not itself prone to invidious action. To be specific, what is there to prevent such action by a democratic state, by a government whose arbitrary and oppressive acts are supported by a majority of the people? If uncontrolled power is intrinsically mischievous, uncontrolled popular power is not less so; and a democratic government exempted from any necessity of being in the right might be as likely to abuse its subjects as would an oligarchical government.[3] Finally, is there any ground for holding that a democracy does, in fact, suffer from abuses of power other than the lawless acts of governments?

II

Consent as a Legitimate Source of Power

Concerning the first of these questions, the legitimacy of consent as a source of power, little need here be said. This is not because the problem is unimportant; on the contrary, it is one to which political philosophers have addressed themselves at great length. It is rather because the theme of my inquiry, which is the relation of democracy to oppressive rule, renders it not strictly relevant. It is sufficient for my purposes to take democracy as an established fact—recognizing, of course, that actual states are always approximations, never embodiments, of their ideal forms—and to argue that no government is democratic in any meaningful sense of the term unless it rests on the empirically determined consent of the people.

This may appear to belabor the obvious, especially when we bear in mind the sometimes neglected fact that consent is often the result and not merely the source of good government. But it is the logical rather than the chronological role of consent that is vital and that is at issue here. And from this standpoint it is well to note that in all other theories of politics consent is also admitted as a necessary principle of government. This is so even where the alternative theory appears to reject consent as a legitimate source of power and to appeal instead to supernatural authority or to force or to the supposed laws of nature.

Consider, for example, the argument in terms of divine pre-

script or sanction. According to some theologians—not least the
Puritans of Massachusetts Bay—a careful and literal reading of
the Scriptures reveals that monarchy and theocracy, even without
the benefit of popular consent, are both approved as legitimate
systems of government. Democracy, on the other hand, is held to
be nowhere ordained by God as a fit instrument of order. Since,
in this view, God's will and not public opinion must prevail,
democracy cannot be said to derive from a legitimate principle
of authority.

Now it is a peculiar fact that those who advance this argument
do so in order to win the acquiescence of the very populace whose
opinions they otherwise scorn.[1] But it is more important to note
that not all who subscribe to God's teachings read them in this
light. Thomas Aquinas, for instance, was prepared to admit that
under certain circumstances democracy is a right form of state;
and some contemporary theologians, like Reinhold Niebuhr and
Jacques Maritain, go further to insist that it is in fact "the only
true political philosophy"; that, to assure justice, democracy and
the principle of authority derived from the will or consent of the
people are not merely "perennially valuable" but are "perennially
necessary"; they are a matter of basic right.[2] Thus, in some theological constructions at least, the appeal to God's will does not
exclude, but builds upon, the principle of popular consent.

Those who look not to consent but to force, who contend, for
example, that might makes right, assert something which is not
only logically untenable but also self-negating. If force is equated
with right, then right changes as force changes. Who has power
is right simply because he has power; he ceases to be right when
his power is overthrown. Then whatever is, is right, not because
it is right but simply because it is. This is to denude the word
"right" of all ethical content. It is to oppose right to weakness
rather than to wrong, which is a logical absurdity.[3] The position
is also self-negating, for the contention that might makes right is
itself an appeal to opinion rather than to force. Yet, in affirming
the superiority of force, it denies the worth and relevance of the
very opinion to which it appeals. Paradoxically, proponents of

the view that might makes right are logically committed to accept democracy (and with it the principle of consent) where it prevails; for democracy by virtue of the fact that it prevails has might and is therefore "right." [4] But all this, as Rousseau well said, is a mass of inexplicable nonsense.

Neither force nor the appeal to divine precept, therefore, vitiates the principle of consent as a necessary source of power. It can even be argued, as I have suggested, that they reinforce that principle. But what of the appeal to nature, to the doctrine of natural law or natural right? Does the nature of man and of his place in the alleged rational order of things prescribe an alternative source of power? An affirmative answer to this question has been set forth, in an ideal sense at any rate, by Plato in the *Republic* and by various neo-Platonists in the modern world. It is not to consent but to reason, to the order discovered in nature by the rational processes of mind, that we are to look for the true basis of authority. And this basis, we are told, is not in what people want or agree to accept but in what is objectively right.

Two difficulties of this position, however, must be noted. In the first place, not all who appeal to nature find in it the same things. Hobbes, Locke, and Rousseau, for example, in contrast to Plato, derived from nature the teaching that men are equal and that it is only through their voluntary consent that they can be said to have moved from the state of nature into civil society. It is only because they have themselves freely willed to constitute and to obey a particular power that this power can legitimately claim their allegiance. According to this version of the natural law or natural right doctrine, therefore, reason and the natural order of things dictate that consent is alone the proper source, if not of truth, at least of power.

In the second place, there is an important distinction between what is theoretically or ideally best and what is practically best. Politics is a practical rather than an ideal science; consequently, what is politically right even by the standards of natural law or natural right doctrines must bear some relation to what is actually possible, to what men will tolerate in the conduct of human affairs. It is meaningless, therefore, to speak of a regime as being the "best" unless it rests in some measure on the consent of the governed. To urge the opposite—viz., that the best regime is that in which the best men rule, and rule absolutely; that wise rulers ought not to be hampered by the unwise wishes of their unwise subjects—overlooks the fact that the few who claim to be wise cannot hope to rule the many who are alleged to be unwise by force alone. They must seek always to persuade the multitude to recognize them as wise, and to obey them freely because of that acknowledged wisdom. Thus, the requirement for wisdom is necessarily qualified by the requirement for consent. The best government—best because it is both desirable and possible—must look in real measure to the consent of the governed. On this point, despite the different orders of precedence assigned to wisdom and consent, classic doctrines of natural right concur with the teachings of modern political philosophy.[5]

Whether we appeal to God or to force or to nature, therefore, consent is in some sense approved as a necessary principle of authority. What the democratic theory does is to outline a system of government which gives maximum expression to this principle. Whether the principle itself is one which can be shown to be intrinsically or objectively preferable is open to doubt; for this rests on philosophical assumptions which, like the doctrine of the equality of man, can be asserted but not proved—at least not in a discussion of political principles per se.[6]

This is not to say that a man can be a democrat only in spite of himself, that he has to endorse democracy in a spirit of despair, that he must hearken to the voice of the people not because he believes that voice to be right or just but because he fears that to do otherwise is to incur the dangers of a revolution. Nor is it to argue that he must, if he is driven by a passion for ethical certainty, resort to the circular argument that the principle of consent is a self-evident truth. All it does is to insist that no man has as a matter of right an inherently superior claim to freedom; that all men, however mean or humble their stations, are entitled to share in the determination of the conditions under which they are to live. But to say this is to say a good deal, as Rainborough's now classic reply to the aristocratic pretensions of Cromwell and Ireton makes clear:

For really I think that the poorest he that is in England hath a life to live, as the greatest he; and therefore truly, sir, I think it is clear, that every man that is to live under a government ought first by his own consent to put himself under that government; and I do think that the poorest man in England is not at all bound in a strict sense to that government that he hath not had a voice to put himself under; . . . that every man born in England cannot, ought not, neither by the Law of God nor the Law of Nature, to be exempted from the choice of those who are to make laws for him to live under, and for him, for aught I know, to lose his life under.[7]

On these *assumptions* (rather than demonstrated truths), consent can be held to be preferable to all other principles of authority. What remains to be considered, therefore, is the relationship between democracy (as the form of state which best institutionalizes the principle of consent) and the diverse abuses of power.

One caution, however, must first be entered. Consent is rarely, perhaps never, unanimous consent. Always there are likely to be some who withhold their approval, not merely to a particular law or to a particular government, but to the state itself and the entire system of social order sustained by the state. I include here anarchists in all political systems, the advocates of oligarchy in democratic systems, the proponents of democracy in oligarchical systems. Consequently, no state can properly claim to rest on universal consent; and with respect to those who—like the anarchists, Fascists, and Communists—withhold their fundamental consent, democracy appears to be, and I believe is, a system of force.[8] From this standpoint, but only from this standpoint, the democratic state can properly be viewed as an illegitimate, and hence tyrannical, power.

For the rest of the community, however, consent remains the binding principle. It is the will not of all but of nearly all men to accept the state and the principles of the social order necessitated by that state. It is their will to accept the government and the laws promulgated by that government even should one disapprove of them; otherwise it would be impossible to maintain that larger political association that can alone secure a system of order and assure the important liberties.

Consent, that is to say, does not require that the government which acts in the name of the state be the government of one's choice. It implies only that the citizen is prepared to recognize as legitimate that government which emerges out of the accepted electoral process to power. Otherwise, the fact that he may have cast his vote for the defeated political party would relieve him of all obligation to obey the laws; and this, it seems hardly necessary to add, is not a principle on which a state can long hope to survive. Nor does consent require the individual citizen to give his specific approval to each of the laws or to each of the actions of a government under the laws. It demands only that he surrender the right of armed resistance when the government imposes restraints that are constitutional but which he finds distasteful.

What I understand by consent in the democratic theory, in short, is the general will to maintain the state, and with it the political processes that make it viable. Where such generalized consent or consensus is forthcoming, democracy can properly claim to rest on a valid principle of authority.[9]

How, then, are we to account for the fact that abuses of power in democratic states are an existing reality and not merely a potential danger? How, in the face of such precautionary devices as the fragmentation and dispersion of political powers, can we explain the emergence, and even more the persistence, in, say, the American democracy of certain undemocratic practices and institutions?

The answer, I believe, turns on the fact that men have misunderstood, or but partially understood, the nature of abusive powers in the democratic state, and have consequently misconceived, or but partially conceived, the problems involved in their control. To make these points clear, it is necessary to define more carefully what I mean by abuses of power, to set forth what I consider to be some of their more important manifestations in the American democracy, and to formulate what I think are some of the measures needed for their control within the democratic state.

III

The Abuses of
Power in
Democracy

If we take a somewhat less than optimistic view of human nature, it is not difficult to understand why abuses of power are always to be found in democratic states. The mere legitimacy of a state in theory is no guarantee that it will not abuse its power in practice. Every community, even one that is democratic in form, dwells always in the shadow of injustice; for men who are free are still men, and if they do not act always as beasts it is still true that they do not act always as gods. In the pursuit of their own interests, or of what they conceive their interests to be, men who are free to choose —even within predetermined limits—will sometimes choose to act not merely wrongly but oppressively: they may endeavor to attain some ends the achievement of which would degrade or harass a portion of the community; in the pursuit of the right ends they may sometimes resort to arbitrary means. And in point of fact— from the standpoint of democratic principles as well as of the subject harmed—this is what men and governments who call themselves democratic have all too frequently done and still do. They have abused and continue to abuse their powers, that is, to infringe upon the rights and liberties essential to and (in a real if not a formal sense) assured by the principles of their political system.

Now by essential rights and liberties I mean here no more than those rights and liberties that emerge out of, and are strictly correlative to, the principle of consent, and derivatively to the principle of majority rule which is the indispensable mechanism for the elicitation of that consent. I leave open here the question as to whether, in the absence of a notion of rights derived from a source outside the state, there can be a genuine or ultimate basis for opposing offensive prescripts of the positive law, for affirming a claim to rights in the face of a political system that flaunts them. Clearly, both secular and theological adherents of natural law or natural right doctrines would insist on a negative reply to this question. But if consent is the sufficient and legitimate basis of democratic government, then those rights at least are fundamental which derive from and are intrinsically related to that principle of consent. A government which fails to respect those minimum rights, accordingly, undermines the very principles on which it presumes to rest.

What, then, are the essential rights and liberties in a democracy? Primarily, they are of two sorts: (1) the rights appropriate to the maintenance of equality, in particular, the equalities of citizenship and of opportunity; and (2) the rights necessary to the maintenance of democracy itself, in particular, the liberties of speech and of political association. Through the latter, democracy maintains—and can alone maintain—that free play of conflicting opinions which makes possible the constitutional responsibility of the rulers to the ruled, which makes government responsive to the governed. Through the former, democracy assures not (as some critics of democracy have absurdly held) the literal equality of all men in all things—viz., in intelligence, talent, achievement, status, power, and the like—but that equal access to public opportunity which enables a man to discover and to prove his true worth, and that political equality which counts each man in his suffrage and his citizenship as one and no more than one. This does not, of course, imply the right of a person to become a member of a private club or of a church society, or to become, say, a teacher in a denominational institution; for such membership is not central to his life *as a citizen*. But it does imply his right not to be barred on irrelevant grounds from an occupation or profession, for these are essential to his opportunities—even, perhaps, to his survival—as a citizen of the democratic state. For this and allied reasons, one at least among the necessary corollaries to these rights merits especial mention: the right to one's safety and security in his own person.

It is true that oligarchical forms of state may, on occasion, recognize one or more of these rights. A Napoleon who holds out to every bearer of a knapsack the possibility that he may someday also carry a marshal's baton immeasurably extends the channels of opportunity, but so long as there is a Napoleon there is no real equality of opportunity or of citizenship—not even if all are equal but one. An enlightened absolutism may, as the age of Voltaire attests, tolerate freedom of speech to a remarkable degree, but not with it that right of political association which by its activity invites the citizens constitutionally to displace the ruling power. The safety and security of one's person may be, if not assured, at least generally unassaulted by paternalistic monarchs or by self-designated emissaries of the Lord; [1] but that security is always contingent on one's submission to the perpetual yoke of guardianship; and there is no security for those who would exercise as well the right to criticize and to remove the government. Only in democratic states are all these rights, in principle at least, constitutionally guaranteed. Only in democratic states is one free both to applaud and to attack the government in power, to join with like-minded men in the effort to make or to unmake that government, to strive himself (if he so desires) to become a part of the ruling power, and not at any time to jeopardize his life or his safety by virtue of his participation in these activities.

Thus, the things that are necessary in a democratic system are but matters of expediency in a nondemocratic system. Whether, for example, the Soviet Union leaves its writers free to say what they will or requires them to conform to a prescribed pattern of production is a matter of programmatic choice and not a principle that implicates the system of government itself. But in a democratic state to impair the right of free expression, or of any other essential right, is to subvert the fundamental principles of the political order. It is to nullify the primary rules of the game. Such action, whether undertaken by private groups or by governments, constitutes nothing less than an abuse of power.

In these terms, the history of democratic states—not least of the American democracy—reveals a considerable disparity between the principles that men verbally espouse and the practices by which they actually live. This is not, it must be emphasized, the easy and all too superficial distinction that men often make between theory and practice; for, at the empirical as distinct from the ideal level at least, there is no such distinction. If a principle is valid in theory, it must be valid in practice; if it does not work in practice, there is something wrong with the theory, or the theory actually involved is different from the theory that is thought to be involved. It is this latter alternative that applies here. The disparity between democratic utterance and undemocratic behavior is not simply that between reference to an ultimate and unattainable ideal, on the one hand, and action within a political system that—even at best —is always but an imperfect approximation of its acknowledged prototype, on the other. It is this in part, to be sure, but it is also more. It is also a disparity that emerges when there is a true conflict of principles—a conflict between, say, the idea of equality and that of inequality, between the rights associated with (because integral to) a democratic state and the denial of those rights as matters of principle in oligarchic systems of government. And this disparity manifests itself most strikingly—and for the preservation of democracy most destructively—in the fact that within democratic communities there are those who, whether acting through legal sanctions by virtue of the governments they control or through nonlegal penalties by virtue of the social and economic power they command, impose punishments which impair, in extreme cases even make a mockery of, those rights of their fellow-men that have been here termed fundamental. By their effective—sometimes malevolent, sometimes unreflective—disregard of democratic principles, they have abused the power entrusted to them.

Now the distinction that is urged here between the abuse of power through the laws (or through the acts of governmental authorities under the laws) and the despotism of individuals or of groups acting outside the government is not one that the literature on tyrannical power has generally viewed as crucial. There is a clear and plausible reason for this. If the oppressive acts of non-legal powers violate the law, the government can suppress them. If they are acts that have the implied or explicit sanction of the government, that government can be held to share or to assume responsibility for such action. In both cases, therefore, the problem of the abuse of power appears to revert to the legally established political power; and it is here, accordingly, that writers on this subject have most commonly focused their attention.

There are, however, at least two difficulties which attend this lack of concern for the oppressive actions of nongovernmental powers. In the first place, it overlooks the fact that in a free society the government lets many things alone, and in some instances it is constitutionally required to do so; hence individuals and groups are free to conduct their affairs in ways to which the government is formally if not actually indifferent. Thus, employers are often free to engage in discriminatory employment practices, nondenominational universities to establish (or in practice to apply) discriminatory entrance requirements, private organizations arbitrarily to exclude disliked individuals or groups from the use of their halls for public meetings, and so on. This may be called the problem of abuses of power within the interstices of the law.

In the second place, it forgets or unduly minimizes the fact that the government may under certain circumstances be unable to control the oppressive acts of individuals and groups even when these run counter to the law. The history of vigilante movements in America, of lynchings and race riots, of the many and varied forms of discrimination that reflect deep-seated prejudices, and the like suggests that even where the government may seek to enforce the law—which in the instances cited it does not always do—the climate of opinion may be such as to foredoom that effort. In some cases, indeed, the temper of public opinion or of public sentiment may actually sustain, where it does not initially compel, the abusive acts of governments themselves. It is public opinion, after all, that determines (through the electoral process) who shall rule, and to what ends. And if legal action takes the form of oppressive legislation, or of the arbitrary and capricious bidding of legal authorities, the public which selects or which refuses to remove those authorities, and which thus signifies approval of the abusive policies established by its chosen officials, cannot escape responsibility. Democratic governments do not move in a vacuum. They respond, as they should respond, to the changing tides of public opinion. Consequently, to subject the ruler to the will of the electorate is no sure protection against oppression unless that electorate is itself determined not to tolerate abusive rule. Where the electorate through its passivity or ardent espousal sustains political infractions of the basic code, it identifies itself with the powers of despotism.

There is another sense in which the oppression of public sentiment—or, as it is often called, the tyranny of public opinion—is sometimes understood. This is that subtle yet pervasive domination over the mind which produces not a man but an intellectual chattel who bears the semblance of a man. It is that spirit of conformity which operates less to punish men for disapproved acts or for the expression of ideas displeasing to the prevailing currents of opinion (though it does this too), than to prevent men by a sapping of the intellect and of the will from ever entertaining or acting upon such ideas. The will of man, said Tocqueville, is not shattered, but it is softened and bent; he is seldom forced to act, but he is constantly restrained from acting; he is neither destroyed nor driven to resistance, but he is led by repeated repressions to surrender the exercise of his own will; and in the end he, and others like him, become little more than a stupefied and enervated people.[2] Among such a people there is no real need to punish divergences from orthodoxy: for on the one hand the enslavement of the mind by opinion—by habituation in doing and thinking what is popularly held to be "right"—has already tended to preclude dissenting ideas; and on the other hand the subjection of the will by a sense of futility—by that despondency of mind that Bryce has called "the fatalism of the multitude," [3] which disposes men to acquiesce in or to submit to the dominant sentiment—renders deviant action improbable. Where, despite this, unwelcome doctrines and actions do nonetheless break through, social disapprobation is likely to repress them by exacting penalties that are often no less, and sometimes more, effective than legal ones.

Now in a democracy, where men are regarded as equals, the tyranny of public sentiment, so understood, may take a special form. Unanimity being impossible, the opinion of the majority rather than of the minority must prevail—not because the majority is necessarily right but because the alternative, the rule of the minority which renders the few superior to the many, is insufferable. But if the majority is to prevail with an easy conscience, it can do so, generally, only if it believes, or convinces itself that it believes, that it is right. Hence, the customary insistence that men should obey the ruling power is defended not simply on the ground that such obedience is necessary for the maintenance of the social order (which is perhaps all that should be claimed), but that it is necessary for men to obey because that ruling power is right. The individual who dissents from the judgment of the majority, who refuses to adhere to the opinions of the ruling power, thereby appears to place himself in an anomalous position. As a democrat, he argues that all men are equal. But as a dissenter, he seems to insist that he knows better than the majority what is right. He implies, or seems to imply, that he (or his judgment) is better than that majority, thereby seeming to affirm the very principle of inequality that he, along with the majority, had previously repudiated. His obstinacy no less than his apparent inconsistency serves only to arouse the animosity of those who are opposed to him and who command the support of the majority. Paradoxically, then, the principle of equality—which is here improperly extended to include moral and intellectual uniformity as well as political equality— enters to reinforce that terrible craving for certainty which all too often results in the effort to suppress disconcerting differences. And it is this intolerance—of heterodoxy in belief and of nonconformity in behavior—that constitutes (for some men) the tyranny of opinion and, derivatively, of majority rule.

We have, therefore, in a democracy, not merely to be concerned with the oppressive acts of governments, but to regard as well the arbitrary and abusive practices of individuals and groups who exercise power through their control of private organizations, and even, perhaps, of that tyranny of public sentiment which sustains them all.

To make more intelligible the nature of these different (yet complementary and therefore overlapping) abuses of power, it may be well to consider them separately and in somewhat greater detail.

IV

Democratic Governments
as Oppressive Powers

Oligarchical governments, I have said, are by nature tyrannical. They derive not from consent but from force and fraud, and they rule, most commonly, for the purpose of serving their own interests. Since their primary interest is to maintain themselves in power— and through such power to turn the laws and the administration of justice to their own advantage—they give to none but the favored few those rights that democratic governments are required to give to all. They comprise, and conceive it proper for themselves alone to comprise, a ruling class.

It is customary to attribute this monopolistic seizure of rights to the malevolence and cupidity of the rulers, and such imputation is not without merit. But it is more accurate to view such despotism as the concomitant of an honest conceit—a conceit by which an oligarchy equates its rule, and the satisfaction of its interests, with justice.

It is not difficult to understand why a ruling class should hold this view, for men who are sincerely convinced of their intrinsic superiority—in talent, in character, in the perception of values that constitute a viable culture—cannot readily believe that they are not more entitled by virtue of that superiority to rule. And once such men ascend to the seats of power, their very removal from the masses of the people—a removal accentuated in time by institutionalized barriers of birth, wealth, place, and manners—makes it impossible for them to appreciate the sentiments and aspirations of the masses. Try as they may, they cannot understand the hearts and minds of the multitude. And in futility no less than in indifference, they finally cease even to attempt it. The inevitable result is that the city of the oligarchs is a city divided within itself: there is the city of the rulers, where men have concern for the desires of their equals and compassion for their afflictions; and there is the city of the ruled, with reference to which the primary interest of the rulers is that it stay ruled.

Now it is a truism that men tend to hold different ideas concerning the justice of their own and others' interests. Rare indeed is the man who affirms as unjust the interests he pursues. As a Christian, he may love his neighbor, but rarely as he loves himself; as an employer, he may be genuinely moved by the welfare of those who labor for him, but not as he is moved by the dividends he seeks to collect and dispense; and as a member of the ruling class, he may admit that the glory of a state is in the multitude as well as in the best of its citizens, but his conception of that glory is derived not from the multitude but from those whom he regards as the best. Thus, whatever it is that one may believe men ought to do, the fact is that men strive to protect and to further their interests as they conceive them. And since, as they imagine, their interests are the true interests of all, their quest and the policies they pursue in line with that quest constitute, in their eyes, the true glory of the state. Here, and here alone, is where they believe justice resides.

Democratic governments, on the other hand, are not tyrannical by nature; for by resting on the empirically determined (rather than assumed or fraudulently determined) will of the people they validate their first claim to legitimacy. But they remain potentially tyrannical in their actions; for in democracy (no less than in oligarchy) diverse interests and diverse conceptions of justice still exist and vie for power, and in the course of that struggle men may sometimes engage in practices and promulgate ideas that are difficult to reconcile with the principles of their political system.

Democracy, it must be remembered, is not a utopia. Within it conflicts of interest are neither eliminated nor stilled. They are rather transferred to a different battleground and the contenders are supplied with different weapons. Where, in oligarchical states, the arena is restricted to a select group that commands the instruments of coercion in sufficient degree to forestall effective opposition to the promotion of its interests, in democratic states that arena is thrown open to all men and to all interests, and the instruments of persuasion are, or ought to be, sufficiently undisturbed as to permit that interest or coalition of interests which can marshal the support of a majority of the people to prevail. Thus, while all men are equal and the interests of all are, in principle, given an equal opportunity to be heard, not all can expect equal satisfaction. So long as there is a conflict of interests—and some interests, though not all, inevitably are in conflict—democracy, like oligarchy, can do no more than strive to protect the interests of some and not of all men. Unlike oligarchy, however, the democratic state makes it possible to secure the interests of the many, or at least of the majority, rather than the interests of a privileged few.

A necessary and important qualification must be entered here, for what makes such conflicts of interest possible, what sustains the state under whose aegis they occur, is clearly a broad and underlying consensus on the fundamentals of the social order. No state —least of all a democratic state—can hope to survive where the masses of the people are not united on and attached to those essential principles, and in this respect there is a common interest at the heart of, and that is furthered by, democratic governments. There are many things—e.g., the preservation of the peace, the maintenance of the vital liberties, the advancement of learning, the cultivation of the arts, and the like—which are advantageous and (avowedly at least) of concern to all; and the commitment to such common values overrides and makes tolerable the lesser conflicts of separate and dividing interests.

Nevertheless, those dividing interests remain, and their proponents struggle (sometimes bitterly) for power. Majorities—even if but temporary and shifting majorities—are formed over against minorities. And in the pursuit of their own interests, aggravated at times by the heat of political passion, majorities—and, where they can, minorities too—resort now and again to arbitrary and oppressive measures. It is not surprising, therefore, that governments representative of and responsible to those majorities should serve as instruments through which such oppressive actions can be effectively imposed.

It would seem unnecessary to catalogue here the ways in which democratic governments—both directly through the laws (or through the bidding of legal authorities) and indirectly through the sanctioned imposition of nonlegal penalties—have behaved despotically toward certain racial, national, and religious minorities. The record is all too clear, whether we look at the Negro, at the American Indian, or at other oppressed minority groups. Thus, while the political worth of the American Indian is no longer computed as but three-fifths of that of the white man, the latter continues (by fraud and by superior force of arms, sanctified by law) to divest the Indian of his lands, to abrogate his political and religious freedoms, and to subject him to various forms of discrimination—ranging from laws forbidding the sale of intoxicating liquors to Indians to laws outlawing their intermarriage with white citizens.[1]

The atrocities to which Negroes were subjected by that peculiar American institution—slavery—are in large part a dim memory, but the myth of their intrinsic inferiority is still widely held, in some quarters cherished, and the discrimination that flows out of and serves by its consequences to sustain that myth is still widely practiced. As a result, not only in the South but everywhere in America the Negro is still (though in varying degree) denied his basic rights of equal citizenship and equal opportunity. He is still denied full access to the ballot box—e.g., by the discriminatory application of literacy tests; despite the recent ruling of the Supreme Court in *Brown v. Board of Education*,[2] he is still condemned in some states to a segregated (and therefore inferior) education; he is still subjected to discriminatory employment policies, to inadequate health and other social services, to inferior housing facilities, and the like. Where the government does not directly deprive the Negro citizen of his fundamental rights, it may do so indirectly through collusion with private individuals or groups. Thus, a legal requirement that all children attend the school in the district where they live, when combined with restrictive covenants that confine the Negroes to a particular school district, effectively (but not illegally) maintain segregation in education; while the frequent failure to indict or (where there is a trial) to convict white men clearly guilty of the murder of Negroes encourages that spirit of violence which causes some of our citizens always to live at the edge of terror.[3]

Racial and national groups such as the Asiatics and Mexicans, including those of American birth, have also been subjected to oppressive rule—most strikingly, perhaps, when an insensitive government evacuated some 110,000 Japanese-Americans from the West Coast during the early months of the Second World War without a trial or hearing or even an allegation that specific evacuees were disloyal or guilty of espionage or treason or other criminal acts.[4] The children of Jehovah's Witnesses are no longer required to commit daily what they believe to be a sacrilegious act, i.e., the salute to the flag;[5] but the children of atheists are today required in many public schools to take "Bible" courses, to recite the Lord's Prayer, and in parts of Kentucky at least to attend classes taught by members of recognized religious orders attired in their clerical garbs. Discrimination against Jews has operated primarily in the social and economic spheres, but infringements of their rights by laws or by governmental agencies or by biased individuals in positions of power are still numerous—e.g., in the admission and subsequent placement of students, as well as in the appointment of faculty and higher administrative personnel, in state and municipal institutions of higher education; in the admission policies of some state licensing boards to the professions; in the failure to enforce laws barring discrimination in housing; and the like.[6]

In all these cases—Indians, Negroes, Asiatics, Jews, etc.—what is involved is an openly avowed or an unstated but effectively pursued governmental policy of discrimination. These are acts—and they are by no means the only acts, or more than a fraction of them—of democratic governments or of agencies of democratic governments, which in one way or another deprive American citizens of their essential rights. Not all in each of the groups mentioned here suffer such disabilities, and there are racial and ethnic groups other than those mentioned here that do. But enough has been said to demonstrate that democratic governments—whether motivated by calculated intent or by prejudice—can and at times do rule oppressively.

THE PROBLEM OF POLITICAL NONCONFORMITY

It will, perhaps, have been noticed that members of the above groups are mistreated and oppressed because of what they are, and not—except for the adherents of certain religious faiths—for what they think or say or do. Few if any consistent democrats would seriously challenge the proposition that restrictions imposed on any group (save, perhaps, children and the insane) merely because of what that group *is* constitute a transgression of basic democratic principles. It is only when the democratic state imposes restrictions on a group for what it says or does that doubts arise as to how far that state can infringe on the rights of such a group without impairing its own principles. It need hardly be added that political nonconformity—to mention an outstanding case in point—is not a hypothetical problem; for in our own as in every age, men who stand at the outskirts of public opinion, who challenge in a marked way the dominant political views, are prone to excite public displeasure and even, on occasion, censure. In a time of crisis, or of assumed crisis, such censure may take the form of suppression. Is that suppression an abuse of power? If it is, can it be justified on other grounds; and if so, on what grounds, and under what conditions?

To answer these questions, we must begin with the recognition that in one respect at least democracy is intrinsically the most dangerous of all political principles; for it affirms as a matter of fundamental right the freedom of all men to voice their dissenting opinions. It is easy enough for a state to tolerate those ideas which endorse the principles of the established order and which are critical—save for secondary matters—only of opposing systems. It requires a quite different temperament, and an infinitely greater degree of confidence in the validity of its principles, for a state not only to accede to a life of perpetual conflict in ideas but to make that conflict the very basis of its existence. This is not to say that democracy—any more than oligarchy—gives dissenters a right to *act* contrary to laws. It is one of the marks of a democracy, however, that it, alone of the forms of state, makes it a primary principle that those who disagree with the fundamentals of the political system or with the policies of a particular government in power have the right both to *plead* for a change in that system or in its policies—to *speak* in opposition to the laws—and to *organize* into appropriate political associations in order more effectively to press for the removal of that government, or for the modification or dissolution of the political system itself. So long as that opposition foregoes violence and moves only in the realm of opinion, seeking through persuasion and the recognized modes of political activity to enlist the opinions and votes of others in its cause, it plays a legitimate and indispensable role in the democratic order.

A state that accepts this principle must accept also its possible consequences, hazardous as these may sometimes appear to be. For by placing no idea beyond criticism, by elevating no principle —including the principle of democracy itself—into a religious dogma that is to be venerated or at least unquestioningly accepted, it submits not only the life of its momentary government but the validity of the state itself to the verdict of public opinion. Thus, whatever its inner confidence or fears, the democratic state must be prepared to live always in a state of ideological siege and political turmoil, even, possibly, of drastic political change.

American practice, however, has not always been in keeping with avowed and necessary standards of democratic conduct. The dissenter, to be sure, has most commonly been viewed with amusement; but he has also, on occasion, been regarded with fear and distrust. He has been treated as a harmless eccentric, but also, at times, as a dangerous enemy. Where, as in the case of a Calhoun or of those contemporary Southern "statesmen" who oppose the Constitution in the name of "white supremacy," the dissenters are representatives of substantial interest groups, they may emerge as minor heroes or even martyrs. But if they speak only for themselves, or for a politically insignificant minority, they are more likely to find themselves objects of calumny, and sometimes of governmental suppression. Thus, in a recent and in some respects a comparable era—the period subsequent to the First World War —radicals of every persuasion (anarchist, Communist, Socialist, and the like) were treated as outcasts and subjected to severe legal (and illegal) disabilities and penalties. Not least among these was the scandalous refusal of the United States House of Representatives and the New York State legislature to admit to their seats Socialists legally and properly elected to office.[7] Even in the period prior to that war political nonconformists such as the anarchists had experienced police harassment and brutality and had often been prevented from speaking in public places; when arrested, they were commonly accorded a type of justice such as Emma Goldman received when, at the close of that war, she was arbitrarily deprived of her citizenship and deported from the United States.[8] And now, a decade after the end of the Second World War, there are disturbing evidences of an even greater intolerance and era of governmental oppression.[9]

The problem today, to be sure, is significantly different from that which existed in earlier times. If we disregard the American South, those who then challenged the first principles of the political system were generally isolated individuals like Thoreau or relatively small and uninfluential groups. Today, we are confronted in addition by highly disciplined and well-organized cadres and political associations, committed in their allegiance not only to antidemocratic political philosophies but, in the case of the Communists as of the disciples of National Socialism only a few years ago, to a viable and antagonistic political system as well. In the service of such a philosophy and hostile power, its adherents (or at least some of them) are prepared not only to battle in the arena of ideas but to resort at times to methods outside the constitutionally recognized rules as well. To the extent that they actually employ such means, a democratic state may legitimately restrict them in its own self-defense; for no state, whatever its character, can be expected to stand idly by and permit itself to be destroyed through treasonable or revolutionary acts. In this respect, freedom for the dissenter ends when he takes that overt step which—whether of violence or of criminal conspiracy or of espionage—endangers the life of the state; for he is then more than a dissenter, he is an active rebel.

But to justify the suppression of treachery or of force is one thing; to validate the suppression of ideas is quite another. Here, as elsewhere, certain distinctions must be drawn and scrupulously observed, or else our principles become no more than verbal apologetics to which obeisance is made only on convenient (and safe) occasions.

I am concerned, let it be emphasized, only with matters of belief, not of action—only with freedom of speech and with the concomitant right of political association, not with overt acts that are intended to destroy the government, or with that speech which in an immediate context constitutes what Justices Holmes and Brandeis termed an "imminent" or "clear and present danger" that violence or other acts of criminality are likely to ensue.[10] The precise line that separates the use of a word from the mob violence or revolutionary action that follows the utterance of that word is, of course, a difficult one to draw, depending as it does not on the word itself but on the special circumstances—of proximity and degree—in which that word is spoken. It makes all the difference in the world, for example, whether one's belief in or advocacy of violent revolution to effect a desired social or political change is made in the pages of a book or in the attentive quiet of a classroom or public lecture hall or in the police-patrolled confines of a Hyde Park or Union Square, on the one hand, or whether it is addressed in flaming words to an armed and seething mob standing before 10 Downing Street or 1600 Pennsylvania Avenue, on the other. However, the difficulty in drawing that line, and the linguistic acrobatics of legislatures and courts in seeking to refine and to apply it, need not detain us here. For what is primarily at stake are forms of speech and of political activity which are admittedly not an "imminent" or a "clear and present danger" but which are alleged to be subversive nonetheless and therefore equally subject to suppression.

In these terms, the first distinction that must be observed turns on the improper and misleading way in which the question at issue is usually put. It is generally stated in the form: How much freedom should be given to those who, like the Communists and Fascists, would use it to overthrow the state and to establish a political system that would deny that freedom to others? The answer of course is: the same for them as for anyone else; for it is the essence of the democratic liberty of opinion that men are free to advocate, and through constitutional means to seek, changes not only in the policies but in the very character of their government.

But the question is one a democrat cannot properly ask; for the query—"Should *we* give *them* (e.g., the Communists) freedom?" —falsely assumes that *they* are not a part of the same society of which *we* are a part, that our faction has a special and superior right to freedom. In this we are like the schoolboy who has been taught to memorize and revere the ringing cry of Patrick Henry, "Give me liberty or give me death," riveting our attention to the liberty-death dichotomy rather than to the word "me." It was the denial of *his* liberty that there concerned Patrick Henry, as it was the denial of *their* liberties that stirred the passions of those who applauded him; no equal care was evinced for the Negro slaves who waited outside the Virginia church to serve as the stepping-blocks for their freedom-demanding white masters to mount their horses.[11] I fail to grasp the great principle that is allegedly served when one battles for freedom only for himself. I am much more impressed by the man who is willing to say, "Give *them* liberty or give *me* death." But in any case, democracy does not and cannot concede that some men have an intrinsically superior claim to freedom. In the democratic state *all* men, whatever their political creeds, have an equal right to speak.

It is said, however, that Communists and Fascists constitute a special threat to American democracy and freedom. That is true.

But it is important to distinguish the sense or senses in which they can be said to be a threat, and what, accordingly, in the democratic scheme of things, is to be done with respect to that threat.

They are, clearly, a threat in the limited or specific sense that every dissenting idea is a threat, a challenge to a particular theory or traditional belief, an incitement to change. They are also a threat in the general and more fundamental sense that they desire to alter the very bases of the social structure, to effect political and economic changes so drastic as to deny to others the very freedoms that make their own activities possible, to do away with democracy and establish a totalitarian dictatorship. These are real dangers, but freedom would be false to its nature if it failed to welcome them. So long as, and to the extent that, the threat is in the realm of ideas, it must be met and refuted in that realm. Otherwise we not only admit our inability to defeat those ideas; we lend our support to the pernicious doctrine that the sword is the proper response to the pen. From this standpoint, censorship and loyalty oaths (or non-disloyalty disclaimers) that seek to curb the expression of such ideas are not merely futile; they repudiate the first tenet of democracy—that no doctrine warrants suppression merely because it is strongly disapproved. Indeed, to suppress an opposing opinion is to forget that heresy—even of the Communist and Fascist varieties—serves a wholesome purpose. As John Stuart Mill reminded us, the heretical view, where wrong, helps us perceive the wholeness of our truth; where right, it enables us to correct injustice and embrace the more valid principle; where partly right, it reinforces our own partial truth by removing our partial error.[12]

The fact that Communists think (and adopt positions) in accordance with instructions from a foreign power—not in the sense that they receive day-by-day telephonic communications but in the sense that they slavishly pursue the policies set by the Kremlin—does not seem to me to compel any modification in this view. As citizens, Communists like all other groups have a right to choose any political god they please. What should concern us is not the source but the content and applicability of their ideas. Otherwise, we are faced by the absurd and impossible requirement that no man may look to an authoritative source for his opinions—whether that source be a church, a philosopher, a parent, or an established government, even his own.

It is, however, a characteristic argument of our time that Communists are unlike other citizens in that they constitute a unique and infinitely greater threat than that which is presented by their ideas. They are held to be a conspiratorial political movement, scheming and acting outside the rules of the game to subvert the institutions or processes of the democratic system. It is argued that by their advocacy of the forcible overthrow of democratic government, and by their conspiratorial activities in behalf of their creed, they rule themselves out of the democratic process, and consequently out of the protection of democratic rights. There is no obligation on the part of a democracy, it is maintained, to tolerate conspiracy, to accord free play to a movement that would corrupt and undermine the conditions of democratic existence.[13]

With respect to this phase of the argument, certain additional distinctions must be drawn. For if Communists are conspirators, they are also heretics; and in attacking their conspiracy, we must be careful not to expunge their heresy. Yet it is generally the case that those who—whether in or out of the government—hold Communism to be a conspiratorial movement have either ignored or badly confounded this elementary distinction that is of their own first making. For in their inability or refusal to distinguish the Communist as conspirator from the Communist as heretic, they have assumed that all who are Communists are conspirators. From Communism as a conspiratorial movement they have moved to a definition of Communism as nothing more than a conspiratorial movement. But these are unwarranted assumptions.

Not all who are heretics are Communists, using the term in its strict sense [14]—e.g., anarchists, Socialists, Fascists, and the diverse factions that look to Trotsky rather than to Stalin (or, since the deliberations of the twentieth congress of the Communist Party of the Soviet Union in February, 1956, perhaps to Khrushchev) as the true expositor of Marxism-Leninism. And while all who are Communists are heretics (at least in those countries outside the Soviet Union and its satellite states), not all who are Communists—and certainly not all who are heretics—are conspirators. For Communism as a heresy is an ideological rather than a political movement; and as a political movement it reflects and builds upon legitimate social forces as well as (and perhaps more than) upon the machinations of diabolical plotters.[15] As a heresy, Communism appeals to millions of people on the basis of its ideas and avowed intentions; and since those ideas touch a multitude of varied things—from highly abstract philosophical principles such as dialectical materialism to concrete and immediate policies such as the removal of discrimination against Negroes in public housing —those who respond to its appeal, even to the extent of joining the Communist Party, do so for a variety of reasons and expectations. Since those who are thus in the Party do not all subscribe to the same things, it does not follow, without specific proof to the contrary, that all subscribe to any one thing, such as conspiracy.[16] Even if it were true, as it is not, that every Communist is a conspirator, the fact remains that he is also a heretic. Consequently, the distinction must still be observed between those of his actions which may be heretical and those which are conspiratorial. The latter may be suppressed, but the former—in so far as they can be distinguished and separated from the latter—never. Hence any legislative measure which in the effort to curb the Communist conspiracy neglects to draw and to respect the elementary distinction between the Communist heresy and the Communist conspiracy is contrary to democratic principle and despotic.

Yet this is precisely the respect in which the American government has pursued deficient principles—as in the Smith Act of 1940, which makes it a crime *to advocate,* or to conspire to advocate, the forcible overthrow of the government, without regard to the special circumstances under which such an attempt to overthrow the government might actually or conceivably take place; as in the McCarran Internal Security Act of 1950, which, in addition to requiring "Communist-action" organizations to register as such with the government and thereby to incur certain disagreeable legal consequences, legalizes the doctrine of "protective arrests"—i.e., the internment of a citizen on the basis, not of unlawful conduct (e.g., espionage or sabotage), but of what it is "reasonably" believed he will "probably" do—in time of emergency; and as in the Humphrey Communist Control Act of 1954, which describes itself as "an act to outlaw the Communist Party" and provides that the Communist Party shall not be "entitled to any of the rights, privileges, and immunities attendant upon legal bodies." [17]

One can, indeed, cogently maintain that the charge of conspiracy, which is all too valid so far as Communist infiltration into governments and the attempt to subvert those governments from within are concerned, has no proper relevance when applied to the communication of ideas; that a conspiracy *to commit* sedition is not in fact a conspiracy at all, involving as it does neither an overt act nor actual speech but the presumed *intent* to speak. It can also be argued that the opinions of Judge Learned Hand in a lower court and of Chief Justice Vinson in the Supreme Court, sustaining the conviction of Communist leaders under the Smith Act, did not establish that the defendants themselves either committed or advocated sedition but only that, by agreeing to assemble, to talk, and to publish at a later date certain ideas that were alleged to be subversive, they "conspired" to advocate Marxism-Leninism, which is a quite different thing.[18]

But it is more important to note the paradoxical fact that the legal sanction given to the conspiracy doctrine may itself provide the factual evidence on which that legal sanction is presumed to rest; for by the processes of what might be called a self-fulfilling definition, the allegation of conspiracy is established not by independent demonstration but by a kind of inverted history. One begins by charging not individual Communists but the Communist Party with being a conspiracy; then a law is enacted proclaiming it to be such; then the Party, in order to survive, is compelled to become a conspiracy even if it had not previously been one. The circularity of this process is made amply clear when we realize that in those countries—e.g., England, France, and Italy—where the Communist Party has not been interdicted as a conspiracy, it functions openly as a legitimate and nonviolent political party, in spite of and apart from the limitations that have been placed on its other allegedly seditious activities or on the conspiratorial acts of its individual members or followers. But where legal, political, and economic penalties are imposed on the Communist Party as a whole, and derivatively on its members, as is done in the United States—e.g., by the Humphrey Communist Control Act—the Party must cease even its legitimate political activities—i.e., holding conventions, adopting platforms (including the expression of nonrevolutionary opinions on all manner of public issues), and nominating and endorsing candidates for public office—and fall back completely on conspiratorial devices. Thus, in seeking to suppress conspiracy, the Humphrey Act fosters and even, perhaps, helps to create it. That, along with the Smith Act, it emasculates the principles of personal guilt and of the "clear and present danger" limitation on free speech, and in effect violates the prohibition against bills of attainder as well,[19] only increases the severity of its infringement on democratic rights.

The evils of outlawing or of suppressing the legitimate speech and associational activities of the Communist Party become more apparent when the repressive principle is extended to non-Communists and anti-Communists who are at the same time disciples of Marx and Lenin. Such an extension is defended by the argument that Marxism-Leninism teaches the revolutionary overthrow of the government (even of a democratic government), an allegation that is true in the sense that this is the ultimate aim of the Communists and can be shown to be so not merely by selected quotations from Marx and Lenin, but by the general tenor of their teachings as well. However, as every competent student of political theory well knows, the doctrines of Marxism-Leninism, like the doctrines of Judaism and Christianity, are by no means unambiguous and consistent; and as with all general principles their application depends on circumstances of time, place, and power. Thus, while Marx repeatedly asserted that the transformation from a capitalist to a socialist society could be achieved only by force and violence, he—and Engels as well—also explicitly said that because of the special conditions which prevailed in England and in the United States, it was conceivable that this transformation could be brought about in those countries by peaceful and legal means.[20] Hence, one can legitimately claim to be an orthodox Marxist and still refuse to advocate violent revolution in the United States.

In the same way, while a disciple of Lenin must reject the exceptions that Marx and Engels had noted and must accept without cavil the idea of revolutionary action to effect the transformation from capitalism to socialism,[21] he can invoke Lenin's own teachings to show that such a revolutionary thrust is to be attempted only when certain conditions make it opportune. "To be successful," Lenin wrote to the Central Committee of the Bolshevik Party in September, 1917, "insurrection must rely not upon conspiracy and not upon a party, but upon the advanced class . . . upon a *revolutionary upsurge of the people* [and] . . . upon such a *crucial moment* in the history of the growing revolution when the activity of the advanced ranks of the people is at its height, and when the *vacillations* in the ranks of the enemy and *in the ranks of the weak, halfhearted and irresolute friends* of the revolution are strongest." Given "all the objective conditions for a successful insurrection," the revolutionary thrust for power is approved. In the absence of those conditions, any effort at a revolutionary *putsch* is condemned.[22]

What Lenin did, that is to say, was to modify the Marx-Engels thesis to accord with his belief that the conditions of "bourgeois democracy" had changed and that peaceful transformation from a capitalist to a socialist society was no longer possible. It can, therefore, be argued—and has in fact been so argued by the twentieth congress of the Communist Party—that those conditions having changed again, the Marx-Engels thesis now applies. The thesis, taken at face value, is thus revealed to be a flexible one: it does not always call for revolutionary change, and where it does call for such change the actual resort to revolution is made to depend always on circumstances.

It does not follow, therefore, that a Marxist-Leninist must advocate the violent overthrow of the government either now or in the immediate future. And in point of fact all those in this country who call themselves Marxist-Leninists, including the Communists, do not *now* do so. The fact is that at least since the end of the last war Communist parties both here and in Europe have given no evidence of readiness to employ force and violence in an effort to overthrow the government—I disregard here riots and skirmishes in Europe which do not affect the general principle—except when they have been in control of the armed potential of the community (i.e., the army, the police, and the key civilian authorities) and have, besides, the loyalty of mobilized mass elements—e.g., Czechoslovakia. By their own actions, and for reasons of Soviet policy and other considerations, the Communists in Europe—even where they have the largest following (e.g., France and Italy)—have steadfastly adhered to a strictly limited strategy of mobilizing public sentiment and legislative blocs against any anti-Soviet policies. At most, their danger to democratic institutions in Western Europe lies in their powers of infiltration, subversion, and *coup d'état* where conditions permit, not in mass revolutionary uprisings.[23] Consequently, if Communists were previously indicted for their unquestioning fidelity to the Soviet doctrine of violence, presumably they would now have to be absolved of that charge by reason of the same fidelity; for by the most recent congress of the Communist Party—the twentieth congress—they have been instructed in no unmistakable terms that they can come to power by parliamentary means.[24] And if this repudiation of armed struggle as a fixed strategic principle is true of the Communists, how much more true is it of the very small and powerless Marxist but non-Communist political organizations such as the (themselves divided) factions that look to the memories of a dead Trotsky rather than to the continuing prescriptions of the rulers of the USSR.

To believe otherwise, to hold that *all* Marxist-Leninists advocate the duty and the necessity of violently overthrowing the government, and that such advocacy is to be translated into surging and bomb-throwing mobs actually rebelling against the government, is to lose all sense of proportion. It is to build inference on deduction on the basis of certain dogmas or general principles selected from the corpus of Marxist writings, much in the same way that a recluse working not from history but from specified passages in the sacred writings might extrapolate an image of Jew or Christian as one who always observes the Commandments, who always does good and eschews evil. But men do not always act in accordance with their own stated principles; and no one who examines carefully even a portion of the very considerable body of Marxist literature can fail to note there the host of exceptions, emendations, and qualifications to otherwise general principles. How, then, can one conclude from an examination of the dogmas another publicly recites, what the true beliefs and character and conduct of the latter (as these may be revealed in a later and particular situation) are?

Yet agencies of the government, by applying the Smith Act in 1941 to a group of "Trotskyites," by placing the Independent Socialist League (a Trotskyite organization) on the Attorney General's list of subversive organizations, and by refusing (until ordered by the Supreme Court to do otherwise) to issue a passport to Max Schachtman, the leader of the Independent Socialist League, have moved on the reverse and demonstrably erroneous assumption.[25] They have alleged that individual conduct is the ineluctable consequence of one's stated beliefs, even more of the principles (whether proclaimed by that individual or not) of the group to which he belongs, and that those stated beliefs (as they appear in Marxist scripture) are absolute and clear and ever binding. And by acting on such false allegations, they have unwarrantedly abused the power entrusted to them.

The problem of the Communist Party member, of non-Communist Marxists, and of the conspiracy doctrine has been dealt with here at some length, because it is at this substantive level that the problem of political nonconformity in our time principally lies. This is not to minimize the very considerable importance of procedural proprieties, for even if repressive steps are to be taken, those steps must accord at all times with constitutionally established rules and procedures. One has only to recall the inexcusable misconduct of some congressional investigating committees in recent years, committees that have violated our traditional standards of decency and fair play even to the extent of effectively (if not formally) reasserting the unconstitutional powers to issue bills of attainder in condemning witnesses who appeared before them and to enact *ex post facto* "legislation" in punishing men for conduct that was not criminal at the time it occurred; or the arbitrary and *ex parte* findings of guilt by the Attorney General in listing organizations thought to be subversive without prior (or even later [26]) hearing; or the indiscriminate extension and use of that list in fields unrelated to its original purpose, so that—like the edicts of the congressional committees—it has become another informal but operative exercise of the bill of attainder; or the denial of due process in refusing to accused persons the right to confront and to examine their accusers or even to know who the accusers and what the accusations are; or the substitution of a presumption of guilt for the traditional presumption of innocence, the invasion of the right of privacy, and the employment of inconsistent and arbitrary standards and procedures in the conduct of the loyalty and security programs; or the importation into American jurisprudence, and the often perverse use made, of the idea of guilt by association (which has now been peculiarly extended to include guilt by kinship, including that of motherhood)—one has only to recall these and other departures from our traditional liberties to realize that the means selected in the pursuit of even the "best" ends are of crucial importance if we are to avoid that exercise of governmental caprice which, when unchecked, proscribes justice and ensures tyranny.[27] That such capricious and arbitrary action was not curbed, and is now but insufficiently beginning to be curbed, helps to explain the many oppressive acts of congressional investigating committees and of governmental officials and agencies in the past decade.

DEMOCRACY AS OPPRESSOR 41

But even if our procedures were beyond reproach, the fact is that we are now pursuing the "wrong" ends. For we have accepted at least two principles which are in basic opposition to the democratic creed. In the first place, we have substituted a system of preventive law for our traditional system of punitive law. This system of preventive law is applicable not to overt acts but to the realm of ideas; it stipulates that men are to be punished not for what they have done but for things it is believed they *may* do; and this conjecture as to what they may do involves a further conjecture as to the effects of that action if and when they do it.[28] In the second place, we have taken the administration of this system of preventive law out of the hands of the courts—where at least elementary due process, if not political impartiality, can be secured—and transferred it to civil and military administrative officials; and in these matters the latter have all too clearly demonstrated that they are distinguished neither for their judicial temperament nor for their special competence.[29]

It is not the quality of the administrators, however, but the fact that they are called upon to administer regulations based upon deficient principles that is the vital issue. For once we concede, as we seem to have done, that it is desirable for the government to prevent the spread of ideas thought to be subversive—and it is to be emphasized again that in proscribing the Communist Party we silence not only its allegedly revolutionary but also its non-revolutionary opinions—then it becomes eminently logical for that government lawfully to read a portion of the human race out of the American community. Men can be criminally punished not for doing wrong but for our fear that they might do wrong, not for personal acts or deeds but for harmful intentions that are themselves inferred from words or imputed words or still-to-be-spoken words. Governments can inquire into all manner of associations as well as into the opinions of individuals. They can deny government jobs to subversives or alleged or suspected subversives.[30] They can maintain a noxious Attorney General's list of subversive organizations. They can evict and exclude Communists and suspected Communists from Federally-aided low-income housing projects. They can even deprive native-born Communists of their citizenship. Governments thus empowered can, in a word, destroy men whose ideas and commitments they loathe by all manner of means short of direct execution. Even the most exacting observance of procedural rights cannot stay the inquisitorial consequences of this invasion of belief; for in the absence of wise policies, good procedures, like good intentions, may serve but to expedite one's passage to perdition. Hence, while it is imperative that the traditional elements of due process of law be restored in the treatment of Communist Party members and followers, as well as of other political nonconformists, the abiding problem remains one of principle.

One last point with respect to the treatment of political nonconformists. Here more than in any other realm—save perhaps that of racial discrimination—the abusive power of the state is exacerbated by nonlegal penalties imposed by private powers with the sanction or at the instigation of the government. Thus, when a political nonconformist acts in a manner displeasing to the government (or to a political or administrative official of that government), but that action being lawful is beyond the reach of formal punishment, it is often the case that the political authority will seek to secure the punishment of that nonconformist through the disapprobation and corresponding action of social powers. This is the principle that has motivated many of the public hearings and pronouncements of congressional investigating committees, especially in recent years. These committees already know—through earlier closed hearings—what the answers of a witness will be; consequently, their purpose in holding later and open hearings is not to gain information necessary for their work as legislators— which it is their legitimate business to secure—but to make that information public and thereby to expose the witness to the outraged sentiments of public opinion and in particular of his employer. In this way they contrive a situation that brings social and economic sanctions—often more injurious than the legal penalties that might otherwise have been applied—to bear on the witness. In effect, they convert nonlegal sanctions into indirect forms of legal punishment. The fact that not all private powers respond to this situation in the same way—Harvard University, for example, withstood the fulminations of an aggressive Senator and refused to expel certain professors who had invoked the Fifth Amendment to the Constitution when declining to answer certain questions put to them by a congressional investigating committee—does not alter the wider fact that those committees have all too effectively succeeded by such tactics in having men punished for lawful but disapproved conduct. There is, I must add, something contemptible and not a little terrifying in this appeal to private powers to come to the aid of a faltering government, when that government also represents itself as a proud and powerful champion of freedom, fair play, and decency.

Before leaving the argument of this chapter, certain cautionary remarks should be made. It is not contended here that democratic governments *must* act oppressively—indeed, I know of no inexorable laws in the conduct of human affairs—or that it is a just characterization of the American democracy to say that it is solely or dominantly despotic. What is argued is that democratic governments can and on occasion do abuse their powers. To sustain this argument, and no more than this argument, it is not necessary to balance the respective acts of democratic and oligarchic governments, or to weigh the relative importance of the oppressive and nonoppressive sides of democracy. It is enough to show, through random or selective cases and incidents, that arbitrary and vexatious rule is not unknown even in a democratic state; and if such abuses of power are real, they cannot without grave peril be ignored.

It may be objected, however, that these are exceptional cases, and that in any case they are but temporary rather than permanent features of the democratic landscape.

The first allegation is true, but to the extent that it implies an identification of "exceptional" with "trivial," it is erroneous; for it then misapprehends the meaning and significance of the exceptional case, which is in some ways the crucial test of a principle. Just as no principle is good that is not good in a time of crisis, so no principle can be counted a rule that is always subject to important exceptions. The problem of minority rights is of necessity an exceptional one, for the minority by definition is comprised of the dissenters to a prevailing view. The conformists, being untroubled, tend to forget that the infringement of another's rights is not only contrary to their own principles; it is a precedent that may serve later to invite the infringement of their own rights. Freedom of speech, for example, is vital primarily to those who object to, not to those who applaud, a given view; and it is most vital to those who object the most. But since those who applaud now may on a later occasion stand to protest, the democrat insists on protesting at all times the invasion of basic rights. For him, the exceptional case is thus transformed into the typical case; it is democracy's ordeal by fire, the supreme test of a principle's capacity to survive.

That these cases constitute but a temporary deviation from the democratic norm is a proposition that is not easy to defend. The problems of racial and ethnic discrimination, of the mistreatment of political nonconformists, and the like have been with us, after all, a long time, some since the very beginnings of the Republic. They are the products or manifestations of deep-seated fears and hatreds, of cultivated prejudices and a narrowly conceived self-interest; and these are exacerbated, not weakened, in a time of crisis. They are the heritage, even more, of historical and institutional factors which render some groups, because, e.g., they are the perceived descendants of markedly inferior or hierarchically low ranks in the predemocratic social orders of the past, peculiarly vulnerable to that prejudice and discrimination.[31] Consequently, while it is doubtless true that some (though I hardly think all) of the particular acts of injustice cited here will, in time, be corrected, others are more than likely to take their place.

It can, of course, be argued that these and other infringements of democratic rights by democratic governments are to be explained in terms of the malevolence or incompetence of the rulers, and not in terms of the principle of democracy itself. As a partial explanation, this is unquestionably true. But it overlooks the fact that there is often much harm in what even "good" men do; [32] and it fails to explain how such malevolent and incompetent men acquired power in the first place. Clearly, democracy—like other forms of state—does not exclude such men from positions of leadership and control; nor does it prevent them from using (or abusing) their powers to deprive other men of their basic rights. To the extent that a democratic system makes this possible, to the extent that it exposes its citizens to arbitrary and invidious measures, it is vulnerable—as a system of government—to oppressive rule.

V

The "Tyranny" of
Public Sentiment

In a democratic state governments are, in principle, the servants, not the masters, of public opinion. They may influence that opinion and even, on occasion, mold it; but in any ultimate sense they are responsive to, because they are dependent on, the will of that majority which decides whether they shall remain a trifle longer in power. To the degree, then, that democratic governments abuse their powers, it is because public opinion—the power behind the power of government—allows them to do so.

It is doubtless the case that public opinion may sometimes tolerate what it does not approve: through indifference or cowardice or despair men have all too often abstained from publicly voicing their thoughts or from taking the requisite action against tyrannical and despised (though powerful) rulers. But apart from the fact that silence or inaction becomes in such circumstances a form of acquiescence, there is the more sobering realization that interest (or conceived interest) and prejudice have led men to acclaim and to maintain in power a variety of petty despots—as the endorsement and reelection of a Bilbo, a Frank Hague, a Huey Long, a McCarran, a McCarthy, a Gene Talmadge, and the like only too well attest. In this respect it is quite proper to speak of the tyranny of public sentiment, understanding by this the attitude or state of mind that sustains and gives impetus to abuses of power by those who possess it in a democratic state.

This implies that opinion, perhaps more than government, is a source of iniquity in a democracy. It suggests, too, that such acts may take other forms than the political alone—e.g., the acts of

private powers—thus raising the question whether public sentiment may not itself create a climate of intolerance so pervasive
and so compelling as to preclude dissident or nonconformist behavior, and thereby render retributive action by the government
unnecessary.

This last question is, of course, the classic problem that oc-
cupied Tocqueville and, through him, John Stuart Mill.[1] For
Tocqueville, there is a type of tyranny in a democracy that springs
not from the actions of men but from their failure to act, not
from their thoughts—whether orthodox or heterodox—but from
their failure to harbor any thoughts at all. It is a tyranny that
exorcises through a sort of prenatal control any upsurge of thought
or of emotion that might lead men to "wrong"—i.e., unorthodox
—behavior. And it derives its strength not from the frequency
of its use but from the fact that it is used, and needs to be used,
little or not at all.

Now it is all too obvious that men do not *want* to do the
"wrong" things. If they could perceive the true values and the
true ways, they would guide their conduct appropriately. Reason,
however, always enters late in life, and to some men it comes in
deceptive forms. Consequently, society undertakes by precept and
by example to accustom its citizens (especially those of tender
years) to the "right" or "proper" modes of thought and of behavior. It teaches them not merely to follow but to approve the
ways of the folk. And for this purpose it has at its command that
supreme instrument of conformity—habit—which in the absence
of and by chronological priority to reflective thought effectively
channels men's wills, their impulses, and their desires into the
pursuit of the "right" things. Society need not, accordingly, force
the individual to think as the multitude thinks; it has already
convinced him. It need no longer suppress the discordant and
irksome notes of dissent, for dissenting voices are rarely or never
heard. It need no longer reproach eccentricity, for there are few,
if any, eccentric men. Uniformity is the rule, and the occasional
exception is almost always quickly and sufficiently controlled by
the power of social disapprobation.

For this reason Tocqueville was led to say that in a democratic society

it will always be extremely difficult to believe what the bulk of the people reject or to profess what they condemn. . . . When an opinion has taken root among a democratic people and established itself in the minds of the bulk of the community, it afterwards persists by itself and is maintained without effort, because no one attacks it. Those who at first reject it as false ultimately receive it as the general impression, and those who still dispute it in their hearts conceal their dissent; they are careful not to engage in a dangerous and useless conflict. . . . public favor seems as necessary as the air we breathe, and to live at variance with the multitude is, as it were, not to live.[2]

And again:

I know of no country in which there is so little independence of mind and real freedom of discussion as in America. . . . as long as the majority is still undecided, discussion is carried on; but as soon as its decision is irrevocably pronounced, everyone is silent, and the friends as well as the opponents of the measure unite in assenting to its propriety. . . . the majority possesses a power that is physical and moral at the same time, which acts upon the will as much as upon the actions and represses not only all contest, but all controversy.[3]

This majority, Tocqueville went on to say, is more than merely preponderant; it is irresistible. For once the theory of equality is applied (as he believed it was applied) to the intellects as well as to the suffrage of men, human pride is assailed and vanquished in its last retreat. Public opinion becomes the arbiter not only of what is lawful or forbidden, but also of what is true or false. The inevitable result is that the same political and philosophical opinions are everywhere entertained; that uniformity governs the conduct and the daily actions of the people. In such a world, Tocqueville argued, tyranny emerges not to imprison the body but to enslave the soul.

The master no longer says "You shall think as I do or you shall die"; but he says: "You are free to think differently from me and to retain your life, your property, and all that you possess; but you are henceforth a stranger among your people. You may retain your civil rights, but they will be useless to you, for you will never be chosen by your fellow citizens if you solicit their votes; and they will affect to scorn you if you ask for their esteem. You will remain among men, but you will be deprived of the rights of mankind. Your fellow creatures will shun you like an impure being; and even those who believe in your innocence will abandon you, lest they should be shunned in their turn. Go in peace! I have given you your life, but it is an existence worse than death." [4]

Tocqueville's thesis does not, of course, imply that legislation need be altogether eschewed, for law does more than provide a punishment after the act. It is also—through fear and moral suasion—a deterrent. Fear of legally imposed penalties is no inconsequential thing; and men who are led by impulse or knowledge to conclusions incompatible with the edicts of the law are not always prepared to suffer the penalties of unlawful action, or even at times of that verbal defiance which may incite public resentment. In a democratic society, moreover, where law is conceived to be the reflection of the popular will, and where that popular will is itself (for all too many people) equated with moral rightness, men tend to look to the law as a standard or guide to right action. Thus law, as a formal expression of public sentiment, serves to ward off dissident ideas and behavior.

Nevertheless, the decisive tyranny—for Tocqueville as for Mill —is not the law but the climate of opinion which initiates or sanctions, and later sustains, the law, and which has recourse to instruments of social control other than the law alone. Always there is an elaborate if informal system of rewards and punishments attached to social approval or disesteem. Always public sentiment can reach into areas that the law cannot penetrate. Potent though the law may be, its natural inflexibility operates as a self-limiting and constricting force. More pervasive and powerful by far is the unseen yet ever-present force of social sentiment.

Does it follow, however, that this force—this play of public sentiment on the minds of men—is in any proper sense a manifestation of that extreme form of the abuse of power that is termed tyranny? Or that it is uniquely a product of democracy? I think not, despite the important element of truth in Tocqueville's analysis.

Clearly, there are pressures for conformity in democratic society, and these pressures can, under certain circumstances and for certain individuals, lead to apathy and despair, even, perhaps, to a withdrawal from any serious concern with or systematic reflection on the moral and political life. No one who carefully and honestly regards the reactions of men to the pressures of conformity in our own time—not least to the useless and degrading loyalty oath [5]— can doubt the reality of this danger, and hence the very real measure of truth in Tocqueville's concern.

Nevertheless, certain considerations make it difficult to accept Tocqueville's thesis as it stands, and as it is equated with the ideas of tyranny and of democracy. It is not at all clear, for one thing, that Tocqueville is correct when he explains this phenomenon of conformity by the fact that democracy is an egalitarian principle. I set aside the question whether America was in fact, at the time Tocqueville wrote, both democratic and egalitarian, as he believed it to be; the inequality of the sexes, the inferior status and condition of the Indian and Negro peoples, and the economic distinctions and political disqualifications that led, among other things, to the so-called Jacksonian revolution offer striking evidences to dispute Tocqueville's easy assumption. The more important fact, however, is that the pressure or insistence to conform is a characteristic of all societies, whether egalitarian or non-egalitarian. Monarchs and self-styled aristocrats, after all, have done more than their share to fill the massive histories of religious and intellectual repression. And if we turn to milder forms of social pressure, it is patent that all societies use, and must use, a certain amount of control if they are to maintain even a minimum system of order. Without some pressures to conform, without some reliance on custom and habit, no society can hope to survive. In this sense, Tocqueville's attempt to relate conformity to the principle of egalitarianism alone is clearly unwarranted. At best, it asserts little more than a truism; for controls in general, and the propensity of the bulk of a citizenry to compel the dissident few to conform, in particular, are almost synonymous with society itself. At worst, it imputes to a particular society exclusive responsibility for an element that is common to all societies; it seeks to establish a causal link between conformity and egalitarianism when, on any fair reading of the evidence, conformity is neither unique to nor distinctive of egalitarianism. For these reasons, the problem of tyranny, or of the abuses of power, must be sought elsewhere than in the mere fact that there are social controls. It must be sought in a particular set of controls, in those controls that deny men the right to break the bonds of custom, to depart (at least in some respects) from the approved or common modes of life.

Not only is Tocqueville wrong when he calls "tyrannical" the indiscriminate pressures of conformity rather than their results, he is wrong, too, when he applies the term "tyranny" to that particular result that Bryce has more properly labeled the fatalism of the multitude. Tocqueville (like some writers today) is disturbed less by the actions of men than by their failure to act, less by their thoughts than by that surrender of intellect and of will that denudes men of their individuality and causes them to cease entertaining any thoughts at all. "The multitude," he remarks, "require no laws to coerce those who do not think like themselves: public disapprobation is enough; a sense of their loneliness and impotence overtakes them and drives them to despair." [6] That no one is driven to despair because no one defies public opinion —perhaps in the knowledge that if he were to defy public opinion he would soon find himself a lonely and futile figure and would thus be driven to despair—is, for Tocqueville, the final confirmation of democratic apathy, of what a recent writer has called "the death by atrophy of the philosophic impulse." [7]

All this, however, does not constitute tyranny. For one thing, Tocqueville fails to see that an inverse relation often exists between apathy and the pressure to conformity. Where there is apathy, there need, of course, be no pressure for conformity; the fact that pressure is required, on the other hand, is generally a convincing demonstration that the multitude offers resistance.

Tocqueville cannot have it both ways: if apathy and withdrawal are the essence of his tyranny of public sentiment, then the resistance that invites suppression is the negation of that tyranny, as must be that insistence on conformity itself; while if the pressure to conform is tyranny, then the greater the pressure the less the degree of apathy and the greater the degree of dissent.

It is for this reason that Bryce's notion of the fatalism of the multitude, which he carefully distinguishes from the tyranny of the majority, is the more useful formulation. Bryce does not make Tocqueville's mistake of equating this idea of apathy and surrender with the abuse of power; he restricts it instead to that disposition of men to acquiesce in the rule of numbers, a disposition especially marked, he believes, in a democratic state where political equality and the alleged leveling down of social eminence render no one man's opinions of special value. All opinions being of equal merit, Bryce argues, disputes can be resolved only by the determination of the majority. In a heavily populated state, this majority is so large as to overwhelm the individual. Consequently, Bryce holds, few men will have the courage to pit their judgment against that of the many. Few will dare to say that the majority, which must by democratic principles prevail, is not also right. And if the majority is right and must prevail, by what "right" can one oppose or censure it? "A man of convictions," Bryce admits, "may insist that the arguments on both sides are after the polling just what they were before. But the average man will repeat his arguments with less faith, less zeal, more of a secret fear that he may be wrong, than he did while the majority was still doubtful; and after every reassertion by the majority of its judgment, his knees grow feebler till at last they refuse to carry him into the combat." [8]

This all too ready acquiescence, even subservience, of the individual to the will of the majority is not, however, as Bryce saw, tyranny. Apart from the fact that not all who are thus subjected to pressure submit to it, the individual who does submit does so of his own will. He is induced but he is not actually compelled to comply. Only where that pressure unfairly and coercively imposes its will upon him—in the sense that it restricts his freedom to dissent and subjects him to severe legal or social penalties—can one properly term it an abuse of power. The unjust exercise of power, that is to say, is one thing; the state of mind which causes one to submit before that power is exercised is another. This latter is little more than a failure of nerve, an abrogation of a man's sense of personal responsibility and of his moral duty to battle for his own opinions. The tragedy is less in the society which engenders this spirit of fatalism and of despair than it is in the weakness of character of the individual who so easily collapses before the forces of social disapprobation.

In this respect a vagrant and a Thoreau, unlike as they are, share a common value: an indifference to or aversion from the esteem of their fellow-men. Neither feels oppressed so long as the society which scorns him lets him alone; neither is victimized if public sentiment merely disapproves of his ideas and conduct and seeks through a variety of pressures to persuade him to "reform." He would suffer oppression only if that society denied him the right to wend his unorthodox ways, only if his heterodoxies were proscribed and his dissident or heretical thoughts were silenced. In the absence of so arbitrary an exercise of power, there is no necessary correspondence, no cause and effect relationship, between the operation of public sentiment and the reaction to it by an individual.

These considerations bring us to another, and perhaps more crucial, difficulty in Tocqueville's thesis, namely, its inapplicability to a heterogeneous and socially fluid democratic society as distinct from a relatively homogeneous and status-fixed or oligarchical society. In a homogeneous and static society characterized by relatively fixed relations, there are few, if any, conflicting interests or conflicting opinions. The dominant view is very close to the universal view, and habit and custom suffice to maintain and perpetuate it. There the weight of social sentiment is normally enough to preclude, or if necessary to ostracize, heretical ideas. With respect to such a society—and Tocqueville, beguiled and misled by the remarkable degree of egalitarianism that he thought

he perceived in America, believed that America was in all fundamentals not simply a homogeneous but even a uniform society—
Tocqueville's estimate of the impact of public sentiment on the
individual would, I think, basically apply. There would, in fact,
be no real problem, and hence no need for the pressures of conformity. The force of custom would cement all the members of
the community into a common mold.

But this is not true of a heterogeneous society such as the American today. There conflicting interests and desires breed both conflicting opinions and a multiplicity of organized groups and associations that bring pressures of their own to bear in defense of
their particular views. In such a society no one set of opinions
can hope to be habitually accepted. Public sentiment can no longer
control the minds and behavior of men through the subtle work-
ings of habit and custom alone, for now there are conflicting
habits and customs, and with them conflicting and competing
loyalties. Conformity to a particular set of opinions, consequently,
can only be achieved through the direct or indirect interposition
of an organized power bloc, which restricts or curtails the normally
wide ranges of opinion in order to compel, if not inner conviction,
at least outer compliance.

Consider, for example, the case of the so-called nonconformist.
He is so styled because he deviates from a pattern of behavior or
rejects a set of beliefs that are widely, perhaps almost universally,
held, and are therefore presumed to constitute an objective and
valid standard for judgment. Does this mean that the nonconformist has no ideas of his own, or that he conducts his life
chaotically? A positive answer to this question would be patently
absurd. Save for a rare exception—perhaps, for example, an extreme nihilist—the nonconformist defies socially esteemed standards only because he prefers to be guided by standards of his own
choosing; he is a man of independent judgments, but his judgments are not independent of his internalized sense of right. More
commonly, the nonconformist is himself as much of a conformist
as those who view him with customary alarm. What distinguishes
him from the bulk of the community is not that he has *no* standard

but that he has a *different* standard, a *different* set of beliefs, a *different* conformity. The Communist may be unorthodox with respect to the overwhelming majority of the American people, but he is quite orthodox, even fanatically so, in relation to his own group. The bohemians of Greenwich Village, the artists and writers of the Parisian left bank, the *philosophes* of the outdoor cafés, even the denizens of the underworld and the members of juvenile gangs—these more often than otherwise conform in dress, in ideas, and in behavior to the standards of their *own* world even as they publicly disdain the standards of the world outside their own.

What is characteristic of a heterogeneous society—particularly one that is democratic in its form of government—is that it provides a refuge for both types of nonconformists by permitting them to escape from a particular group and to unite (if they so desire) with others of their own kind. The dissident (of the second and more common type, at least) is not then the lonely and impotent man of Tocqueville's imagination: as a member of a group, he has achieved both a sense of identification and a dedication to an ideal; more than that, if the group is welded together—as it commonly is—by a conviction not only that it is right but that, because it is right (or because history is on its side), it will prevail, he finds in that association the will to withstand even the contempt of, and the penalties exacted by, the majority. Valuing the favor of his group, he holds lightly the disfavor of the multitude outside. Under such circumstances, neither the public sentiment that is arrayed against him nor the indiscriminate pressures that are brought to bear upon him are particularly important; nor can they be said to constitute tyranny; for he can and does ignore the one and escape from the other. They become important only when they are given organized form and are so directed as to deny him any effective possibility of refuge.

The problem of tyranny in modern society, that is to say, in so far as it relates to the operation of public sentiment, is largely one of permitting or excluding conflicting loyalties and conflicting memberships. If a complex and heterogeneous society were left to its own devices, the diversification—given the industrialization and urbanization of modern society, perhaps the increasing diversification—of interests might well lead to a proliferation of groups and, with them, of the places of refuge available to heretical thinkers. It is true that the proliferation of groups may increase not only the number of places of refuge but also the number of refugees. Conflicts of interest and of opinion, after all, generally initiate tensions and resentments where they do not exacerbate those already in existence for other reasons; and such antagonisms, when combined with a lack of respect for the right to be different, explain only too well the impulse to suppression. In this sense a heterogeneous society may abet rather than limit and restrain the pressures for conformity. But by providing nonconformists with places of accommodation, a heterogeneous society also encourages and protects them. The task of those who would impose conformity to a particular idea (or set of ideas) and a particular way of life, consequently, is not simply to elicit but to direct the force of public sentiment. It is to channel that sentiment behind such pressures as organized groups may be able to marshal in order to destroy the nonconformist organizations and to silence their opinions. And the test of their success in this venture can be more or less estimated by the degree to which the individual dissident is in fact precluded from forming any attachments or from speaking publicly and in unison with others of his kind.

Whether such pressures need take the form of legal or of non-legal sanctions is not my concern here. Clearly, if maximum effectiveness is to be achieved, both forms are required. What is of concern is the recognition that these pressures come not from some vague and amorphous (if nonetheless real) state of mind called public sentiment, but from the actions of men, sometimes acting singly but most commonly proceeding through the infinitely greater power that resides in organizations. It is this form of the tyranny of public sentiment, not the type that Tocqueville and Mill and some of their contemporary disciples speak of, that counts and that is paramount today. But in this form public sentiment remains but a *source* of the abuse of power; it is not that abuse itself.

For these and other reasons, Tocqueville's idea of the tyranny of public opinion and, derivatively, of the tyranny of the majority has little relevance to a democratic society like the American. Tyranny is not to be sought or found in the principle of egalitarianism, or in the mere insistence on conformity, or in the indiscriminate pressures that are imposed in the effort to bring that conformity about, or in the apathy and despair that may enervate a body politic. It exists only where there is an actual denial of democratic rights—such as the rights of free speech and free political association—by organized powers, governmental and nongovernmental alike.

In the preceding chapter we considered some of the ways in which democratic governments have abused, and can abuse, their powers. It is time now to inquire into the oppressive acts of private powers.

VI

The Abuses of

Private Powers

Men are governed, I have suggested, less by the Platonic idea of reason than by interest and will; consequently, they seek power not to secure freedom but to secure those freedoms that appear to them most likely to promote their interests.[1]

For this purpose, political power is primary. It alone gives universality of control within the state, thereby enabling its holders to maximize the conditions for the pursuit (and presumably the satisfaction) of their interests. It also invests their acts with moral approbation; for when self-interest (and even, perhaps, prejudice) is translated into law, it somehow acquires—in a large sector of the public mind, at least—ethical sanction. One need not himself accept this customary identification of law with right to recognize that law to most men is more than the expression of power; it is sanctioned and therefore legitimate power; it is power that when exercised comes to be regarded as morally right. As a result, political power has an importance that other forms of social power cannot override.

This, however, is not to suggest that nonpolitical power is consequently of little significance. On the contrary, those who command economic or other forms of nongovernmental power are in a position to influence and under special circumstances even to control the operations of political power. And where, as in a democracy, the state accords a considerable degree of freedom to nonpolitical associations, those associations can employ their powers to do directly what they might otherwise require the law to do. In the first case, their efforts—if successful—take the form of laws; and to the extent that these may be oppressive they are the oppressive acts of governments rather than of private powers. It is the second case, therefore, that is of concern here; for when men have power apart from (though not necessarily in conflict with) the power of government, and are free, even within a stipulated or restricted range, to employ it in the furtherance of their interests, they may on occasion use it in such a way as to violate the democratic rights of others. Where they do so, they can be said to have abused their powers. And where, because there is no real alternative, such abuses of power must be borne, there oppression in its worst (because permanently degrading) form resides.

This last point requires a word of comment. Clearly, some individuals and groups are ill disposed toward others and unfairly discriminate against them. In an essentially free society, the latter need not despair, though they may feel aggrieved. They can shrug off this denial of their right to an equal opportunity and look elsewhere—for other employers, other landlords, other universities, and the like. This being so, the discriminatory act (or acts) is oppressive only in the narrowest or most rigorous sense of the word. In the larger perspective it can well be regarded as little more than a slight, for the victims are not bound by it. But sometimes the discriminatory act (or acts) is committed by a private power bloc that has a monopoly or near-monopoly of the places of employment, education, and accommodation, or by individuals and groups acting without premeditated concert but sharing the same attitudes and indulging in the same arbitrary uses of their power. Then a common pattern of controls is imposed that has the same effect as if a single gigantic monopoly had imposed them. In such cases, the discrimination cannot (apart from the exceptional individual who by unusual fortitude or fortune overcomes what is to other men an insuperable set of difficulties) be escaped. It must be lived with. In such cases, not governments but private powers are abusive; and for the individual who is thus degraded the abuse is not the less resented for the knowledge that it comes from private rather than from governmental powers. Indeed, the knowledge that his government sits idly by and seems by its indifference or ineffectual measures to sanction an evident wrong only makes that government, in his eyes, a partner in the crime. Where the government goes beyond this to give encouragement and positive aid to those private powers, where the collusion between governmental and nongovernmental powers is a real and effective one, the individual is subjected to a measure of oppression so severe as to render pretentious any claim by that society that it is a free state.

This interrelationship of governmental and private powers has already been noted in the course of our discussion in Chapter IV. Here, to avoid undue repetition, it might be well to call attention to some of the forms that such arbitrary and iniquitous action has taken, rather than, as in that earlier discussion, to the type of victim abused.

PHYSICAL VIOLENCE

Consider, in these terms, the resort to violence (or to the threat of violence) to deprive men of their elementary rights of speech, of suffrage, of equal opportunity, even of survival. The long and sordid history of the white man's treatment of the American Negro—the kidnapings, whippings, acts of bodily mutilation, and murders—is, of course, a familiar tale. What ought to be remembered, however, is that this treatment is by no means restricted to Negroes in the American South and to the ancient, if not very venerable, past. The white mobs that used violence to keep Negroes from occupying homes in housing developments built for them in Detroit, Michigan, in 1942, and in Chicago, Illinois, in 1953 and 1954, for example, make it clear that racial prejudice and discrimination can take on equally clinical forms elsewhere in this country. And the slaying in 1955 of a Negro minister who in defiance of open threats was the first of his race to register to vote in Humphreys County, Mississippi, and of a fourteen-year-old Negro boy who was alleged to have "whistled at" or "obscenely looked at" a white woman in another county of that same state—

a state which is distinguished for having lynched more mob victims (nearly 600) in the last three-quarters of a century than any of its sister states in the South—indicates that even today the Negro's right to life, in Mississippi at least, is often a matter of white whim or caprice and not of principle.[2]

If it be said that murders and other criminal acts by private powers—whether by individuals or by groups—cannot be prevented but can only be punished, the answer surely is that while this is partly true, it overlooks the fact that with respect to disliked or "inferior" groups that which is formally illegal may be informally the customary and approved pattern of behavior. No one, for example, was arrested for the shotgun slaying of the Negro minister; the two men who were indicted for the murder of the Negro boy were, after a farcical trial, quickly acquitted; the Detroit police aided the white mobs and arrested Negroes; and police and court action in connection with the Chicago rioters was woefully weak.

In Louisville, Kentucky, in 1954, when the home of a young Negro veteran who had moved into a white residential neighborhood was first fired upon and then bombed, the law officers arrested, tried, and secured a conviction against, not those who had thrown the bomb, but the white man who had purchased the house and then deeded it to the Negro. He was found guilty of *sedition* and sentenced to a term of fifteen years at hard labor.[3]

At the University of Alabama in 1956, a lone Negro woman, Miss Autherine Lucy, the first of her race to be admitted as a student to the University,[4] was assaulted by an egg- and rock-throwing mob of one thousand or more white students and townspeople. The police dealt with the situation not by curbing the hoodlums but by removing the Negro woman. The Board of Trustees voted first to suspend, and then (after a court decision ordering that she be readmitted) to expel, not the students responsible for the outrageous assault, but the victim. The state legislature, far from condemning, commended the action of the Board of Trustees. And in what may well go down as a classic example of shocking political collusion, the governor of the state, when appealed to for additional police protection, refused and said: "We are not excited. It is normal for all races not to be overly fond of each other." [5]

And in Columbus, Ohio, in 1948, to move away from the area of racial conflict, a Communist newly resident in the city found that he, his wife, and his children were accosted and threatened, his home was stoned, broken into, and pillaged, and his books were confiscated. When the forces of law and order were asked why, in the light of the Communist's petition to them for protection after he and his family had been threatened, they had not furnished it, the Chief of Police blithely replied: "Columbus is a peace-loving and church-going community, and the city administration is not going to tolerate any Communists." [6]

It is needless to multiply examples. The pages of American history are replete with illustrations of such nongovernmental acts of violence: by white men over Negroes, Indians, and Mexicans; by nativistic groups over immigrants; by employers, or their imported professional strikebreakers and local vigilance groups, over employees; by union racketeers over union members and by union members over strikebreakers, especially when an attempt is made to break the picket line; by "patriotic" groups over political radicals—e.g., anarchists, Socialists, and now primarily Communists; by the members of one religious sect over those of another.[7]

Ugly as all this is, it does not, however, warrant a conclusion that physical violence is a dominant or inescapable feature of the American democracy, or that illegal acts of violence are generally left unpunished. On the contrary, apart, perhaps, from the American South, physical violence is by and large a minor and generally diminishing factor in American life; a Mississippi or Alabama Negro can, presumably, flee to New York City's Harlem or to Chicago's South Side; and law enforcement officers seem, on the whole, to move adequately against individual or mob acts of violence, at least where racial and other minority group conflicts are not involved. What it does show is that under certain conditions, in certain communities, private or nongovernmental powers can with relative impunity resort to physical violence to deny some citizens their basic democratic rights. To the extent, however small, that this is so—and with respect to certain groups it is larger than considerations of human decency can allow—it constitutes a primary abuse of power in a democratic no less than in an oligarchical state.

ECONOMIC SANCTIONS

Violence, being both crude and a little dangerous, is not always the most effective instrument of oppression. Economic sanctions or deprivations that can achieve the same results have the further advantage of being both lawful and, superficially at least, blameless. By some psychological quirk that we cannot pause to examine here, men often think themselves guiltless who do not injure another by themselves perpetrating a crime or by directly wronging him, but who indirectly destroy, or aid in destroying, him either by having an intermediary commit the unsavory act or, what is usually more to their taste, by simply failing to act at all.

I do not refer here to the man who delegates to a subordinate the unpleasant task of informing an employee that he is fired from his job; this may be no more than a manifestation of timidity, rather than of oppression. What I have in mind is the more pointed case of the owners or directors of a corporation who shift responsibility for immoral action to an abstract entity or its agents, thereby depersonalizing the exercise of abusive power and exempting themselves (at least in their own eyes) from responsibility for its unjust deeds. From this standpoint, it is not the owner but the personnel manager (or the director of industrial relations) who refuses to employ or, if employed, to upgrade Negroes and Jews, or who hires guards and imports strikebreakers with a more-than-usual competence in the wielding of clubs and lethal weapons. It is not the university president or the member of the board of trustees but the admissions office which excludes or sets rigid quotas for members of certain minority groups. It is not the stockholder and dividend receiver but management which establishes company towns and maintains a near-feudal system of employee relationships.

And even where it is a particular person who is responsible for refusing a Negro, a Jew, or a Communist a job or an apartment, does this make him culpable for the misery of the injured applicant? Are there not others who can give him what he requires? Surely the distance between one's refusal to do any of these things and the misfortune of the individual or group who cannot obtain them is sufficiently great to absolve the former of a personal sense of guilt.

The answer to this attitude, I would suggest, is that it is wrong. Economic power gives to those who possess it the legal right to withhold from others what they need but cannot by their own means obtain—e.g., access to land and to the means of production. Consequently, the refusal to do something may in a particular instance deprive an individual not simply of an available opportunity but of a necessity. Economic power also enables its possessors to use it in a coercive way to achieve a particular objective. Where this calculated use or nonuse of economic power impairs the democratic rights of citizens—e.g., the rights of speech, of political association, of equal opportunity, and the like—it constitutes an oppressive act.

In these terms, I hold oppressive those economic acts which force (or seek to force) men to cease legitimate political and social action—as in certain Southern states, for example, where some white employers are dismissing Negroes who actively seek enforcement of the desegregation decision, and where white bankers, wholesalers, lending agents, and others are foreclosing mortgages, refusing credit, and boycotting members of the National Association for the Advancement of Colored People and any others who oppose segregation and the so-called Southern way of life.[8] In some labor unions, sometimes by constitutional requirement but more often by tacit agreement or by custom, Communists, Negroes, and some foreign-born workers (particularly those of East European or Oriental origin) are excluded from membership or from acquiring apprenticeship status, or are denied the full benefits of union membership and rights established by collective agreements, particularly with respect to such matters as upgrading and seniority. Businessmen have similarly discriminated against Communists and members of racial and religious minority groups; and of those who have sought to eliminate such discrimination some have seen their employees go on strike protesting the employment of Negro workers or demanding the dismissal of a fellow-worker who had invoked the Fifth Amendment to the American Constitution when refusing to answer questions put to him by a congressional investigating committee.[9]

The dismissal from employment of one who invokes the Fifth Amendment is, by this time, a commonplace in the academic and business world. It is, of course, the application of an economic penalty for what some men consider to be an improper political or moral act, and rests, among other things, on the dubious assumption that the government is incapable of dealing with those who do not do what it legitimately asks them to do, and that it is then the obligation of private powers to reinforce the inadequate hand of the state. But to drive men out of their chosen work for such reasons is not only to convert the employer—whether this be a university, a manufacturing or commercial establishment, a motion picture company, a newspaper, or a press association— into a law enforcement agency; it is also to impose a political requirement for employment that in effect abrogates the employee's lawful freedom to speak or not to speak, and that makes it difficult, if not impossible, for him to find employment—in his own or another field—elsewhere.[10] In this respect, it does far more than merely impair the employee's right to an equal opportunity; it endangers his very ability to survive.

Examples of economic practices that vitiate the democratic rights of citizens can be multiplied endlessly. In almost every aspect of our economic life, members of certain minority groups find that they are either excluded from opportunities afforded to others or are subjected to discriminatory practices that impair their ability to exploit the opportunities that are open to them. In medicine, for example, to take but one of the professions, a Negro is still excluded from most medical schools and admitted to a very few others on a highly restrictive basis; he is denied membership in many state and county medical associations and is not admitted to practice in many of our hospitals. Restrictive covenants are no longer enforceable in a court of law, but they are still written; and one who would sell or rent his home to a Negro or an Oriental or a Jew may find that he can do so only at the risk of losing his job or having his place of business boycotted. A blacklist is currently very effective in keeping alleged "subversives" from being employed, particularly in the entertainment industry.[11] And an overwhelming number of manufacturing and retail establishments throughout the country have long maintained exclusionist or discriminatory practices in relation to the hiring and promoting of members of minority groups—restricting Negroes, for example, to nonskilled or nonprofessional jobs.

These and innumerable other instances suggest that the deprivations of private economic power can be as cruel and as coercive—as despotic, if you will—as those imposed by violence. That some men are deliberately subjected to both, not for rational cause but for their lack of foresight in selecting their parents and the place of their birth, or for their belief not that the Constitution of the United States should be overthrown but that in Mississippi and elsewhere in the South it should be applied, constitutes a defilement of the democratic principle of liberty and of the equalitarian creed.

Violence and economic sanctions do not, of course, exhaust the forms of oppression utilized by private powers. Patterns of social segregation and discrimination also serve to humiliate "undesirable" minority groups and to maintain them in an inferior status. Such patterns are too numerous and varied to permit detailed illustration here—examples range from the simple agreements and practices of real estate boards and operators to exclude members of "undesirable" groups from preferred neighborhoods (a technique that has effectively kept Negroes, for instance, in squalid quarters of the city), to the elaborate and systematized code of etiquette that governs interpersonal relations in the South.

That such patterns and techniques have been immensely successful in their discriminatory effects, no honest observer can deny. And that, along with the use of economic sanctions and the resort to physical violence, they have one crucial point in common—the isolation and subordination of allegedly inferior groups—is all too clear.

There is a nice question of logic here: for if these groups are truly inferior, no denial of equal opportunities is necessary for them convincingly to demonstrate their inferiority; while if equality of opportunity is arbitrarily limited or denied, the suspicion is inevitably raised that in the absence of such a limitation the allegedly inferior groups might come to stand on an equal or superior plane to their oppressors. But in matters of despotism, as in many other things, not logic but a compound of prejudice, interest, and will prevails.

Nevertheless, if a democratic state is necessarily committed to the proposition that equality of opportunity is a right seriously to be pursued and not merely verbally to be affirmed, the denial or limitation of that right by private powers cannot be ignored. It is true that equality of opportunity is not the only value that a democratic state seeks to assure, and that in a particular situation this equality may come into conflict with another value, notably liberty. Both values, as Myrdal and others have noted, are major elements or norms of the American creed; and it would be a happy state indeed that could maximize the enjoyment of both of them. Unfortunately, if equality of opportunity is to be assured, the liberty of the individual to make choices, to discriminate—at least in those areas that affect another man's right to an equal opportunity—may have to be curbed. I do not mean to suggest that these norms are always in conflict with each other; clearly, the freedom of the individual to select his friends or his occupation or his religion or his political party has no necessary—and may not have even an incidental—relation to the right of other individuals to make the same choices and to have the same opportunities. I argue only that where they do come into conflict with one another

—as in the decision of an employer or of a university not to employ or to admit members of certain minority groups—there one must give way.

Whether, in all such cases, the principle of equality must prevail over that of unfettered liberty is no easy question to answer; for here, as in so many matters, the very complexity of social life does not permit easy mathematical reduction. Always there are vast areas in which experience remains the only guide, in which the establishment of broad principles cannot settle concrete problems. But if we bear this very fact in mind, then we see that the opposing claim—that the liberty of voluntary associations (of private governments, if you will) is *always* paramount—is bereft of all meaning. Both principles have a valid claim; neither has an exclusive one. Consequently, there may be certain conditions under which the equalitarian principle may have the greater claim—e.g., the curtailment of segregation and the limitation of the power of an employer to do as he might wish with respect to the hiring and working conditions of his employees.[12] With respect to such things, and because the insistence on equality of opportunity does not adversely affect the *political* liberties of the citizens, the American democracy has in fact abridged the freedom to discriminate.

However, as the evidences cited in this chapter make plain, the abuses of private powers have not all been curbed. In part, this is because some private powers are intrinsically too strong to be controlled by countervailing private powers. But in part, too, it is because democratic governments play an ambivalent role: while they check some oppressive practices, or the oppressive practices of some private powers, they leave others alone; in some cases, in fact, they not only sanction, they encourage and even (at times) cooperate with the wrongdoings of private powers.

For these and other reasons, the problem of the abuse of power (if we may still, in the traditional vein, call it a single problem) remains; and in remaining it stands to plague and to challenge the democratic state.

PART TWO

Democracy and the Control of Power

VII

The Limitations
of the American
Democracy

Traditionally, the democratic reply to the challenge of power has turned on the principle of responsibility: for if a democratic government abuses its powers, the people can, through their suffrage, dismiss that government and replace it with another; while if oppressive acts are committed by private powers, the people can, through that government, restrain or even (in some cases) destroy those powers. But the principle of responsibility is a double-edged sword: it enables a people to remove an oppressive government, but it indicts a people that fails to do so. Consequently, if abuses of power exist in the democratic state, either the people (who ultimately govern in those states) are responsible for those abuses or they are overcome by other powers, in which case the system is not democratic, or not fully so. I shall argue here that both of these alternatives are significantly, if only partially, true of the American democracy.

To begin with, it is a fact that the people do, in considerable measure, control or direct public policy. In part, this is because the framers of the American Constitution, while openly disdainful of the "common" people, did not think it wise to exclude them altogether from political power. But in part, this is also to be accounted for by the development of institutions and practices contrary to the design of the framers. The rise of the national political party and the reforms of what is generally called the

Jacksonian revolution [1] are but the more dramatic of many changes that have taken place in American political life since 1789—changes which have moved the control of public policy materially closer to the will of temporary and shifting majorities.

The rule of the people remains, however, but a partial rule. Madison might fear the "sinister views" of minority factions and say sincerely that "a dependence on the people is, no doubt, the primary control on the government"; but he—and the rest of the framers of the Constitution—was far more impressed by the dangers to a government that is too dependent on them. The excesses of the minority, he thought, would easily be curbed by the power of the majority, exercised through regular vote. But who or what would curb the excesses of the popular will? Who or what would stem "the superior force of an interested and overbearing majority"? Not, surely, enlightened men; for enlightened men would not always be at the helm. Nor, even, a sense of self-restraint; for the fallibility of man's reason, together with his pursuit of self-interest—a pursuit which, Madison believed, would bias judgment and corrupt integrity—would operate to the disregard of the public good. It was necessary, therefore (or so he and the framers insisted), to look to "auxiliary precautions," to establish institutional obstacles—e.g., federalism and the separation of powers—that would effectively limit or prevent the majority from having its way.[2] And it is surely a tribute to American perversity (perhaps to our strength as well as to our political irrationality) that the evolution of American institutions has been such as to extend both the rule, and the curbs—e.g., judicial review—on that rule, of the majority.

As a result, the American political system is characterized by an ambivalence or political schizophrenia in which the majority is both directed to rule and is restrained or prevented from doing so. The principle of responsibility is simultaneously both affirmed and denied.

Now by responsibility I mean here no more than the accountability of the rulers to the ruled. To be real, this accountability must give men the power as well as the right constitutionally *to dismiss,* not merely to approve, their government. This, of course, requires a system of free and periodic elections in which, unanimity being impossible, the choice among opposing candidates or political parties must be determined by the will of the majority; and the majority, it seems hardly necessary to add, is a majority not of all but only of those who happen to express themselves at a particular time.

Thus stated, the principle of responsibility appears to be a simple one. Actually, it is exceedingly complex, all the more so when it is applied (as I mean to apply it here) to the problem of abuses of power. This is not to question the principle of responsibility, or to allege that the American system is, on the whole, an oppressive one. It is rather to argue that the American system—however meritorious it may be on this or on other grounds—does not check *all* capricious and iniquitous acts. It is also to point to certain intrinsic limitations to the principle of responsibility as well as to some limitations that are imposed on it by the specific institutional arrangements—e.g., federalism and the separation of powers—that are allegedly designed to give it effect. Even where the political system approximates a full realization of the principle of responsibility, it may still be used to uphold rather than to remove an oppressive government. Where it is employed, its application in a particular situation may be such as to serve as a restraint on *political* oppressors only, neglecting thereby the oppressive acts of other—but not necessarily lesser—men who exercise power in other fields. Finally, the facts of political life may make it all too clear that, whatever the stipulated lines of political and administrative responsibility may be, in practice only those political despots who occupy the highest rather than the intermediary places of power are likely to be seriously affected by the interventions of the popular will.

Let us consider these several points in turn.

INTRINSIC LIMITATIONS TO RESPONSIBILITY

Consider, first, the inherent or natural limitations of the principle of responsibility. Of these, two at least are of commanding importance. One is a limitation that derives from the fact that responsibility can be applied only to the broad or general ends of public policy, and not to its specific details. The other derives from the fact that responsibility, which in principle resides in the will of the people, is lodged in practice in the will neither of all nor of the citizens nor even of the eligible voters, but at best in the will of a particular and temporary majority.

What does it mean, for example, to say that a people can dismiss a government? Does this imply that they can thereby readily overturn fundamental policies or secure the reversal of a particular measure? If this is its meaning, then only occasionally have the people in fact been able to achieve this result—e.g., in the United States in the election of 1932 and in England in the national election of 1945. In the common run of events this is not likely to be the case. All too often the major political parties are agreed on a specific measure or policy. All too often, and notably so in the American political system, disagreements do not divide but cut across party lines. The result is that the removal of a government carries no necessary assurance that its successor will proceed in a markedly different direction.

Political parties and their candidates do not, after all, save under the most extraordinary circumstances, submit themselves to the electorate on the basis of their positions with respect to any one issue; instead, they seek to be judged on the totality of their actions and views. Consequently, a voter who is asked to choose from among the two or three major possibilities afforded to him by the American (or the British) political system can seldom expect to find a candidate or a party whose opinions are similar to his own in all regards. His choice is necessarily a qualified choice. He prefers Mr. A to Mr. B because *in general* Mr. A is closer to his own views; but he would prefer someone more like himself to the settled-for Mr. A. And if he waxes enthusiastic about Mr. A, it need not follow that he does so because of a fortuitous coincidence of political ideas. In 1952 very few people indeed knew what Mr. Eisenhower's ideas were, as in 1932 hardly anyone, least of all the Democratic candidate for the presidency, had a clear notion of where Mr. Roosevelt was going or how he intended to get there. Yet, in both cases, millions of supporters were supremely confident—as were the candidates themselves—that the unstated or unknown objectives would be achieved.

What elections in a democratic state do, therefore—particularly in the American democracy—is to determine, primarily, *who* shall rule, and only secondarily what shall be done. And with respect to what shall be done, elections do no more than determine the *broad* ends of policy; they do not, as they should not, settle questions of legislative and administrative detail.[3]

The principle of responsibility is limited, secondly, by the fact that in practice democratic governments are not and cannot be held accountable to the will of *all* of the people. Clearly, not all of the people can express themselves; nor, even if they could and were to do so, would they display any unanimity of sentiment. Where conflicts of interest abound, there differences of doctrine and of loyalty follow. Clearly, too, responsibility cannot be lodged in a literal majority of the people, or even in a majority of those who are interested, for in every modern democratic state a considerable portion of the population (interested and otherwise) is excluded from the suffrage on what are alleged to be "reasonable" grounds—e.g., immaturity as measured by chronological age, mental deficiency, lack of citizenship or of a prescribed period of residence in a particular locality, illiteracy, conviction for certain heinous crimes, and so on. A very large proportion of the eligible voters (in local elections it is commonly more than a majority of them) fails through negligence or indifference to exercise its right of suffrage. And in certain parts of the United States, eligible and willing voters who are also members of certain minority groups are often prevented by diverse (and sometimes unlawful) means from doing so. As a result, the majority of those who actually vote in an American election has always been a minority of the total population and generally a minority even of the eligible voters. If, for practical reasons, we insist that such a minority shall in fact be considered a majority, as in some cases we must—e.g., because of the disqualification of, say, minors—we must at the same time recognize that this is a convenient fiction and not the application of an absolute majoritarian principle. This is all the more true where the election turns on a plurality rather than on a majority of the voters; for then the minority which prevails is confronted by an opposition which, *as an opposition,* commands the support of a popular majority.

Moreover, if we assert, as we should, that responsibility in a democratic state must still be sought in the will of the majority rather than in that of the minority—even if this majority be but a majority of the actual voters and thus a minority of the eligible voters or of the body politic—how often shall a government chosen by such a majority be required to submit itself for popular judgment? To say that it ought to be neither too seldom nor too often is a platitude that obscures rather than clarifies the issue. And if it is not every year but every few years, can we maintain that a government that arrives at and acts upon decisions that result in its being turned out of power at the next election had the support of the majority at the time it took those steps?

To these technical difficulties we must add a more general complication—namely, the fact that in a complex political system the structure of political responsibility tends to become so elongated and dispersed, the distance between the citizen and the official or policy he would like to affect tends to become so great, that one can meaningfully speak of responsibility only by glossing over the helplessness of the individual enmeshed by the vast web of political relationships.

These are not the only perplexities that bedevil those who seek to locate responsibility in majority rule, but they are sufficient perhaps to make clear that those who think in terms of a rigid dichotomy between absolute majority rule and some form of minority rule, and who would therefore exclude any third possibility, are guilty of a gross oversimplification.[4] It is conceivable that such a stark choice would confront the citizens of a small and homogeneous community organized into a direct democracy, with the opposing forces (if they exist at all) aligned into two and no more than two camps; but as soon as one moves into a highly diversified society such as America is today, the will of the majority—or, as is so often the case, of a plurality—can no longer directly formulate the rules under which a people are to live. All that the majority can do is to elect a representative government— necessarily comprised of a few—to formulate those rules; and it does not necessarily follow that a majority which selects and thereby approves a government approves too *all* of the rules which that government then proceeds to formulate. It is quite possible, in fact, that the legislative decision, though it reflect the views of a majority of the representatives, will in any one case be opposed to that of the majority of the people; for majorities that are formed for one purpose—e.g., to choose a government—do not, in a diversified society, remain majorities for each of the many different purposes which that government may then seek to carry out. The widespread criticism in England of the Conservative government's action in Suez in October, 1956, is a dramatic illustration of this point; as is too the bitter denunciation by many of those who supported Mr. Eisenhower both in 1952 and 1956 of his failure to carry through his pledged commitments—e.g., to reduce the national budget, to provide significant tax relief, to reduce the "welfare" activities of the national government, and the like.

The majority in a democratic state, consequently, is a shifting rather than a fixed and permanent majority, and its "rule" is limited to the expression of a yea or nay with respect to the general rather than the specific policies of a government. This being so, the idea of majority rule in a democratic state must be understood to mean not rule by the majority in any literal sense, but rule by a government accountable to the majority, which is a quite different thing, especially since the majority is one that is formed only for that particular function, only at that particular time, and only out of that part of the people that then happens to express itself at the polls. It is for this reason that some commentators, while they insist on majority rule, insist even more on what has been called the majority *principle* or *process*—i.e., that process of group competition out of which, through the free exchange and organization of opposing opinions, majorities and minorities are formed and continue to vie for power.[5] But this is a large theme, to which we shall later return.

INSTITUTIONAL LIMITATIONS TO RESPONSIBILITY: ON THE FRAGMENTATION AND DISPERSION OF POWERS IN AMERICA

Whatever intrinsic limitations there may be in the application of the idea of majority rule, a democratic system should at least not interpose any additional obstacles of its own. Yet, what is striking about the American democracy is that, while the people accept (or at least verbally affirm) the principle of self-government, of government by the consent of the governed, they have imposed limitations on themselves which impede its realization; they have devised institutional arrangements which hinder and at times effectively block the translation of public opinion into public policy.[6]

It can, I think, be argued that this insistence on self-limiting institutions reflects an uncritical acceptance of traditional practices rather than a discriminating assessment of contemporary needs, and that where careful scrutiny leads to its approval it is most commonly because such arrangements are deemed to be more conducive to one's interests than is a problematical alternative.[7] But it is enough here simply to note that in this respect Americans are less assured and more suspicious of themselves than other democratic states are of their own peoples; for no other democratic state has made it so difficult for a majority to come to power or, when in power, to rule.

In the British system, for example, the lines of responsibility are relatively simple and clear. It is true that the persistence of "rotten boroughs" and the election of parliamentary members from single-member districts by pluralities rather than (in some cases) by majorities make it possible for a political party with a minority of the national electoral vote to secure a majority of the parliamentary vote (as in 1951). But more commonly a popular majority determines the legislative majority, which in turn selects the executive. A committed and well-disciplined political party assures the executive of continuing legislative support and the legislature of viable cabinet responsibility. And while there is an aristocratic second chamber, it lacks the power—with but mild exceptions—to stay the government's hand; nor is there a co-ordinate or superior power such as the American judiciary to prevent the government from having its way.

In contrast, the American political system seems almost cha-otically to blur the lines of responsibility. Elections are regularly held to discover the will of the people, which (presumably) is then to be translated into the law of the land. But Americans have shown themselves to be marvelously adept at manipulating voting districts in such a way as to give disproportionate representation to minorities and thereby to distort what is still (if euphemistically) called the will of the people. As a result—even if we set aside the notorious county-unit system of Georgia—rural groups, though a minority, dominate urban and industrial majorities in the heav-ily populated states, e.g., New York, Illinois, Ohio, Pennsylvania, and Michigan. And everywhere—save for a thinly populated state like Nevada which comprises but a single congressional district— the lines are drawn so as to give preferred minorities an undue share of the national legislative power. In the American Senate, perhaps the worst "rotten borough" system in the democratic world, the disproportions are so extreme that one voter in Nevada exercises as much legislative power as some ninety voters in New York, and a bloc of Southern Senators holds a degree of power totally incommensurate with the number of constituents those Senators are supposed to represent.[8]

Gerrymandering, however, is only one of many efforts to con-ceal rather than to discover the popular will. This is further and no less effectively achieved by a system of staggered national elec-tions, in which different majorities speaking at different times elect those who at a particular moment control the bicameral legislature and the presidency. Now if the purpose of an election is to convert a popular majority into a legal or controlling majority— and if this is not its purpose it can hardly pretend to be the instrument of a democratic state—in what sense can we speak of responsibility when we fulfill this purpose in so far as the lower chamber is concerned but deny it with respect to the upper chamber by limiting the number of Senatorial seats at issue at that same election to only one-third of the membership? Under such circumstances, the majority (if it is a majority) that gives control of the lower chamber to a particular political party may be a different majority from that which judges one-third of the Senatorial candidates, different again from the majority which two years before may have put the leader of the opposing party into the White House, and different yet again from the majorities which determined the composition of the Senate at two previous elections. It is not at all uncommon for the party which controls the House of Representatives to find itself confronted by a Senate in control of the opposing party, or for the party that controls both branches of the legislature to find that the presidency is in antagonistic hands. Should those who control the executive and legislative branches of the government be men of the same political *identification,* it does not necessarily follow that they share the same political *persuasion;* for the lack of party discipline permits legislators even on crucial issues to cross party lines. And even if there should be sufficient party consensus or legislative-executive rapport to produce agreement on a particular measure, there is still the ever-present possibility that a hostile judiciary will hold that measure unconstitutional.

Who, then, represents the majority will—the Democratic President or the Republican Congress in 1947–48? the Republican President or the Democratic Congress in 1955–56? the Democratic President and Congress or the Supreme Court in 1933–37? Which majority is it that controls, or ought to control, the government in such cases? And if the answer is not readily forthcoming, as it assuredly is not, wherein lies the principle of responsibility?

The problem is further complicated when to these obstacles to majority rule we add other limiting (and in operative effect essentially undemocratic) devices. There is, for example, the rule of seniority in the American Congress, which not infrequently gives the chairmanship of a powerful legislative committee to one who, because he comes from a stable political district and therefore one that does not necessarily reflect the changing tides of public opinion, may be opposed in all major respects to the majority of his own party. There is the filibuster, which in the American Senate enables a determined minority to block majority action, and which has, in recent years, been the most effective weapon of Southern Senators determined to block Federal legislation designed to further the civil rights of Negroes. There is the electoral college, which by a peculiar and nonrepresentative method of computing votes makes it possible for a man to be elected to the American presidency not only when he has but a plurality of the national popular vote, but even when his leading opponent may have an actual majority of that vote.[9] There are the cumbersome provisions for amending the Constitution, which enable a minority, provided it can secure the support of one-third of the members plus one in either chamber of the Congress or the support of a majority in one-fourth of the states plus one, to prevent any change in the formal document itself.

These and other impediments to majority rule make it plain that, whatever the principle of responsibility may logically be held to imply, in the American system it does not imply that the government shall be responsible in any thoroughgoing sense to a determinate majority. It does not imply that the majority shall have its way. It does not even imply that there shall be a serious quest for the elicitation of majority will. What it does imply is a distrust of majority rule and of the principle of political responsibility in so far as this is attached to the idea of majority rule. It does imply that however we explain, or to whatever source we impute, the persistence of oppressive power in the democratic state, we cannot legitimately attribute responsibility for that oppression simply to majority rule; for in the sense that I have defined the term here, the majority neither "rules" nor completely controls the government that rules in its name.

Nor, given the American institutionalization of the idea that tyranny is best prevented by the fragmentation and dispersion of political powers, could this be otherwise. Federalism, which is a theory of political organization that divides powers between two governments, both operating over the same individuals in a given territory, though commonly with respect to different things, is preeminently designed, as Dicey noted, for a people that desires union but not unity.[10] The constituent states want still to be *states,* even though their sovereignty (if I may employ that much-abused word here) is now but a partial one. They value their individuality. They give but a qualified allegiance to the greater community. Consequently, if the union is not to be endangered or disrupted by internal conflicts, it is ordinarily the mark of wisdom for the greater power to abstain from coercing the constituent states on matters concerning which the latter feel deeply and uncompromisingly.[11]

This, however, is a relevant argument only where the constituent states represent fairly homogeneous sets of interests motivating the great bulk of their populations. Under such conditions, a conflict of values between a constituent state and the national government would involve distinct sets of interests clearly opposed and embodied in their respective political units: the constituent state would represent one set of interests, the national state, another. But if, as is quite generally the case, there are divisions or conflicts within the constituent state no less strong or important than those that apply in the first relationship, the insistence on the higher claim of the constituent state serves only to promote the special interests of the group that happens to control the government of the constituent state. To sacrifice a real political or economic or social interest of an important (albeit a minority) section of that state's population for a fictional geographic interest is then not necessarily a sign of wisdom; it may be no more than a surrender to expediency. Where the issue at stake is more than a matter of conflicting interests, where it involves basic democratic rights, such a surrender (or the argument for such a surrender) attacks the very principles of the federation itself. For it is these democratic rights, constitutionally guaranteed to *all* citizens—of state and nation alike—that are the meaning of the federation. Without them, the federation would have no legitimate claim to the loyalty of its citizens. Without them, the federation's very survival would be perpetually in question; for it would then rest on the most shallow of all possible grounds of allegiance—the passing whims and conveniences of its members.

Consider, in these terms, the dramatic conflict that today seems to pit nation against state in terms reminiscent of that great conflict a century ago. I refer to the problem of desegregation in education and, ultimately, in all phases of civil life in the American South. The Southern states, whatever their pretense to the contrary, are not internally united. They are themselves dual communities—divided at the very least into separate societies of Negro and of white citizens. For the national government to abstain from coercing the governments of those states is to permit those governments, now in the exclusive (and in some cases oligarchical) control of the whites, to continue to coerce their Negro citizens. For the national government to compel the Southern states to cease this unlawful oppression is to coerce their governments, and perhaps the bulk of their white citizens, in turn. But if coercion—whether by political, economic, or moral means—is thus an inescapable factor in the resolution of the conflict, the question is no longer one of coercion or no coercion; it is, instead, a question of who is to be coerced—the white or the Negro citizens?

Here the principle of federalism is no real guide. On the contrary, it confuses the issue by producing two majority wills; and it distorts the meaning of democracy by seeming to insist that the majority will of the smaller or constituent state shall prevail over the majority will of the larger or national state, even though the national majority will includes the will of the minority within that constituent state. Clearly, if all our citizens are equal in their political rights, this is an intolerable solution. And if not equality but the dignity of the individual or the fulfillment of personality, say, is the key value at stake, the argument still flounders; for the personalities of our white citizens have no greater claim to fulfillment than do the personalities of our Negro citizens. But it is surely enough to do no more than adhere to the principle of democracy itself to recognize that we cannot properly approve the majority process as it operates at the level of a constituent state and disapprove it as it operates at the level of a federal state.[12]

In any case, federalism, whatever its other merits or difficulties, serves here only to undermine the principle of political responsibility.

Similar considerations are raised by the American application of the separation of powers doctrine, by which I mean not the division of powers between governments but the distribution of powers among the various branches of a particular government, most commonly among the legislative, executive, judicial, and (some would contend) the administrative branches.

It would seem unnecessary to inquire here into the origins of the separation of powers doctrine—to ask, for example, whether Montesquieu was in fact the primary source from which the framers of the Constitution had derived this idea,[13] or whether Montesquieu had correctly read the British practice from which he purportedly adapted his formulation of the doctrine [14]—for what is important in this context is only its relevance, or more accurately its irrelevance, to the principle of responsibility. I say irrelevance because, while the idea of responsibility requires, at the very minimum, a political mechanism that will effectively translate public opinion into public policy, the separation of powers doctrine requires, and in American practice has achieved, a political mechanism designed to obstruct if not to deny that purpose. Whatever the intent, this is the ineluctable meaning of such institutions as bicameralism and judicial review.

I referred earlier, if briefly, to the incoherency of the bicameral idea in a democracy. Here it is necessary to add a word or two more, for of all political notions few are so plainly at odds with the principle of democracy and few rest on so many erroneous assumptions. Bicameralism assumes, for example, that a nation consists as much of artificial geographical units as it does of persons; but in giving equal representation to such units it gives disproportionate representation to the persons within those units; thus, equality of representation to states means inequality of representation to citizens. Bicameralism assumes, again, that there are but two interests to be represented—place and person; but why should we not give representation to function or occupation, say, instead of, or in addition to, geography? Why not a tricameral rather than a bicameral system, and so on *ad absurdum?* Bicameralism assumes, too, that if the voice of a single chamber is the voice of evil, the voice of a second chamber will set it aright. But the second chamber may agree with the first, in which case the mischievous act represents a collusive enterprise. If, on the other hand, the second chamber disagrees with and successfully checks the first, it may well be a triumph of error over wisdom rather than the reverse. Long ago the Abbé Sieyès wisely observed that if the second chamber agrees with the first, it is superfluous; while if it disagrees, it is obnoxious. For these and other reasons, notably the inaction produced by deadlock and producing in turn a vacuum of political power (of which I shall say more in a moment), bicameralism ill accords with the principle of democracy.

Nor is judicial review any the more acceptable; for, whatever the immediate policies of the Supreme Court, it is intrinsically an undemocratic institution. The judges are not chosen by the people, nor are they removable by them; yet the judges make law as if they constituted a legislative body or sat as a continuing constitutional convention. The fiction that judges simply apply and at most interpret but do not make the law is one of those myths that, though repeatedly exposed, tenaciously dwell among the unburied dead. Clearly, the Court makes law through negative action, determining by its invalidation of statutes the contours or limits within which public policy shall flow. It makes law through positive action, so interpreting statutes, and even constitutional amendments, as to effect significant changes in them. And it makes law even through inaction, rendering its own judgment, in effect, when it refuses to review a case and thereby affirms the ruling of a lower court—a practice that has the additional advantage of avoiding the issuance of a perhaps controversial opinion. In all these cases the Supreme Court is determining, or sharing in the determination of, public policy; yet it is a court neither representative of, nor responsible to, the people over whom that policy is to operate. That the translation of public opinion into law should thus be subjected to the review, and on occasion the veto, of a judicial aristocracy is surely one of the great anachronisms of a supposedly democratic society.[15]

I have dwelt, though briefly, on bicameralism and judicial review because they bring into sharp focus the conflict between the separation of powers doctrine (at least as it is institutionalized in the American system) and the principle of political responsibility. The latter seeks to control power by holding the rulers accountable to the ruled; the former seeks to control power by fragmenting it and then pitting one power unit against another. This has the inestimable advantage of curbing, or making it possible to curb, the mischief that might otherwise be committed by, say, a corrupt and despotic power. It also helps to prevent that noxious concentration of powers that renders freedom uncertain, because so completely dependent on the whim of one who is at once prosecutor, judge, jury, and jailer—all in relation to "laws" that he himself has enunciated and can arbitrarily change. Without a tranquillity of mind that comes to a man from the certainty of his safety—a tranquillity that none can possess when those who hold power can abuse it with impunity—freedom is a precarious and perhaps meaningless thing. In this respect, and to the degree that it does in fact lessen or remove the fear of oppression that always besets men when confronted by the wielders of power, the separation—and more importantly the general fragmentation and dispersion—of powers is not only a desirable but a necessary precondition of freedom.[16]

Unfortunately, the separation of powers doctrine also introduces other mischiefs of its own. For it is by no means clear that power conferred in one place is an adequate check on power exercised elsewhere. If the powers agree, such a check does not enter; if they disagree, the greater power will have its way. This is readily evident where the powers are unequal, but it is no less true where the powers are formally or seemingly equal. For if they are equal in fact, deadlock results; and power, far from checking power, simply checks a new or particular power that is attempting to deal with an already existing (perhaps nonpolitical) power. The checking power, that is to say, maintains or creates a void in which an old or different power remains or becomes dominant. Thus, if the American Congress (assuming unity of action from the bicameral legislature) sought to check the abuses of a business corporation or of a labor union or of a religious power group but was restrained from doing so by the check of the executive, the power vacuum created by the inaction of political power would be filled by the nonpolitical (i.e., the economic or religious) power group. And where that nonpolitical power group acted despotically, the separation of powers doctrine would have the result not of controlling power (and thus securing the endangered liberty) but of fettering political power so as to leave other (nonpolitical) power groups free to destroy that liberty.

It is not enough, consequently, to think in terms of the dispersion of legal or political powers alone, for political power cannot—in a democratic system at least—exhaust the vast areas of social action. Always there are those who would invade the rights of others, and political power, no matter how potent, is never the only way by which that can be done. Political power remains, however, a primary means of curbing that transgression, whether that transgression is the work of private or of lesser political powers. Hence, to restrain the uses of political power by an involved system of checks and balances may, in a particular instance, prevent rather than further the control of a particular oppressive act.[17]

When, therefore, James Madison—and the considerable number who share his views even today [18]—looks to majority rule to

restrain the tyranny of the minority, but then, through the fragmentation and dispersion of powers, sets limits on and obstacles to
such rule, he in effect defeats the very purpose he set out to achieve.
For if the majority does not rule, we have once again to fear the
tyranny of the minority. Or if the majority can rule in some things
but not in others, we have still to fear the tyranny of the majority
in those things where it is presumably free to have its way. Or if
the majority which checks the minority is itself checked by the
minority in turn, the inaction that ensues is inaction only in the
political sphere; nonpolitical powers are then free to wend their
devious and sometimes despotic ways.

As a result, the fragmentation and separation of powers may
check some abuses (or potential abuses) of power—e.g., of an
arbitrary and otherwise unrestrained executive. But in doing so it
introduces other oppressive possibilities—e.g., abuses of power by
the Supreme Court. And in doing so it generally impedes, even at
times curtails, the translation of public opinion into public policy. It militates against the idea of majority rule. It circumvents,
where it does not effectively deny, the principle of political responsibility.

RESPONSIBILITY AS A SOURCE OF OPPRESSION

It would be a grave error to infer from this that if only the
majority did rule, or if only the majority were in fact able to hold
accountable the government that rules, abuses of power would be
unknown in the democratic state. For one thing, it does not follow
from the circumstance that the majority is not assured that it will
always have its way, that the American system does in fact always
prevent it from having its way. Franklin Roosevelt did not have
his way in *all* things in the early years of the New Deal, but he did
secure *some* things; and with the collapse of the Supreme Court as
a resisting force in his second term, he was able to achieve a number of additional purposes. And surely it cannot be denied that
his was a government selected and supported by a majority of the
people.

Secondly, there is no reason to believe that majorities are less driven by prejudice and considerations of private interest than are minorities, or that they will be more solicitous of their opponent's fundamental rights. It is not, after all, a minority that has discriminated against the Negro, that has oppressed the American Indian, that has undertaken to wipe out the constitutional rights of political nonconformists such as the Communists. Nor are they minorities that, within their states, sent as their elected representatives to Congress such men as Senators McCarran and McCarthy. It is all very well to say, as some writers do, that when a majority acts this way it acts contrary to its real or true interest. But in this respect, as Mill rightly observed, majorities are surely no better or worse than oligarchs and kings; they determine their conduct not by what their interest is but by what they suppose it to be.[19] It is not necessary here to insist that this cannot be otherwise, that men habitually—if not always—pursue their immediate and apparent interest rather than their real and ultimate interest, or, more accurately, than what others conceive their real and ultimate interest to be. It is sufficient in this context merely to note that majorities, like minorities, can and on occasion do uphold (and even, at times, applaud) the iniquitous acts of their rulers.[20]

It is true that a strong sense of tradition, an abiding respect for the common ways, will frequently serve to deter such oppressive action. Men are not, ordinarily, quick to defy, or to sanction the acts of others who defy, the approved values, the fundamental precepts of the common code. They respect the established modes of behavior; they insist on a proper observance of "right" procedures, even, one must add, when the purposes for which those forms are utilized are in seeming incompatibility with the traditional goals. This, surely, is what Tocqueville had in mind when he insisted both on the necessity of forms and on the force of tradition if the excesses of democratic power were to be curbed.[21]

But whatever may have been the impact of these and other factors as a mitigating force, they have clearly not eliminated abuses of power from American life. The reasons for this are undoubtedly many and complex, but central among them are surely the multiplicity and instability of traditions in America. Where there is a great diversity of groups, there is not one but a multiplicity of traditions, some of which stand in direct opposition to others. Thus, a tradition that teaches one to respect and to treat decently (i.e., equally) all men, without regard to race or religious affiliation, is countered by a tradition that teaches one to regard some men as intrinsically inferior to others and to treat them not equally but each according to his kind. And where there is great social and occupational mobility, so that men born into one group will in the course of their lives generally pass through and into others, the sentiments that bind them to one another and that guide their conduct tend to be those of the particular group to which they momentarily adhere, and not simply those of the larger community to which they are also attached. There is still, of course, this sense of the greater community, but it is no longer deep and firmly rooted. The qualities of friendship, of shared experiences, of a commitment to common values, are dissipated in all too great a measure by the vast size and complexity of America, by the lost ties of neighborhood and of community.[22] In their place, or at best alongside them, we find the loyalties attendant on insulated group memberships and the antagonisms that beset competitive group relations. To derive from this complex of conflicting and changing traditions the notion that *tradition* will serve to check abuses of power is to fly in the face of all logic as well, indeed, as of American history.

I return, therefore, to the real if uncomfortable fact that the principle of responsibility, even when accompanied by a substantial measure of majority rule, is no necessary curb on despotic men.

THE LIMITATIONS OF "POLITICAL" RESPONSIBILITY

The principle of responsibility is limited, further, by the fact that its application in a democratic state is restricted, on the whole, to *political* officials, and to the oppressive acts that those officials might, through the offices they control, themselves commit. Unless, therefore, those political officials undertake to curb the oppressive acts of men in other realms of power, or the principle of responsibility is itself used to govern the internal affairs of nongovernmental organizations, the idea of holding rulers accountable to the ruled is of no consequence in what are deemed to be nonpolitical fields.

Now the term "political" is, to be sure, an imprecise one, and I do not mean to narrow it unduly here. Clearly, it includes those civil officials elected by the people, as well as those who are in turn appointed by them. Customarily, it does not (in the American democracy at least) embrace those who exercise power from a focus other than the state, who function in what we normally consider a religious, educational, or economic association. As a result, the descendants of Henry Ford, of Du Pont, of Rockefeller, and the like, assume and exercise control over vast economic empires not by virtue of popular elections (let alone merit) but by hereditary right, by the perquisites of a modified dynastic tradition; and there is no principle of responsibility by which they can be removed at the displeasure of those over whom their power is exercised. Consequently, if they—or others in like positions— were so to use their power as to abrogate the democratic rights of their employees or of other individuals affected by them (say with respect to freedom of political association or equality of opportunity), the purpose for which political power is rendered responsible could be achieved only by the countervailing force of another power—perhaps a labor union, perhaps the government.

If it is a labor union or some other private association, there is no assurance that its power will prevail over that of the oppressor; or that, if it does prevail, it will not be oppressive in turn. It is true that some private associations—e.g., some labor unions, consumer cooperatives, and a very few churches—utilize democratic procedures to hold power within their own organizations responsible; but in the broad sweep of American life these are so atypical as to constitute not even a feeble promise that the abuses of private powers will thereby be controlled. And there are always, of course, technical considerations that militate against the wholesale application of the principle of responsibility in nonpolitical realms. Even those who, like Harold Laski, argue most vigorously for "economic democracy" do not really mean that they want plant managers and specialists of various kinds to be chosen by popular vote of the workers or of the consumers, who are themselves to be organized for this purpose into opposing political ("economic"?) parties.[23] Nor do those followers of John Dewey who speak of "educational democracy" mean to suggest that students should decide by ballot who are to be the professors, what the courses, and what the nature of a curriculum or a degree. Clearly, neither the idea of countervailing power nor the idea of internal democracy (at least as it has thus far been applied in America) has proved sufficient to foreclose the abuses of private powers.

If we turn to the government, its power is all too likely to prevail, but only at the cost of increasing the extent and degree of power in the hands of political officials. To increase a grant of power is not necessarily to abandon it, or even, in a particular situation, to make its control more difficult. On the contrary, in any given situation this may be the indispensable and thoroughly safe means to correct an evident injustice. But it does carry with it certain dangers that always attend an *undue* concentration of power, and it does not escape the limitations we have already noted with respect to the principle of responsibility in the American democracy.

Hence, so far as the control of power is concerned, this much in any case is clear: the principle of "political" responsibility—or the limitation of the principle of responsibility to political government—does not (in the American democracy at any rate) adequately curb the abuses of nongovernmental powers.

BUREAUCRACY AND THE LIMITATIONS OF RESPONSIBILITY

We come, finally, to the last of our limitations on the principle of responsibility, a limitation that turns on the fact that even within the political sphere there are lesser officials—i.e., those who occupy what might be termed the intermediary offices of political power—who are not, and who cannot without excessive difficulty be, effectively controlled.

In the broad sense, of course, administrative officials—whether in independent regulatory commissions or in executive agencies (or, *mutatis mutandis,* in private organizations)—lack the power of ultimate decision. They may initiate and influence the enactment of legislative measures, but they cannot by themselves turn their proposals into law. They may interpret the laws they are to administer, sometimes in such a way as substantially to modify them; they may even enact subsidiary regulations that have the full effect and force of law; but their acts and their interpretations remain subject to legislative and executive, not to speak of judicial, review. In a real sense, too, the bureaucracy, by virtue of its fears of legislative investigation and budgetary curtailment, no less than by its own innate pride and its allegiance to the values of the larger community, cannot always be said to be unresponsive to the popular will.[24] For these and other reasons, it would be misleading to suggest that administrative officials are wholly or even largely exempt from responsible controls.

Nevertheless, there is a sense in which the remoteness of the bureaucracy—or of certain portions of the bureaucracy—from both the indicated superior officers and from the public that is affected by it is in some cases such as effectively to remove it from ready direction and control. This is especially true where the bureaucratic unit—which seeks not simply to achieve the ostensible purpose for which it was created, but also to increase the power and prestige of its officials—successfully surrounds itself with an aura of secrecy, so that few know or can feel competent to judge what that particular unit does.

It is a first fact of politics, after all, that whatever the administrative charts may show concerning the hierarchical or pyramidical structures of power, the lines of responsibility are informally rather than formally determined.[25] In some cases, indeed, they are so convoluted and successfully hidden as to make it almost impossible for the outsider to discover whether they exist at all. Consequently, for a president or a cabinet minister, for example, merely to enunciate a policy is sometimes a most ineffectual thing. His subordinates, if they disagree with it, may sabotage it. If they are carrying on an activity in a manner disapproved of by that superior, his official instructions to them to cease such activity may meet with verbal acquiescence but actual neglect. And where bureau chiefs, division heads, and members of regulatory commissions find that they are largely ignored, or that they are not being held strictly to account, they often tend to go off in directions of their own choosing, or, what is sometimes worse, not to move at all.

If we add to this familiar fact of indifference or sabotage, the destructive impact of secrecy, we can see that the principle of responsibility is not always realized. The problem of secrecy is, of course, an old problem, bedeviling democratically elected ministers and absolute monarchs alike; for rulers—at all levels and in almost all areas of activity—have ever been (in some measure at least) the prisoners of their administrators. Those who hold the power of ultimate decision are not infrequently embarrassed by the fact that they stand, or believe that they stand, as dilettantes before the awesome knowledge of their experts. Those experts, in turn, not only cultivate the myth of their own expertise but, through a natural reluctance to admit to error, seek (as Max Weber said) to increase their superiority by keeping their knowledge and their intentions a mystery.[26] As a result, the petty tyrannies (not to speak of the many errors) of bureaucratic officials who operate in and control the vast intermediary levels of policy making are sometimes hidden from the eyes of those who might otherwise proceed to correct them.

In effect, then, the bureaucracy can and at times does act independently of, even in opposition to, the popular will. And to the degree that it does so, it limits or defeats the principle of political responsibility.

Consequently, whether we identify the principle of responsibility with absolute majority rule or with a majority system that provides for some form of qualified majority rule, the problem of oppression remains. There are some abuses of power that, by the very nature of things, the principle of responsibility cannot by itself render easily amenable to control. But there are others that, by the institutional arrangements of the American political system, or by the willing acquiescence of the governed, we do not —and perhaps do not want to—control. There are some respects in which majorities cannot, in any absolute sense of the term, be formed. But there are others in which, by contrived and customary means, we keep majorities from being formed.

Thus, the idea of responsibility, which is by all odds the central principle of democracy, is in some measure corrupted. The people do not rule, at least not in the sense that a simple majority can have its way and not in the sense that the lines of political and administrative responsibility are unimpeded and readily susceptible to popular control. To the extent that they may be said to rule, to the extent that a majority (or a qualified majority) can be said to have succeeded in translating its will into law, the people have not always ruled democratically; they have sometimes upheld rather than dismissed the despots who acted in their name.

As a result, we are confronted by a tragic dilemma. If the people are indeed responsible for abuses of power by governments and by private powers in a democratic state, the institutional arrangements that limit or impede popular (or majority) rule may help to curtail those abuses. But if such institutions are established, the people (or the majority of the people) no longer rule, in which case it is hard to see what claim the state has to being called democratic. We cannot logically have it both ways. We cannot insist both on majority rule and on impediments that limit or prevent the majority from ruling. If majority rule, if democracy, endangers liberty by giving free rein to the forces of popular despotism, does it follow that some form of minority rule will not produce oppressive measures in turn? Clearly, such limitations on majority rule as the American system has already produced have not staved off all the abuses of political and of private powers.

This is not, however, to say that those limitations have staved off none of them. It is quite possible to argue that in the absence of legislative and judicial checks, the executive in America might have proved—in some cases at least—to be no less oppressive than an absolute monarch, and that in certain instances it was only a judicial veto that prevented the despotic impulse of a Congress and a President (when acting in concert) from becoming law. But in guarding against such abuses of power, or the possibility of such abuses of power, the American system has introduced other abuses, or the possibility of other abuses, of its own. The history of the Supreme Court with respect to social legislation—to take only the period from the Civil War to the time of Franklin Roosevelt— is, after all, a dismal record of sanctioned abuses of power; [27] and it is the federal system that has enabled some states to deny to certain of its citizens elementary civil rights.

The dilemma, then, reasserts itself. If the majority rules, there is a real danger that it may rule oppressively. If, to remove that danger, we prevent the majority from ruling, we abrogate the principle of democracy and thereby impose a system of oppression that derives from a government based not on the consent of the governed but on that of a minority. However we resolve this dilemma in our own minds, the fact is that the American democracy has failed to resolve it. The American system attempts to combine both principles, which is logically and (in the strict sense of the term) factually impossible. Consequently, what the American system does is to espouse both but to practice neither. It vests a measure of responsibility in the people, not because the people are held to be infallible, but because there is, in democratic terms, no suitable alternative. But it also vests an effective power of restraint in variously formed minorities; it accepts, even if ambivalently, the principle of minority checks on majority rule. This, whatever else it may be called, is not the principle of responsibility. Nor has it eliminated the danger or the reality of abuses of power.

VIII

The Futility of
Withdrawal

"In a country with an oppressive government," John Dewey once wrote, "everyone is either hammer or anvil." [1] Since few can be the former and none would be the latter, some have sought an escape from the dilemma through withdrawal.

It is easy to show, however, that withdrawal is not a solution to the problem of oppression but merely what the word itself implies—namely, an escape from it; for while it is conceivable that any one person or group may, through flight or selective abstention, attain physical release from, or an inner peace that is indifferent to, even tyrannical action, such an achievement does not affect the principles of democracy that are here at stake. And it is these principles, not the forms of subjective action through which a very few individuals might hope to escape, that constitute our focus of interest. I do not, of course, deny the advisability of withdrawal for an individual or group in a given situation. I argue only that such withdrawal, as a matter of general policy, neglects or negates democratic principles. This can easily be shown if we consider the consequences of such efforts at individual or group withdrawal from oppressive situations, whether on a total or selective basis.

Take, first, the physical withdrawal of the individual (or group) from the hand that oppresses him. For a T. S. Eliot or a Santayana or a Gerhart Eisler, who flees from what he conceives to be the oppressions of a democratic state in order to live amidst the aristocratic vestiges of England, Spain, and Italy, or in the assumed benefits of a Communist-controlled East Germany, such an act of withdrawal may well appear to be a flight to freedom; as indeed it was (at least temporarily) for the Mormons who migrated to Salt Lake City and (somewhat more permanently) for the hundreds of thousands of immigrants who came, and who continue to come, to the United States in order to escape the barbarisms of despotic oligarchical governments in Europe. But the removal of some men from an oppressive situation does not necessarily ameliorate the conditions of those who remain behind, though it may, of course, under certain circumstances do so; nor does it put the refugees themselves beyond the control—and the possible oppressive measures—of their new governments.

Or again, if we consider the American Negro, who remains after a near-century of legal freedom the most obvious and, in view of the very considerable number of Negro political refugees in the United States today, the most serious contemporary illustration of the problem, we find that this conclusion is more than amply sustained. For the Negro who flees from a Southern state to a Northern city may find, in the first instance, that he has simply transferred his problem to his new environment. Chicago, New York, and like cities are indeed havens of refuge in comparison to numerous Southern communities, but they are not devoid of their own iniquities; and the Negro who escapes to them may find himself subjected to political and private acts of discrimination that, while infinitely more tolerable than the discriminatory acts he had previously experienced, are not altogether compatible with the larger principle of equality to which a democratic state is necessarily committed. It is altogether probable, in fact, that a sudden influx of Negroes into already congested areas may reproduce in the new environment attitudes of hostility and practices of discrimination no less oppressive than those which they experienced in the South.

Let us grant, however, that his escape is a successful one—either because he now lives under a lesser form of oppression or under no oppressive system at all.[2] Still, the crucial dimensions of the problem remain. What is more, they might in fact be worsened. For, by depleting the Negroes who remain in the

South of their numerical strength and thus impairing their political (and perhaps economic) capacity to resist, those who flee may in effect help governmental and private powers in that region to perpetuate their oppressive rule.

I return, therefore, to the proposition that individual or group withdrawal—in the sense that I have employed the term here—is no solution to the problem of abuses of power in the democratic state. It focuses on persons, not on principles; and by neglecting the latter it renders all the more difficult the correction by democratic means of abuses with respect to the former.

The difficulties attendant on individual or group withdrawal are no less serious when applied to that extreme form of concerted withdrawal that we call secession. It is true that in a given situation a particular group may, by separating itself from an established state, escape what it conceives to be the oppressive measures of the latter and achieve a greater degree of freedom. This was dramatically illustrated by the secession of Roger Williams and his followers from the Puritan theocracy of Massachusetts Bay and by the secession of the American colonies from England. But as the abortive effort of the Southern states to secede from the Union a century ago made clear, the line between secession and rebellion is a thin one, and is drawn only by the victor. It is not, therefore, always a practical thing. Under modern conditions, in fact, it is (in America at least) well-nigh inconceivable.

But even if secession were a real alternative—and I set aside here the disastrous economic consequences of such a step—it would be no solution to our problem. The seceding state, after all, would at best escape the oppressive acts of the larger state; it would not correct or mitigate that oppression. Moreover, in the specific situation in which we now find ourselves, it is only the Southern states that might contemplate such an act of secession. Were they successful, they would escape not oppression but checks on their own oppressive acts; and this would render the argument for secession absurd.

What is true of seceding states is true also of seceding groups;

for mass withdrawal, far from attacking the abhorred system, serves it instead as a sort of safety valve. By permitting troublemakers and other dissatisfied persons to leave, the oppressive power is often able to achieve another lease on life. Mass withdrawal may thus help to perpetuate rather than to change an existing abuse of power.

There is, finally, a form of withdrawal that is selective in character. A person withdraws, but only from some things.[3] He refuses, for example, because he is a "good" man and regards politics as a vulgar and degrading business and political "bosses" as despots, to participate actively in the conduct of public affairs. Or, because he is a Negro living in certain areas of the South, he stays away from the ballot box lest, by that action, he expose himself to physical violence and even death. Or, because he believes that there is no possibility of checking a particular form of oppression, he yields it an outward or seeming obedience, but subjectively he retains his serenity, he achieves an inner peace of mind. He distinguishes what Simmel, for example, has called the objective and subjective life-elements; he separates his personality from his work, or from the tyrannical situation in which he finds himself. He is thus able to subordinate himself without suffering internally depressing and degrading consequences. He can, Simmel suggests, "actually tolerate a treatment which, if it really concerned his ego and feeling of honor, would move him to the most desperate reactions." [4] Through these and other means of selective abstention the individual withdraws (or seeks to withdraw) from the abuses of power.

To the extent that this achieves the desired results, to the extent that the individual can in fact remain indifferent to a particular abuse of power or system of oppression, the consequences of selective withdrawal are substantially the same as those we have noted with respect to total individual withdrawal and to mass migration. Since, apart from the most extreme forms of totalitarianism, what is demanded is not one's agreement but his acquiescence, an abstention from or outward surrender to a system or particular act of abusive power is normally sufficient to leave that power undisturbed. The individual may feel unaffected, but so does the power that oppresses him. His action (or inaction), therefore, does not weaken or endanger the oppressive government; on the contrary, it but helps to maintain it.

It is questionable, however, whether selective withdrawal can be said to work. Take, for example, the "good" man who refuses to participate in politics. He does not, strictly speaking, withdraw from oppression; he withdraws only from a particular manifestation of it—i.e., the political—not from all of it. He participates in other realms or areas of power—e.g., the economic, the military, the religious, and the like—where arbitrary and unjust acts are by no means unknown, and where his own participation may have been instrumental in producing them. In the larger and more important sense, however, he can withdraw at most from the direction, but not from the costs, of political power. He is still a member of the state, and as such he is still affected by its decisions. In this respect the teaching of Socrates remains both relevant and vital: that he who refuses to rule always runs the danger of being ruled by someone who is worse than himself.[5]

Or take the case of the individual who seeks to achieve an inner indifference to outward forms, who would be serene even in the midst of turmoil. Under certain conditions, this can probably be achieved—especially where the oppressive demands put upon him affect only part of his life, and then a less important part, as would be true in an extreme sense of a priest in a monastery. But under such conditions as the Negro in the American South finds himself, for example, this cannot be done. He may withdraw, but others will not; and since he is part of an identifiable group he will be affected by the actions of other members of that group. He will suffer the penalties visited upon all of them, even though he may have done nothing himself to merit such treatment. For his sin is not that he does something but that he exists.

This being so, selective withdrawal does not solve the problem of oppressive rule, any more than does individual or group withdrawal. They all leave unaffected the abusive aspects of existing powers; hence, whatever the success of the person or persons resorting to them, they do not touch the heart of the political power system. They neglect or negate rather than reinforce the principles of democracy as they are expected to function in the real world.[6]

So much for the futility of withdrawal as a means of redressing the state's violations of democratic principles. Can withdrawal, whether by an individual or a group, be any more effective in combating the abuses of *private powers?* Here, clearly, an individual (or a group) suffering from this discriminatory treatment has somewhat greater latitude of action, and in some cases can, by availing himself of the opportunity, effectively weaken the oppressive power so as to render its despotic impulses insignificant.

Thus, a member of a minority group who is denied access to a college, medical school, or private place of employment can seek and perhaps find it elsewhere; and it is entirely possible that the private power involved may discover that, as a result of its discriminatory practices, it suffers more—both economically and in its moral and intellectual reputation—than it gains. This, it would seem, is at least part of the reason for the very marked gains that members of minority groups have achieved in the educational and business worlds in recent years. However, the individual or group who seeks to mitigate such an abuse of power cannot hope to do so if his reaction is solely to withdraw from that situation and to apply elsewhere; for discriminatory practices by such business and educational institutions are frequently perpetuated by other clients who support the discrimination. It seems hardly necessary to add that the advances I referred to above are the result not of withdrawal but of concerted action against such discriminatory conduct.

In short, because the state is an all-inclusive organization, the individual cannot escape from its controls except by migrating from the country. Private powers, however, are partial powers, and for this reason the individual can more easily escape from them. But the extent to which such withdrawal can affect these private powers obviously depends on whether or not they are competing powers or real alternative powers or whether, on the other hand, they are in some way interlocked. Where they are interlocked, the opportunities of escape dwindle—as is evidenced, for example, by the fact that the inclusion of a man's name on a particular "blacklist" may effectively exclude him from employment in that industry, or by the fact that a physicist fired from the government or from a university as a security risk is not likely to find employment in private industry. Thus, while the general principle remains a valid one, its particular relevance depends always on the specific set of circumstances.

For these and other reasons, the consequences of withdrawal from the abuses of private powers may be essentially the same as those of withdrawal from the abuses of governments; for he who escapes (or who seeks to escape) through withdrawal does so only at the cost of leaving those powers undisturbed. He does not assail them; nor does his departure necessarily weaken them. On the contrary: so far as those private powers are concerned, his act of withdrawal may constitute a welcome gesture of compliance or, what is hardly of import, a futile gesture of defiance.

IX

The Appeal to
Right Principles

If withdrawal is but an escape from, rather than a solution to, the abuses of power in a democratic state, it need not follow that oppressive government is inevitably the order of the day. Withdrawal, after all, is but one of many ways in which men can react to the abuses of power; other choices remain always at hand.

Two such alternative reactions are the appeal to right principles and the appeal to the right man. The failure of the American political system to eliminate abuses of power, it is sometimes argued, is to be explained by the fact that it looks only to institutional controls. The framers of the Constitution lacked confidence in men, or, more precisely, in the probability that good men would always rule in a democracy. They sought, therefore, to curb the anticipated excesses of power by resorting to institutional rather than to moral restraints. They sought to prevent evil or stupid men from carrying out their narrow designs, not by showing them that those designs were in effect (if not in intent) injurious to the public welfare—for such a revelation would be ineffectual in the face of moral or intellectual inadequacy—but by making it impossible for them to have both the opportunity and the power to indulge their selfish wills. In establishing such institutional controls, the framers succeeded (perhaps more effectively than they anticipated) in limiting the powers, and therewith the despotic inclinations, of governments. But it is not altogether clear that in doing so the framers always kept in mind the fact that they too were not angels but men, subject to the same (or the same type of) prejudices and interests that gave them concern when present in others. Consequently, for them to believe (or to pretend to believe) that they could establish "good" institutions to control "bad" men—i.e., men who in the narrow pursuit of their selfish interests would hinder the advancement of the common good—was to ignore (or at least to minimize) the fact that those institutions were themselves conceived and were to be administered by interested and selfish men. Hence, even with the best institutions in the world, the problem would still remain.

It is true that the authors of *The Federalist* were not prepared to carry this argument to its logical extremes. Despite their generally pessimistic view of human nature, they believed that not all men are governed by considerations of self-interest alone. They thought that some men at least are sufficiently dedicated to rise above the passions and narrow pursuits of the multitude. But unless it can be shown that such men (or reasonable approximations thereof) actually were in control of the writing of the Constitution and of its subsequent amendments (formal and informal alike), and that such men have continued to determine the policies of the state, it is futile to expect good institutions to emerge and to be properly run. To warn, therefore, as Madison did, that enlightened statesmen would not always be at the helm is not necessarily to conclude, as he did, that our best hope lies therefore in good institutions; for in the absence of such enlightened men, the helm may be improperly steered and the institutions corrupted and destroyed. It is rather to emphasize the necessity of procuring and appointing such enlightened men, and of keeping them in power. Such, at any rate, is the contention of those who look neither to withdrawal nor to "good" institutions but appeal instead to wise (i.e., enlightened) and therefore virtuous rulers—men who know what the right principles are and who can therefore be expected to apply them with prudence, or who, though lacking this knowledge, possess other qualities of excellence that set them apart from ordinary men and commend them as "good" rulers.

Both definitions are, to be sure, variations on the same theme—

the appeal to wise or good rulers. But the first, by identifying that wise ruler in terms of his knowledge of and adherence to the right principles, looks less to personality than to ideas; while the latter subordinates ideas to the character structure or personality of the man himself. I shall examine the second of these appeals—that to personal excellence, or what I shall call (more broadly) the right man—in a succeeding chapter. Here I want to consider only those schools of thought that appeal, ultimately, to right principles.

Of these, one seeks to control abuses of power by invoking the principle of democracy itself. Others look instead to a principle outside of and allegedly more fundamental than that derived from agreement alone; they appeal to revelation, to tradition, to a secular natural law or natural right doctrine, even to intuition.

THE APPEAL TO DEMOCRACY

That a real commitment to democracy will do much to limit the excesses to which even democratic governments and peoples are prone cannot, I think, be denied. For democracy implies, among other things, a belief in the equality of men (as I have heretofore defined this term); consequently, one who is a practicing democrat cannot consistently indulge in or sustain others who indulge in the discriminatory practices that contravene the equalitarian creed. Democracy implies, too, that the *way* in which men adjust or resolve their differences is of crucial importance, that conflicts of opinion as to what constitutes the right moral and political ends are not to be resolved arbitrarily—i.e., by fiat of a stronger or allegedly superior group—but are to be mediated and temporarily adjusted through a political process that builds on the free exchange of opposing ideas and on the periodic resort to the ballot box; accordingly, those who accept democracy must respect the principle that men are not to be penalized merely for holding or for expressing nonconformist views. Thus, the appeal to democracy is no more than the quite legitimate demand that men practice what they preach, that they not merely seek to understand what democracy is but that they observe its values in their day-to-day relationships.

As such, the appeal is unexceptionable. But it is also largely ineffective. For it overlooks the fact that interests and passions, not principles, are the primary movers of men, and that a charge of logical inconsistency does not bite very deep. This discrepancy between faith and deed can be accounted for, among other things, by the fact that people can grant or espouse a principle without seeing its ramifications in practice; or by the curious fact that men who are aware of the inconsistency remain, all too often, untroubled by it. They seem to have little difficulty in compromising their creeds and in discovering new rationalizations when it is convenient for them to do so. They are not overly disturbed by the intrusion of facts contrary to their prejudices, for there are always *some* facts to reinforce their prejudices; and since, in any case, the real grounds on which they hold their beliefs are not the grounds alleged—since it is their attitudes rather than their opinions that are at stake—the exposure of false charges, of misinformation, of illogical reasoning, of moral schizophrenia, and the like leaves those attitudes unaffected. This is why the informed are hardly less prone to prejudice and inter-group discrimination than are the uninformed, why consistency of thought and action is regarded in many quarters as but a foolish hobgoblin of little minds.[1]

This is not to say that the appeal to democracy is a completely ineffectual one. Always there are some men, even if but a few, who would be guided by the light of reason, who respect principles and seek to act in accordance with them. But even for such men it is not altogether clear that the appeal to democracy is an effective bar to oppressive action. For one thing, such an appeal remains always but an invocation of general principles, and as such it cannot resolve particular issues. For another, it is less an appeal to a principle than it is an appeal to a procedure.

Clearly, men may agree on a general principle and disagree as to its particular applications. What, for example, should a democratic society do with respect to the Communists? One group would outlaw the Communist Party and put its leaders in jail. Another group would tolerate them as a political party. Yet both groups, oddly enough, invoke a common principle—democracy—to sanction their respective positions. What, again, should be done with respect to the desegregation of American Negroes in the schools? One group insists on immediate and uncompromising desegregation. Another is adamant in its opposition to this, terming the Supreme Court's ruling on desegregation an unjust and even illegal act. Still a third group urges what it believes to be a moderate course, accepting desegregation in principle but delaying its application in time, hoping that such a middle ground will conciliate the extremes, or at least prevent a violent rupture between them. And all three groups, despite their differences, claim that theirs is a democratic solution to the problem. In some cases such a claim is doubtless no more than a shameless act of duplicity. But it would be manifestly unfair to allege that this is so of all who make this claim. Thus, the appeal to democracy remains an insufficient solution to our problem. We cannot say that the remedy for oppression is simply a return to democratic principles, for the very people who are guilty of oppressive acts often commit those acts in the name of democracy itself.

This is all the more true when we recognize that democracy is a principle of government that looks primarily to a method or process through which conflicts in moral and political ideas can be negotiated. It establishes a procedure for the tentative resolution of disagreements; it does not formulate an answer to such disagreements. Consequently, the appeal to democracy is an appeal not to a fixed and final solution but to a method through which a solution—admittedly tentative and experimental in nature—can be obtained. It is true that majorities do not always decide wisely, and that the right method can therefore be said at times to produce a wrong result. But so long as the integrity of the method is respected, that result remains subject to continuing inquiry, to criticism, and to the possibility of change.

What is relevant to our purpose here, however, is not the virtues or demerits of the democratic method as a source of philosophic wisdom, not the rightness or wrongness of a particular result, but the fact that the procedure may, paradoxically, lend itself to the disavowal of democratic rights, and thus to abuses of power. It is conceivable, to take an extreme possibility, that a temporary majority may vote democracy out of existence by outlawing opposition parties or by canceling elections. It may utilize the *procedure* of democracy to destroy the *principle* of democracy. In this event minority groups would, of course, be free to rebel; for the state having ceased to be a democratic state, the rulers have no legitimate claim to popular obedience. But if the majority which takes this action is an overwhelming one, so that the outlawed political party (say the Communists) or the excluded minority group (say the Negroes in the American South) has no effective alternative open to it and must therefore submit, the majority can delude itself (as it all too commonly has) into believing that through democratic procedures it is preserving democratic ends. To the extent, therefore, that the appeal to democracy is an appeal to procedures without regard to the values implicit in them—values which they are clearly designed to promote—it provides no necessary bulwark against the abuses of democratic power.

THE APPEAL TO REVELATION

The fact that a real or professed faith in democracy per se is insufficient to prevent departures from the democratic principle has led some theorists to seek the remedy in the inculcation of a more universal and binding principle. Such a principle, they maintain, cannot be force, for force—even that superior force which is designed to curb the excesses of a lesser force—always requires control in turn. Nor can it be, in their view, a form of nonpolitical power, for another power—e.g., economic power— is (a) itself often oppressive and thus in need of control, and (b) in any ultimate sense, despite occasional successes to the contrary, dependent on that greater power of law reinforced by force which resides in the hands of the state. Nor, finally, can it lie in any system of institutional controls, for apart from such limitations as were noted in an earlier chapter, the crucial fact (from the standpoint of these theorists) remains that institutions as such never exercise power; it is always men in charge of institutions who have power. The essential solution, it is therefore argued, in so far as it is possible to speak of a "solution," must be sought instead in a moral code. "It can only be found," says one writer, "in the establishment and general recognition of criteria for the use of power and of obligation to observe those criteria." Such criteria would establish politics on a firm and viable foundation, for to men of good will they would provide "decisive ethical inhibitions" on the use of power. They would suppress the irrational law of tooth and fang. They would foreclose tyranny.[2]

The most obvious—and, historically, the most widely accepted —source of such ethical criteria is, of course, revelation. I have in mind here not that direct communication with the deity which affords some men what they think is an immediate and personal insight into God's will, but that understanding of supernatural teaching which is revealed to man through organized religion. It is true that men differ in the gods they acknowledge, and hold consequently to somewhat different principles. It is also true that some men deny that there are gods, and hold consequently that there are no revealed principles. But to both these objections the holders of the true revelation have what is in their view a sufficient answer. They insist, on the one hand, that the differences between religions have been emphasized out of all proper proportion and that, in essence, the similarities among them are sufficiently overriding to warrant the recognition of a common heritage, "the Hebraic-Greek-Christian tradition." [3] They assert, on the other hand, that where real differences can be said to exist, whether among believers or between believers and unbelievers, such differences do no more than demonstrate that *the others* are either mistaken or perverse, and probably both. History being in their eyes but "a dialogue between God and man, with God taking the initiative and man either fleeing or responding to His call," it becomes clear that "man does not belong to himself but to God who created him." [4] The essential meaning of political life (as of history) is thus the restoration of true personality, a task which can only be achieved if we understand, with Xenophanes, that the one God in his formless transcendence is the same God for every man, and that "the truth of man and the truth of God are inseparably one." [5]

From this standpoint, abuses of power can only be controlled by man's submission to divine truth, to God's will. From this standpoint, it is the tragic failure of secular democracies—and the explanation of their oppressive acts—that they have reversed this elementary principle and have confounded God's will with man's will. They have forgotten that the will of God is a rational will, and that it is, consequently, not what men will but what they *rationally* will that can alone claim legitimacy. For this reason, men who speak of freedom, who affirm (as theological adherents of democracy affirm) that "democratic forms and institutions find their essential and ultimate meaning in the preservation and enlargement of human freedom," must understand that what is here meant by freedom is not Hobbes's absence of restraints. This, in their view, is but the vain and empty freedom to do what one wants, even if what one wants to do is wrong. Freedom properly understood, according to this view, is *rational choice,* which "requires both knowledge of the good and the will to choose the good when known." [6] And such knowledge, it cannot be emphasized too often, derives not from man but from God; for man is not an autonomous being but the creature of God. In this respect (among others) adherents of this view but echo the teaching of Augustine, who held that the good, the moral strength, that is in man comes from God; but the sin, the evil, the moral weakness in him—these are his own.[7] Consequently, political action that expresses simply the will of the people or of the legislators rather than of reasoned deliberation and right judgment—i.e., judgment according to the revealed dictates of God's will—is not truly law; and a democracy which gives priority to the former rather than to the latter is to that degree corrupted and debased. It tends to become a tyranny.[8]

To forestall this corruption, to prevent this abuse of power, it is necessary, therefore, in this view, to return to God, to guide our conduct by that absolute morality which, through revelation, teaches us to do good and avoid evil.

Now it is incontestable that men who are genuinely committed to such an absolute morality will not knowingly do what it enjoins as evil and avoid what it specifies as good, and if this were the purport of the natural law teaching no one would say it nay. But to leave the doctrine in such general terms is not, surely, to carry us very far; for then, even more than the appeal to democracy, it provides no specific solutions to concrete problems. We can all agree to do good, to be kind, to act justly, and the like, yet disagree sharply on the proper policy to adopt with respect to the Franco dictatorship in Spain, or with respect to the segregation of the Negro in the American South and in the Union of South Africa, or with respect to the Communists in France or in the United States. In the name of Christianity and of a theologically-rooted natural law, men of good will have taken opposing sides on these and other actual political issues. Their commitment to religion, to God's will, has not provided them with clear and determinate answers to specific questions. Nor, indeed, can it do so; for whatever the universal validity of their alleged inviolable ends, there cannot be any universally valid rules of action. On the contrary, within the framework of their absolute morality the utmost flexibility in the choice of means is necessarily allowed.[9] And while, with respect to such choices, the teaching of natural law does not sanction the use of "bad" means, the definition of what constitutes a bad means is itself left up in the air. In any case, the wide discretion that is retained in the selection of diverse means to prescribed or, more commonly, ambiguous ends—for it ought never to be forgotten that in the realm of politics a given end is itself generally instrumental to other ends and is thus itself a means in turn—leaves room for great differences in conduct.

Since, therefore, the principle of natural law, however forcefully it may urge us to do good and avoid evil, affords no specific guidance to those who accept it, it can hardly be said to resolve the problem of abuses of power.

It is worth noting, moreover, that the appeal to revelation is attended by other and no less serious difficulties. Suppose, for example, we grant that the right principles are those revealed by God. The obvious question then is, which god? Each group vigorously asserts that its god is the only true god, but apart from a dogmatic reiteration that this is so, it can offer no *proof* to substantiate its claim; nor can it *disprove* the opposing claims of others. The contest is shrouded in mystery and can be penetrated only by those who possess the right faith. But which faith?

To ask these questions here is not to invite an answer satisfactory to theologians, but to call attention to certain political implications of the controversy. For in a state rent by competing theologies—by competing gods and competing principles—the alternative to the supremacy of the right theology is either compromise, indifference, or war. The last is a remedy that may kill the patient and still not cure the disease; for conflicting religions have a way of surviving even the holiest of wars. Since, moreover, the appeal to war is not an appeal to the right principles but to force, which is the very thing that the right principles are supposed to suppress, it aggravates rather than resolves the problem of abusive power. Indifference or neglect—letting religion alone —is the political denial of that principle which the adherents of this view urge as the only solution to oppression. It may make for peace; it may even permit the several religions to flourish; but because it also precludes the guidance of human affairs by the "right" religion it remains, or ought to remain (in the eyes of theologically-oriented political thinkers), an abortive approach to our problem. Compromise, of course, is in this view utterly useless; for it mixes wrong with right in all sorts of disharmonious blends. True, it may enlist the support of the less rigid or less orthodox followers of a particular religion by giving them some recognition rather than none at all; but in any ultimate sense it waters down the "right" principles and thereby affords no true guidance, no sure control, to the abuse of power. We are left, then, with the only proper solution—the dominance of that "right" religion which alone has the "right" principles. But which religion is it to be, and how shall its rightness be determined?

Clearly, the appeal to revelation but opens a Pandora's box of many difficulties, difficulties which are further complicated by the fact that democracy as a principle of government is designed to further two at least of the unacceptable alternatives—namely, compromise or indifference. A democratic state does not, to be sure, preclude the dominance of a particular religion or religious group—witness the place of Protestant Christianity in the United States—but because it gives a measure of political power to those who are committed to an alternative religion it makes it difficult for any one religion to have complete (i.e., undisputed) sway. For this reason, those who insist on the appeal to the "right" principles frequently end by rejecting the principle of democracy itself.[10]

In this respect the advocates of the appeal to revelation, where they are both rigorous and sincere, are often the necessary opponents of freedom, at least as that word is understood in democratic states. By freedom the latter mean the right of an individual to choose, whether or not this choice is the "right" or the "wrong" choice. But by freedom the former understand only that choice which is the "right" or "rational" choice—i.e., that choice which accords with God's will. For them, it is not freedom but rightness that is the crucial value. Consequently, they are prepared, with Rousseau, to force men to be "free." Unlike those who might foolishly (because erroneously) submit to Rousseau's secular general will, however, men would now (in this view) "really" be free, since they would now act in accordance with their "true" will—i.e., the will of God, which is their will if they could but apprehend it and perceive its proper application to a particular set of circumstances. In this way coercion or restraint becomes, in Orwellian fashion, freedom, and freedom becomes doing not what you want to do—i.e., what you *think* you want to do—but what you *really* want to do, which is what you ought to do, which in turn is what God commands you to do. Whatever the theological merits of this position, this much at least is clear: that it involves an authoritarian rather than a democratic solution to the problem of freedom in political society.

This point requires, perhaps, a special word in emphasis; for what is at issue is not the validity of the source from which the divine teaching is alleged to emanate but the right of those who profess this "right" teaching to impose it on others. It is clearly compatible with democracy for one to maintain a belief in revelation and to seek to *persuade* others to accept the principles that comprise that system of belief. It is, however, a quite different matter for the believer to insist on his right to *coerce* others into acting according to those proclaimed dogmas. Conversely, it is incompatible with democracy for a believer automatically to refuse to abide by the decision of the majority which goes contrary to his "right" principles.

In these terms the attempt to translate revealed truths into political maxims raises certain difficulties. One can, of course, point to the historical fact that a revealed religion such as Roman Catholicism has been able to live with relative equanimity under a monarchy like that of Louis XIV, a dictatorship like that of Franco, and a democracy like that of England and the United States. For, whatever its statements concerning social and political justice, the Catholic Church has shown that it can get along with any regime that lets Catholics practice their religion—preferably as the sole religion, but if necessary as one among many. Since the word of God is revealed not directly to the individual but indirectly through the organized church, those who control the church can alone proclaim the revealed teaching and thereby control the believers.

But what if the believers are few, or what if those who once believed or who profess to believe are led astray? In the latter case, if we are to take Thomas Aquinas seriously, heretics are "to be not only excommunicated but even put to death." [11] Such extreme treatment, however, is not generally practiced by democratic states. Nor does it affect the unbelievers. Consequently, an alternative means must be found for controlling them. This has led some Christian writers to urge that the state commit itself to the authoritative promulgation and protection of their particular morality, even as applied to those who reject it. This does not necessarily mean that a ruler must be a Christian in his private beliefs, but that he must rule, if he is to rule "rightly," as a Christian. The Christian God being a jealous God, it is not enough for a state to let Christians live in an essentially non-Christian world; the "right" state must forego such democratic license and restore what T. S. Eliot, for example, calls the idea of a Christian society.[12] Thus only, argue the adherents of this view, can abuses of power be controlled.

But the price of such control—setting aside the question as to whether it can in fact be effective—is of course the abandonment of democracy itself. And as such, the appeal to revelation evades rather than solves the problem of how to control abuses of power *within* a democratic state.[13]

But the question as to whether the appeal to revelation can in fact be effective is not one that can lightly be set aside. For so long as the appeal to revelation approaches the problem of the abuse of power on an ethical rather than a physical plane, it cannot effectively control those who do not share the same morality. As a Catholic spokesman for this school admits: "The natural law is a moral law the subjects of which are physically, though not morally, free to violate it in defiance of the sanction which such breach invokes." [14] This, of course, makes it possible for those who would abuse their power to do so, either because the pleasures of oppressive rule exceed (in their judgment) the punishments that await them in a presumed afterlife, or because they do not believe that the moral disapproval of a different god (or of the church that professes to speak in his name) is sufficient to offset the approval of their god, or because they do not admit to the validity of such conceptions as heaven and hell at all. This is why the moral appeal of a Gandhi, say, can hope to be successful when applied to a country like England, where the rulers share essentially the same morality which Gandhi invoked, and be unsuccessful (in all probability) when applied to a ruler like Hitler or Stalin. This is why, too, the appeal to revelation is insufficient to bind "bad" rulers, why it fails to induce that restraint in the possessors of power as to lead them to exercise it only in accordance with the "right" criteria.

THE APPEAL TO TRADITION

The appeal to tradition is in one sense improperly included here, for it is not, fundamentally, an appeal to principles at all. By substituting tradition for principle, it denies that principles —or the search for principles—can provide a rational guide for political conduct. But by that same substitution it implies too that the study of tradition—of "that body of knowledge which is bound up with prescription and prejudice and authority" [15]— is the best of all possible paths to political wisdom and virtue; and in this respect it offers tradition itself as the right principle by which human affairs ought to be—as in fact (in this view) they essentially have been—controlled.

From this it follows that the appeal to tradition can be a surrender to oppressive power or an attack on it. It surrenders to oppression where oppressive behavior is clearly a part of the established ways—e.g., the treatment of the Negro in the American South. It attacks oppression where oppressive conduct contravenes the established codes, the recognized patterns of behavior—e.g., the castigation (if belated) of Senator McCarthy by the United States Senate. In the former case, the appeal to tradition, by validating the customary abuses of power, fails to curb those oppressive practices of democratic governments and peoples that concern us here. In the latter case, despite the very real sense in which it sometimes impels some men to do the "right" things, or at least to feel uneasy when they do or permit others to do the "wrong" things, it suffers from all the difficulties that bedevil other appeals to the right principles, notably the appeal to revelation.

For the appeal to tradition is nothing if not a form of the appeal to revelation. It argues that a principle or rule is validated not because it accords with God's will but because it is the cumulative fruit of the past. It thus assigns a value to the past (as others do to God) simply because it is the past (or God). It does not reason about this; it simply affirms this to be so. The past is said to be the only true source of wisdom; it is therefore held to be the only true guide to the conduct of human affairs. Those who look to divine revelation say that because God is wise, his dictates are wise. Traditionalists say instead that since the past is wise, its rules are wise. Logically, the argument is the same: it is an appeal to faith, to a special authority, not to reason.

But just as there are many gods—it was, after all, the same Xenophanes who believed in a single god who observed that everywhere the gods are made in the image of man: that among the Ethiopians, for example, the gods are black and snub-nosed, among the Thracians they have blue eyes and red hair, and so on—so there are many traditions. And just as men pick from among the gods such as may please them, so men pick from among the multiplicity of traditions those traditions that are most congenial to their interests and pleasures.

This raises the nice question, which traditions are traditional? The answer is clearly a subjective one: some men desire some among their present institutions, and term them traditional; others desire different practices to be enshrined, and term those traditional even as they reject the others for being contrary to tradition. Both groups, of course, are in most cases right; for tradition is nowhere monolithic. The past yields many and contradictory readings, and what one selects as his official text is generally his present heart's desire. Thus, if he appeals to tradition, both authoritarian and democratic forms of state may commend themselves. If he resolves this conflict by adopting his own national tradition as the right tradition, then he may still have to resolve conflicting traditions within his own national tradition. Is the American tradition, for example, an egalitarian tradition, or one that sanctions discriminatory treatment with respect to certain minority groups? Is the American tradition one that encourages dissenting political opinions or one that at best tolerates but ridicules and otherwise penalizes that dissenting opinion when it is deemed to be noxious? Clearly, the answer is both an affirmative and a negative one, changing according to the different periods and circumstances of historical time, and depending always on which sector of the country and which economic or racial class, say, is being asked to respond. The same duality (or multiplicity) of traditions presents itself for a whole catalogue of issues—e.g., slavery, prostitution, the inferior status of women, the resort to violence or to war, and so on. And in this respect the appeal to tradition, like the appeal to revelation, provides no standard by which conflicts among traditions can be resolved.

The appeal to tradition is plagued, of course, by still other difficulties. The most obvious is that, just as it does not reason about the content or validity of its general rules, so it does not reason about their application to concrete issues. Even if we were agreed that the inferior status of women, say, is contrary to the American tradition—and I regret to say that it is not— we would still have to agree on the empirical changes that are required if such inequalities as do exist are to be obliterated. Such an agreement, it is plain, cannot be derived from tradition; it must emerge instead from men's rational judgments as to what is the best (i.e., the most effective or least harmful) way of realizing this objective. Another difficulty derives from the fact that tradition can, even at best, yield no more than a description of what men did and how (in some cases why) they did it. It can even, perhaps, reveal the consequences of their alternative practices. But it cannot tell us whether men *should* have done what they did; it cannot tell us which of the alternative consequences is better. These remain value questions that tradition can illuminate but never by itself resolve. For such a determination we must look elsewhere.[16] This underscores still a further difficulty of the appeal to tradition; for if we appeal to antiquity as the great repository of wisdom, we ought not to forget (as John Stuart Mill somewhere said) that our own is the oldest and hence, by this standard, the wisest age.

THE APPEAL TO A SECULAR NATURAL LAW OR
NATURAL RIGHT DOCTRINE

Akin to the appeal to revelation but differing from it in one crucial respect at least is the appeal to secular theories of natural law or of natural right. These theories differ (sometimes considerably) in the meanings they give to such words as "natural" and "law" in the term "natural law," [17] as they differ too in their specific delineations of the content of that natural law; but common to them all is the appeal from the positive law to justice, from the law that is to the law that ought to be.

Now the distinction between the *is* and the *ought* is a vital and necessary one, and those who oppose existing injustices and plead for social change are, whether they will it or no, committed to it.[18] Thus stated, however, the distinction remains a commonplace one, arguing little more than that men should do good rather than evil. It is still necessary to determine the nature of the good, to produce a standard and a body of definite rules that will tell us what men should do. If the principle of democracy is that standard, then the conflict is not between the positive law and justice but between a particular legislative enactment that is adopted and perhaps enforced as a part of the positive law, and a more general and universally binding principle that is also a part of the positive (or, if you will, of the constitutional) law. That some men, even judges, should confuse the two or at times hold erroneously that the first when contrary to the second is really not contrary to the second—e.g., half of the Supreme Court's many contradictory decisions on matters involving the due process clause or the clause providing for the equal protection of the laws —simply shows that men are sometimes mistaken or even unenlightened or wicked; it does not disprove the legitimacy of the appeal. And in this sense it is perfectly proper, indeed essential, to condemn the abuses of governments or of private powers by appealing to what ought to be, e.g., the principles of liberty and equality in a democratic state.

But this is not, customarily, the sense in which natural law and natural right theorists—especially those who are at the forefront of the natural law revival today—invoke the term; for what they mean by justice is a body of principles external to and (because more fundamental) possessing a higher validity than any political or legal principle as such. By natural law or natural right they have in mind a concept of rights and duties derived from and expressive of the principles of human nature itself, and of that larger order of nature within which the distinctively human plays its appointed part. They appeal to nature as a rational order in which all things have a fixed and ascertainable end. This end, this order, is not, in their view, something to be invented by man. It is not the product of someone's fancy or prejudice. It is not a collection of precepts established by the willful and arbitrary commands of an individual or of a sovereign power. It is, on the contrary, an objective reality that is already there. It is antecedent to man and even transcends man, and as such it is beyond the capacity of man to alter or to command. It exists only to be discovered, and when discovered to be obeyed.[19] In the words of one of its more articulate spokesmen: "All natural beings have a natural end, a natural destiny, which determines what kind of operation is good for them. In the case of man, reason is required for discerning these operations: reason determines what is by nature right with ultimate regard to man's natural end."[20] Thus conceived, the appeal to a secular natural law or natural right doctrine differs from the appeal to revelation only in that it substitutes "nature" for God and "reason" for revelation.

Now the contention that nature is a rational rather than a chaotic and essentially irrational order is not a self-evident truth. It may be, as Walter Lippmann, for example, terms it, "a necessary assumption";[21] but if it is no more than this, then clearly there is warrant for dismissing it, as Santayana in one place does, as but "an imaginative presumption."[22] If it is to be taken seriously, it must do more than appeal to man's will to believe; it must be established by the same principle of reason, by the same objective standard, to which secular natural law philosophers otherwise appeal. In other words, the *assumption* that there is a rational order must itself be sustained by reason. Yet it is precisely at this point that secular and theological adherents to natural law divide: the latter contending that no explanation of the universe can be proved without invoking an objective reality (i.e., God) that is outside that system; the former asserting that the very principle (reason) which explains the system constitutes the objective proof of the rationality of that system. The one is a direct appeal to faith. The other is a circular argument because, like all value theories, it rests on certain unproved assumptions; it appeals, ultimately, to an alternative faith. Lippmann seeks to build on the element of faith common to both of them by ignoring the *differentia specifica* which forces them into opposing camps. But in doing so he too abandons the court of reason for the court of belief. Thus, while he admits the need for the successful demonstration of the rational order, he is compelled at the same time to admit that its principles cannot be verified empirically. He seeks instead "to repair the capacity to believe"; repeatedly he asserts that with respect to these principles "we have to believe in them." [23] But the capacity or will to believe is not an appeal to reason; nor is it a convincing demonstration of the truth of what is believed.

Lippmann and other proponents of this view attempt to circumvent this difficulty by invoking the authority of the rational and "decent" man. Men being what they are, not all men are held to be competent or rational or motivated by good will; not all, says Lippmann, are "the people of light and leading." [24] Consequently, it is only to the perceptive few that we can appeal in the name of eternal reason. Among such men, Lippmann holds, there can be no doubt concerning the validity of the principles of natural law. Their validity is grasped because

They are the laws of a rational order of human society—in the sense that all men, *when they are sincerely and lucidly rational,* will regard them as self-evident. . . . They are the terms of the widest consensus *of rational men* in a plural society. They are the propositions to which all men concerned, *if they are sincerely and lucidly rational,* can be expected to converge. . . . The highest laws are those upon which *all rational men of good will, when fully informed,* will tend to agree.[25]

Concerning this proclaimed certainty, two things at least must be said. One is that while questions of justice may all be matters of opinion, no one in practice seriously argues against the view that one opinion may be better founded than another. Not every claim to rational insight is necessarily evidence of the rationality of the claimant. And in this sense Lippmann can legitimately hold that the reason of the wise man (where he is known) is superior to the ignorance of the fool. But also to be noted is that by Lippmann's own construction we are enmeshed in a circular argument that begs the very point at issue, namely, what is the test of the rational man? It would appear, if I read Lippmann and others of this school correctly, that the rational man is one who perceives the principles of the rational order, and that the principles of the rational order are those perceived by the mind of the rational man. Conversely, according to Lippmann, those who deny these principles would appear to be willfully irrational and insincere.[26] This is a *reductio ad hominem* that may please the believers in natural law, but it hardly accords with accepted canons of logic.

Let us, however, set aside the question of the authenticity or validity of this allegedly objective moral code. Let us recognize, with one of the more philosophical of the defenders of the natural law doctrine, that there is a difference between a substantive code and a science of principles, and that to apply principles as circumstances require is not to disprove the general method or rule. Let us admit, too, that the tendency to note differences rather than similarities among peoples has generally led to an exaggeration of the variability of social judgments.[27] Let us assume, finally, that a few wise men—the natural law or natural right theorists— have now correctly read the precepts of the natural order or of human nature and stand ready to guide us in the conduct of our political affairs. Can we conclude from all this that they can, in the light of their knowledge, exclude abuses of power from the democratic state?

The answer is that they cannot. In the first place, the adherents of a natural law or natural right doctrine, in the effort to prevent abuses of power, may require the state to cease being democratic. Suppose, for example, it were determined that divorce is contrary to the principles of natural law or of natural right but that, despite this, a legal majority of the people want to make it one of their rights and elect a government pledged to enact it into law. If the right of divorce is a matter for political decision, and if a democratic state is required to adjust its political policies according to the results of its established procedures, then the legal majority must be permitted to have its way. But natural law (or natural right) is unconcerned with democratic rules of procedure; it looks rather to the character of the results. Consequently, in the instance cited, the guardians of the natural law can perform their function only by interfering with, and checking, the will of the majority.[28] When translated into direct political terms, therefore, it is difficult to see how a democratic state can adhere to natural law precepts unless the overwhelming bulk of the people accept them. But they do not—either because some of them accept an alternative rendering of that natural law or because they are not concerned about such matters. In the absence of the consensus that Lippmann and other adherents of natural law postulate, either the will of the majority prevails, in which case natural law has failed to control "improper" or oppressive action, or the will of the natural law guardians prevails, in which case there is an end to majority rule and to democracy. If we substitute for divorce such issues as segregation and the treatment of political nonconformists, we readily see that an autocratic regime may in a particular situation (perhaps even in general) prove more responsive to a natural law doctrine than does a democratic state.[29] If, then, we wish to retain democracy, and the democratic process leads to a result incompatible with the natural law teaching, we must deny the right of the natural law guardians to prevent that democratic result from coming into being. We must abide by the will of the majority, even if that will is, by natural law standards, wrong.[30]

But suppose, in the second place, that not only are the natural law theorists right, but that the people are overwhelmingly in accord with them, so that the question of maintaining a democratic state is not at issue. What, then, is the natural law solution to concrete issues such as the problem of political nonconformity, or of academic freedom, or of desegregation and miscegenation in the American South? What insight can natural law give us that will enable us to deal "rightly" with the troubles of our time? If the adherents of natural law theories recognize, as they do, that it is the part of wisdom to adapt natural law principles to changing circumstances, it follows that even among those who appeal to natural law there will be disagreement as to its particular applications. In this respect, the appeal to natural law suffers from the same disability as the appeal to other "right" principles, such as revelation and tradition. For it is an appeal to general maxims only, and general maxims do not decide concrete cases, do not dictate specific rules of conduct.[31] These depend, among other things, on the knowledge men have of a particular situation; and since men, even wise men, differ in such knowledge, as well as in their capacities to reason, the particular interpretations and applications of nature that they bring to a specific case may result in wide disagreements. Thus it is that on any number of specific questions—whether of civil rights or of public housing or of education or of foreign policy—a natural law theorist may find himself aligned with a positivist in opposition to another natural law theorist. When a Reinhold Niebuhr, a Bertrand Russell, and a Walter Lippmann find themselves sharing a near-identical position on certain issues in opposition, say, to a self-proclaimed moralist like John Foster Dulles, who in turn is often at odds with himself, it becomes all too clear that natural law does not speak in a uniform voice to all who listen.

In the third place, the appeal to natural law, like the appeal to revelation, has no effective means of securing obedience to its rules. If the appeal is only to reason (or to conscience), as it is, what is to be done when reason (or conscience) fails? What is to be done when the rulers violate the canons of the natural law,[32] when they act despotically? It is no real answer to reply that the rulers, if they are committed to natural law, will not act this way. For on the one hand, not all rulers are likely to be committed to, or to go beyond a mere verbal commitment to, natural law—did not Socrates say in despair that in the real world philosophers would never be kings, nor kings philosophers? And on the other hand, even wise men—i.e., those who "know" the natural law—do not always act wisely. It is utterly untrue that right knowledge *always* produces right conduct: there is a psychological and sociological component to power that often leads men who rule to do so in accord with their self-interest, just as there is a moral component that leads them to rationalize this action so as to make it appear an unselfish and proper one.[33] If, then, rulers act contrary to the natural law, those who adhere to the latter must be prepared to resort to force to see to it that those rulers modify their ways. The appeal to force, however, may not only lead to their own destruction; it violates the very principles by which they seek to live. And there is no solution outside of force, since a democratic election may return those wrong rulers to power and the appeal to reason, to natural law, has already proved insufficient to bind those rulers. The net result is that the appeal to natural law (or natural right) is a self-defeating one, except in those rare cases where the rulers act in a manner satisfactory to those who judge them. But this, of course, is not the problem. The problem is rather, what shall be done to curb those rulers when they do *not* act rightly, when they rule oppressively? And to this question, the appeal to natural law gives no adequate answer.

One last point ought, perhaps, to be made. This is the evident fact that all appeals to natural law or natural right, whether through revelation or through reason, must be mediated by men. And since men differ, in their reason as in other things, conflicts are bound to occur not only with respect to the application of the natural law but with respect to the very meaning, the interpretation, of the natural law. Such conflicts cannot be resolved by the appeal to reason (or to God), for the conflict is one of competing reasons, of competing gods. It can be resolved only by choosing among men, by accepting the reason of some men as superior to the reason of other men. But those who make this choice are themselves men, who by the very assumption of the right to choose imply a belief in the superiority of their own reason over that of the competing parties. We are thus enmeshed in an unending circle of claimants to right reason, and the circle cannot be broken by reason alone. Rather than permit a resort to mutual slaughter, democracy provides a mechanism whereby this conflict can be submitted to the judgment of the market place for a peaceful and tentative resolution. The judgment of the market place may, of course, be "wrong." But in the face of otherwise irreconcilable claims to "rightness," it has, among other qualities, the inestimable virtue of maintaining social peace, *and* of enabling the rival claimants to continue to press their claims. Those, however, who insist on political conformity to *their* higher law, to *their* particular rendering of natural law or of natural right, jeopardize this peace; they affirm, in effect, that where persuasion proves insufficient to control men's conduct it is incumbent on them, as the defenders of the natural law, to compel those others to live "rightly." The consequence is, that in seeking to curb the abusive acts of those who, in their judgment (which is the "right" judgment), rule "wrongly"—i.e., oppressively—they are prepared to impose an oppression of their own. For the very act of imposition, and of the concomitant denial of the right of those who differ from them to rule, is an abrogation of democratic principle.

Thus, the appeal to natural law or to natural right may involve both an invitation to mutual slaughter and a denial of democracy —no longer, be it noted, in the name of the right principle but in the name of those who claim to know which is the right principle.

THE APPEAL TO INTUITION

"Just as theology moulds and guides the beliefs and behavior of the faithful, strengthening and affirming their *intuitive* perceptions, so, in politics, theory is not an objective analysis of what exists, but a normative system of concepts which ought constantly to direct the citizens towards ends to which they are *intuitively* committed." [34]

Here, succinctly stated, is the beginning of a paradox which, while seeming to deny the appeal to a right principle, actually affirms it, only (in the last analysis) to deny it again. It recognizes, to be sure, that ultimate values—i.e., those values which are held to comprise justice—are not to be derived from some allegedly objective standard, for in this view there is no such standard. It seeks instead to achieve justice "only insofar as the complex of interests and institutions is made answerable to the citizen's *intuitive sense* of fitness and proportion." [35] But it insists too that there are ultimate values, and that through intuition—i.e., through a form of direct and immediate revelation or apprehension rather than (as in the case of divine revelation of or a secular natural law) through some mediating agency such as an organized church or a body of wise men—men can discover what those values are.[36] And in this sense the appeal to intuition is held to be more than merely an appeal to subjectivism. By appealing to that inner ethical check, that sense of decency, that is said to be intrinsic to man, it appeals to that subjectivism that is "right." Clearly, the person who appeals to intuition would not do so if he felt that it would lead him to erroneous or absurd conclusions. He appeals to it only because he is convinced that it will lead to certain preconceived (and correct) answers. Thus, the intuitionist is, in this view, a man of principle. He invokes intuition not because intuition is itself the right principle but because he believes that an intuitive grasp of things will reveal the right principles.

It is difficult to see, however, how such an appeal can serve to curb the excesses of arbitrary rulers. Since it does not reason about doctrines, since it substitutes a purely subjective method of arriving at the right standards for those standards themselves, it does not provide any criteria by which rulers can in fact be guided. Suppose, for example, that X condemns Y's intuitions as arbitrary or trivial, and alleges that Y's actions, which are based on those intuitions, were taken without adequate regard for their immediate or ultimate consequences. Suppose, further, that Y denies the validity of such allegations and asserts in reply that those charges are in fact an appropriate description of X's intuitions and recommended actions. How, in the intuitionist scheme of things, is this conflict of intuitions to be resolved? Neither intuition can claim superiority over the other, for it is the intuition of the individual making the judgment that is the supreme arbiter. Nor can it be another intuition that may be called in or that presumes to judge the conflicting intuitions, for there is always another intuition that might judge the situation differently, in which case the ground would be laid for summoning still another intuition to enter, and so on in infinite progression. In the intuitionist scheme of things, moreover, the man who intuits the right principle, who perceives or apprehends the right course of action, is right, even if the intuitions of others are arrayed against him. For the intuitionist knows not only the correct principles governing his behavior and his obligations; he knows also that he himself knows them.[37] Consequently, he is not required to provide a means for public verifiability of his intuitive knowledge; he does not need to tell us how he obtained this knowledge, or why it is right. It is enough that he *feels* or *apprehends* it, that it is part of the direct and immediate data of his consciousness, that it is felt as a power of insight and control.

Thus, the issue is taken out of the realm of principle, out of the realm of reason, and is reduced to the simple question: which man intuits the right doctrine? If the reply is that it is the intuiting man, then the ruler who is led by his intuition to embark on a program of oppressive action is justified in whatever he does. And while those who are led by different intuitions to an alternative or opposing position may condemn him, and by their intuitive standards be right in doing so, they have no legitimate basis for interfering with him. For each man, in the intuitionist theory, can claim to be the right man.

This, however, leads to palpable absurdities; and the intuitionists who seek to save democracy from the evils that attend it do not, of course, accept such a conclusion. They distinguish, instead, between right and wrong intuitions, between right and wrong men. To the extent that they do so, the examination of their doctrine is properly the subject of our next chapter. But to the extent that they do so, they clearly abandon the appeal to intuition for a criterion outside of it. They clearly admit that intuition cannot by itself resolve the problem of abuses of power.

X

The Appeal to
the Right Man

Now at least from the time of Socrates, in whose ideal state philosophers would be kings, the appeal to the right man has played a major role in systematic reflections on the control of power. For if the right man does rule, Socrates argued, neither institutional nor other controls—e.g., law—need to be employed. Because he is the right man, he will do the right things: he will rule wisely; he will establish or, where it is already established, he will perpetuate that order in human affairs that best approximates or achieves justice and that secures liberty.

The problem, then, for those who hold this view in democratic states, is not whether the right man should rule, but how he is to be discovered and how he can be assured the reins of political power. Or, to formulate the problem in negative terms, how can we identify and exclude from power those who are the "wrong" men, those who are likely to rule badly and unjustly, those who—because they are, for example, "authoritarians" at heart—may if they achieve positions of power violate the very principles of the democratic state and thereby endanger its existence?

A preliminary—and perhaps crucial—difficulty must be noted. The appeal to the right man may not be altogether compatible with the appeal to democracy. If, for example, the right man is subject to democratic controls, primarily to the principle of responsibility, he may be removed from or not elected to office, in which case democracy is revealed to be a form of state in which the "wrong" man can rule by popular approval. If, on the other hand, those who appeal to the right man insist that the right man rule, or that the wrong man be excluded from political power, without regard to what the people want, then the state which adopts their view ceases to be (if it formerly was) a democratic state. Most political philosophers who have looked to the leadership of the right man for political salvation have seized the latter horn of this dilemma. With Plato and Santayana—to take but two from among the more noted of such writers—they have mocked democracy's trust in public opinion. They have derided what they have contemptuously called the rule of the common (by which they mean vulgar) or average (by which they mean inferior) man. They have appealed instead to a form of the aristocratic state—to a political order in which those few who allegedly know what is right will also, precisely because they "know" (i.e., have wisdom), follow the path of "virtue."

This is not the place to discuss the easy assumptions and many fallacies of the aristocratic appeal to the right man,[1] for, whatever its merits or deficiencies, to the extent that it departs from or negates the principle of democracy it offers no solution (and is therefore irrelevant) to our central problem, which is the control of abuses of power *within* the democratic state. When we turn, however, to democratic expositions of the appeal to the right man—to the doctrines of men who, like Harold Lasswell and Karl Mannheim, take the position that only through a reliance on the right man, and a concomitant rejection of the wrong man, can democracy hope to prevent or to escape from abuses of power— we encounter other, and scarcely less serious, difficulties.

For one thing, who is the right man, and who the wrong man? How, and by what criterion or set of criteria, is such a man to be identified or defined? Secondly, will a reliance on the right man, or a repudiation of the wrong man, really eradicate oppressive rule? On the one hand, the right man may succumb to and be corrupted by the normal temptations of power, in which event he ceases to be the right man, or may in retrospect be held never to have been the right man. On the other hand, he may, to retain his office, yield to the pressures of public opinion; he may give the people what they want, or what they say they want, and in this event, should the demand be, say, for oppressive rule over a despised minority group, he would no longer fulfill the purpose for which as a right man he was called. If either of these eventualities were to be realized, we would find that we had but traveled a full circle: for we began by looking to the right man to prevent and even to eliminate the ravages of oppressive rule, and we end by looking for some means to rid ourselves of the man who is no longer the right man, and who may in fact have himself become the worst of oppressors.

To make clear that these are real and probable difficulties and not merely hypothetical horrors, it is necessary to consider each of them in turn.

THE DEFINITION OF THE RIGHT (AND WRONG) MAN

Despite the bitter judgment of the writer of Ecclesiastes, who warned that "there is not a just man upon earth, that doeth good, and sinneth not," [2] some of those who would save democracy from its sins have looked yearningly for a just man, one who would do good and commit no evil. Such a man, in traditional political thought, was not merely the competent but the superior man; he excelled all others by virtue of his merit or achievement.

Merit, to be sure, is an ambiguous term, and has been variously defined. In some constructions it has been equated with learning or wisdom; in others, with that technical training or experience that produces what is commonly called expertise; in still others, with certain intrinsic qualities allegedly associated with blood and breeding; and in others, again, with the prescriptive sanction of a higher authority such as God. Each of these qualities is susceptible, in turn, of different definitions. Thus, while learning to the ancient Greeks meant philosophy, to what is perhaps the dominant strand of contemporary American opinion it means knowledge of such applied sciences as medicine and law; and this knowledge is generally associated less with scholars in the law schools, say, than with practicing lawyers, especially those who for one reason or another have attained a place on the Supreme

Court. Similarly, the term "achievement" is not without considerable ambiguity: for one who has acquired great wealth may not enjoy great fame; one who has achieved fame may not also be wise; and one who is wise may remain always in poverty and relative obscurity. Which is the greatest achievement?

It need not follow, of course, from the fact that traditional political philosophy has produced no agreement as to who is the superior or right man, that there is no such man. One among the many divergent views may prove, ultimately, to be well grounded. One among the many claimants may emerge as "the" right man.

But the dilemma referred to above would still remain to bedevil those who appeal to this right man. For if, on the one hand, they place him beyond popular control, they move out of the realm of democratic theory into the never-never land of what they choose to call aristocracy—a world that can appear real only to one who seriously believes that some men at least are, if not perfect, uncontrolled by passion and by the pursuit of self-interest; that some men are, indeed, possessed of so compelling a sense of duty and so abundant a measure of intelligence as to be motivated only by what is advantageous to all and to be unaffected by the corrupting influences of power; that such men are, consequently, to be unhesitatingly entrusted with the lives and destinies of other men. Unfortunately for such a belief, it ignores certain inconvenient historical truths, not least among them being the fact that the very existence of democracy is to be accounted for as a reaction against the demonstrated incompetence and tyranny of "aristocrats" and other self-styled superior men. Not all who have affirmed the aristocratic theory have had the honesty and courage of Santayana, who, while he dared to hope, admitted too that good government—from his aristocratic point of view—has never yet existed (and perhaps can never exist) in this world, that all past aristocracies have in fact been artificial and corrupt.[3]

If, on the other hand, the appeal to the right man is limited to an exhortation to the people to select a particular man or type of man on the ground that he is the right man, it is an appeal not to the wisdom of the right man but to that of the popular will, in which case it is the judgment of the latter that is at stake.

Another form of the appeal to the right man, however, has emerged in recent years. This appeal eschews the language of morality—of right and wrong, of good and bad, as ethical terms— and seeks instead, in line with what is conceived to be the approved method of modern science, to use such terms only in relation to a stipulated goal. If that goal is the preservation (or the achievement) of democracy, and more immediately the control of oppressive power, the right man is not one who is abstractly the best or most virtuous man but one who is specifically committed— dedicated, if you will—to the attainment of that goal. He shares "democratic" values, he avoids abusing his power, not because it is fashionable for him to do so or because it may happen to serve his convenience or his purposes, but because he *must,* because he really wants to, do so. He is so constituted, in fact, that he cannot (or at least is unlikely to) think or act otherwise. This is because, in the language of the theorists of this school, he is a "democratic" as distinguished from an "authoritarian" personality; he has the "right" type of character structure.

It would be misleading to imply, as do some of the more extreme formulations of this view, that the appeal to democratic personality altogether neglects or moves outside of the institutional framework. On the contrary, it is most commonly an appeal to personality precisely because that personality is held to be in accord with a particular institutional framework. Thus Mannheim, one of the more sophisticated exponents of this "scientific psychology," assumes as an underlying premise of his argument "a correlation between social organization and personality pattern." He draws a dichotomy between democratic and authoritarian types of personality and between democratic and authoritarian societies, and insists that only where we have *both* a democratic social structure and a democratic man can we hope to realize the good—i.e., the democratic—society.[4]

A like argument is advanced by Lasswell. Ideally, Lasswell believes, human freedom requires the elimination of power; it means a world "in which coercion is neither threatened, applied nor desired." Since, however, there is no likely probability that power will be eliminated, the immediate task is to curb its destructiveness, to prevent it from interfering with or deviating from the "network of congenial and creative interpersonal relations" that, in Lasswell's conception, constitutes democracy. To guard against such "antidemocratic and destructive" deviations, he would have us rear, choose, and support "leaders with the personality formation appropriate to democracy." He would have us look not to their beliefs but to their adjustment; and this, of course, makes democratic leadership a function not simply of popular desire but of social psychiatry—"the social psychiatry of democracy." "What is needed," Lasswell insists, "is a *National Personnel Assessment Board* set up by citizens of unimpeachable integrity which will select and supervise the work of competent experts in the description of democratic and antidemocratic personality." For unless we support the one and reject the other, "the equilibrium essential to sustain the democratic commonwealth cannot be maintained." [5]

Now the contention that in every society there are some men who are visibly—i.e., impressionistically—more prone than others to resort to arbitrary or "authoritarian" methods is, I think, unexceptionable; as is too the conclusion from this fact that a democratic society, if it is intelligent, should not select cruel and vicious men in the hope that upon attaining power they will succumb to the father-instinct and become shepherds rather than wolves, that it should look instead to the leadership of "decent" and reasonably stable persons. None would dispute such a position. But if I understand Lasswell and Mannheim correctly, their argument goes further than this. They would have such men selected, or at least initially screened, by "scientific" methods— i.e., tests, questionnaires, interviews, and the like—that would, because they are "scientific," admit of little or no error. And this is quite a different thing.

In the first place, the difference between a "democratic" and an "authoritarian" personality is sometimes not in how he behaves but in how he is treated. In this respect Shaw's conversion of Eliza Doolittle from a flower-girl into a duchess attests to a greater insight than that simplistic psychology which mechanistically reduces adult conduct to its alleged infantile origins, or equates it with a particular type of character structure. No one who has seen the products of prison or reform school brutality, or who has witnessed the frustrations and anxieties imposed on administrators by the formalized routines and other pressures of a bureaucratic system, can doubt that personality is as much molded by the situation in which a person finds himself as it is by the imputed compulsiveness or aggressiveness of his neurotic nature. If, then, a so-called "authoritarian" personality is thrust into a "democratic" environment, it does not necessarily follow that his personality will remain unchanged.

In the second place, it is not at all clear just what a "democratic" or an "authoritarian" personality *is*. Despite the urgency (let alone the confidence) with which Mannheim and Lasswell and others of this school plead their cause, they have nowhere adequately spelled out the specific nature of these conflicting character profiles or personality types. It does not carry us very far, for example, to say, as Lasswell and Mannheim do, that the democratic personality is tolerant, cooperative, and secure, while the authoritarian personality is domineering, resentful of criticism, more prone to resort to violence and other forms of pressure, and burdened by social anxiety. These are, for the most part, tautologous terms; they hide rather than reveal meanings. They also overlook the fact that few if any individuals are in all the facets of their being consistently the one or the other personality type, that nearly every man exhibits a complex of both "democratic" and "authoritarian" behavior traits. It is not unusual, then, for many who are "democratic" in their social relationships to be "authoritarian" in their family or professional life. It is, to revert to our first point, the situation and not the so-called personality type that is often crucial.[6]

It follows, thirdly, that if we do not know with "scientific" precision what a democratic or authoritarian personality *is*, and if what any one person *is* depends on the dynamics of a situation as much as, and perhaps more than, upon some static character trait or set of attitudes, then any attempt to test or to measure an assumed and fixed personality "type" is bound to be ambiguous or meaningless. And if we turn from the work of a sociologist like Mannheim and a political scientist like Lasswell to the tests, questionnaires, and interviews of the professional social psychologists and psychoanalysts, we find that this is precisely what occurs: the tests do not measure what they purport to measure; the evidences do not *prove* the existence of a definite "democratic" or "authoritarian" personality type.

This is true whether we take as our point of departure the simple though politically meaningless definition of the authoritarian personality given by Erich Fromm—that the authoritarian personality craves power over men but at the same time esteems it in others and longs to submit to it [7]—or the more complex if somewhat contradictory definition given by the authors of *The Authoritarian Personality* (perhaps the most influential of recent studies espousing this point of view)—that the authoritarian personality is rigidly conventional but is also cynical and destructive, is unimaginative and opposed to the subjective but is also disposed "to believe that wild and dangerous things go on in the world," holds to a deterministic view of man's fate but is also preoccupied with sex and power, and so on.[8] Neither definition is very helpful, for they describe or delineate features that can be found in some measure in nearly every man and hence do not enable us to discriminate among men. Since, moreover, both Fromm and the authors of *The Authoritarian Personality* employ an approach to personality that focuses on attitudes or predispositions rather than (as Mannheim in one place urges [9]) on behavior, they run into a larger difficulty—namely, the inability to distinguish (and consequently to measure) opinions or ideology from character. If we add to these limitations the failure of both contributions to take adequate account of the varying intensities with which such attitudes or predispositions may be held, and to relate them to the dynamic situations in which they may emerge or in which they may be present but subdued, we see that neither work can be said to carry us very far toward a "scientific" understanding of what the "authoritarian" personality is.[10]

Lasswell, indeed, in commenting on *The Authoritarian Personality*, argues that such a concept as the "authoritarian" personality—which he here defines as the "power centered" or "power oriented" man—is more properly applied to *followers* than to *leaders*, or to those who play comparatively minor rather than major roles in the power structure; conversely, he suggests, "all top leaders in democratic or totalitarian regimes . . . tend to be recruited from fundamental personality patterns that are not primarily oriented toward power." [11] If this hypothesis is valid, it would seem to negate his own earlier thesis as well as to cast into disrepute the entire notion of the appeal to the "right" personality (and the concomitant rejection of the "wrong" personality) as the indispensable corrective to the abuse of power.

THE RELEVANCE OF THE RIGHT MAN

It may, however, be argued that these strictures are not permanently binding. I have, after all, conceded that the *idea* of an authoritarian personality has a certain plausibility as an impressionistic or intuitive-apprehending, if not scientific, fact. Consequently, it may be said, refinements in testing techniques may in time enable us to verify such impressions and reduce them to demonstrable facts. They may help to isolate what is intrinsic to character structure from what is part of the total environment. But whether or not they succeed in doing so, it can be argued, the important fact remains that the authoritarian personality—however men may differ as to its definition—can in some measure be detected even now; hence, this awareness properly becomes, or should become, a guide to political action.

Now the possibility that refinements in testing techniques and in other devices will be achieved is hardly to be contested. Nevertheless, two problems at least will still plague those who hope to demonstrate through such means the validity of a particular personality typology. One problem derives from the curious but not surprising fact that while the concept of the authoritarian personality has received much attention and can be held to rest on some "scientific" evidences, the concept of the so-called democratic personality hangs very much in the air, and is more likely to remain there. For however difficult the task of defining the authoritarian personality may be, the description of those character traits or attitudes that constitute the democratic personality is a most dubious and controversial—because unscientific—undertaking.[12] The other problem stems from the fact that the line between the individual and the social cannot be effectively drawn. This, of course, was precisely the point on which Mill's otherwise admirable essay *On Liberty* floundered, and it is by no means evident that psychologists and sociologists since his time have succeeded in establishing a legitimate principle by which to differentiate that which is intrinsic to man from that which is inherited or acquired from society. I do not mean to imply by this that personality cannot be distinguished from culture; for the two, while not separable, are not the same. I argue only that the individual, be he conformist or rebel, is so much a product of his society that his attitudes, values, and behavior are always in some measure socially conditioned; they are always a reflection of his cultural environment. When we add to this the very great complexity, the continuing mystery, of personality itself, we see that no psychology can hope through an analysis of individual character alone to establish a particular typology of democratic and authoritarian personality.[13]

Let us, however, set these objections aside. Let us grant, in the face of our ignorance of future events, that a meaningful distinction may be drawn between democratic and authoritarian personalities, and that adequate tests will be devised to tell us into which category our various political leaders or would-be leaders belong. Can we then really expect the eradication of oppressive rule?

The answer, I fear, must still be negative, and for two reasons preeminently. On the one hand, abuses of power are not simply a consequence of some psychological quirk or defect in the ruler; they are also the product of conflicting interests, of long-sustained prejudices, and of established traditions. On the other hand, the right man, once in power, is not likely always to remain the right man. Contrary assumptions, while not wholly false, are insufficiently true to warrant the high expectations that some men have placed in them.

Consider first the view that men who abuse power do so primarily (in some formulations of this theory, exclusively) out of evil intent or vanity or madness. The list of tyrants who meet this view is a long but not an exhaustive one; Attila the Hun and Hitler and others like them are known, after all, only because they were, even among tyrants, unusual men. But, more importantly, the abuses of power that disfigure democratic states are customarily of a different order. They derive not merely from the caprice or malevolence of those who come to power but also, as we have seen, from the fact that those who rule, like the factions of the people who support them, tend all too often to pursue their own narrow or selfish interests; that rulers tend all too easily to identify the good of the whole with the material good of their class or of some special portion of the whole, such as their families and themselves. Thus, unless it can be shown that personality stands in some necessary—or even approximate (understanding by this a highly probable)—relation to policy, so that the right man will by virtue of his "rightness" act justly (i.e., in a way that transcends particularity of interest) and the wrong man will by virtue of his "wrongness" act unjustly (i.e., in a way that sacrifices the rights of the many, or even of the few, to greed and ambition), the appeal to personality is no solution to our problem.

This cannot be shown. There is no demonstrable relation between "democratic" or "authoritarian" personalities and policy such that authoritarian men will line up on one side, and democratic men on the other side, of each conceivable issue. The lines of ideological division do not respect those of personality, whether we look at a particular issue such as desegregation or at more general questions of domestic and foreign policy or even at the basic problem of the form of state itself. Indeed, if the theory of the authoritarian personality is a valid one, it is precisely among authoritarians that the greatest ideological divisions are likely to occur; for here the driving force is said to be not ideology but ambition, the craving for power, and in this context policies will be supported or opposed not in terms of their relation to one's character structure but in terms of their utility as steps along the pathway to power. The shifting positions on policy questions taken by Communist political parties in all democratic states at the command of the rulers in the Kremlin, most strikingly at the time of the Nazi-Soviet pact and again at the demise and subsequent denuding of their "great leader Stalin," are a continuing illustration in point; as are too the autocratic methods sometimes employed by democrats in combating those whom they deem to be authoritarians. On the other hand, persons of quite different dispositions may well behave in a more or less uniform manner, as is evidenced, for example, by the wide diversity of personality characteristics to be found in any political movement, including a democratic one.[14]

In fact, to argue that there is a causal relationship between democratic personality and social role is to imply that the specific undemocratic practices in this country—many and varied as they are—could all be eliminated merely by placing men with democratic personalities into positions of power. But this, surely, is a fanciful expectation. History is not made by the impact of personalities alone. A Carlyle may look to the ablest man in loyal reverence, and decry any institutional or other restraints that lesser men might seek to put upon him. But politics in a democracy is more than a matter of heroes and hero-worship. Other influences are also at play: the individual must come to grips with the interests and traditions of parties and pressure groups no less than with the established organs of government; he cannot ignore social conditions and the power of nonpolitical organizations; he must look to the will, however erroneous he may believe it to be, of the electorate which put him in power, and which can vote him out. He is bound, in a word, by historical, political, and economic forces that are not of his own making and that are often beyond his effective control. Consequently, even if the ruler should be the right man, the right personality, it does not follow that he can, in a democratic state, do what he conceives to be the right thing.

Nor should he be permitted to do so. If it is the business of a democratic state to give the people what they want, to satisfy their stated desires rather than their objective needs (i.e., what some allegedly wise men conceive their needs to be), then it is the function of the government to meet, not to negate, that demand. This is why, in principle, all the people, and not just a few of them, are given political rights. They need those rights, as Mill said, not in order that they may govern, but in order that they may not be misgoverned.[15] And for this purpose it is not the right or the outstanding man, not the so-called democratic personality, that is required, but the representative man—who is sensitive to the changing tides of public opinion and will faithfully seek to translate them into public policy. This is not to imply that a democratic leader ought never to attempt to mold or to change public opinion, that he ought never to be more than an effective recording device for the popular will. But it is to say that however much he may essay a leading role, he ought not, by and large, to act contrary to the judgment of his constituents. So long as he fulfills this role effectively, it is no proper concern of the public what manner of man he is. In this respect it is the part of wisdom to distinguish, so far as one can, the ruler's public life from his private character.

All of this is not to deny that evil or stupid men can cause great harm, and that those states are fortunate that can keep such men out of power. It is only to argue that since tyrannical policies are not necessarily the result of wrong or authoritarian character structures, those policies can neither be removed nor prevented by a remedy that looks to personality alone.

This conclusion is reinforced when we turn to the second of our two major objections to the relevance of the right personality: that the right man is also prone to do great harm. In part, this is because the temptations of power may sooner or later corrupt him, in which case he ceases to be the right man. But in part, too, it is precisely because he is the right man that he may do wrong things.

For if the right man is "right" in the moral sense of the word, and is moved by his intelligence and good will to correct the injustices that exist about him, he is sometimes apt to resent those of lesser talents or firmness of character who disagree with him and who would impede his work. Rather than risk failure, rather than have to say later, as the utopian Communist Wilhelm Weitling bitterly said: "If all had followed me as the children of Israel followed Moses out of Egypt, I would have succeeded," [16] he may endeavor to silence or to override dissent and to impose his own right judgment. Unhappily, in a world of conflicting moral codes, the right man is right for himself and perhaps for some others, but not for all men; and for those whose judgment is at variance with his own his coercive rule is as wrong as it may, in a particular situation, be oppressive. This is not, let it be understood, to argue that it is impossible to obtain a "right" man (i.e., right to those who so conceive him) as a leader in a democratic state, or that it would be undesirable to have such a right man rule. Nor is it to contend that such a right man could not, under any conditions, succeed both in remaining a right man and in ruling wisely. It is only to insist that such a right man *may*, in a particular set of circumstances, insist on having his own way (i.e., the "right" way) even if this requires him to act contrary to the popular will or to violate basic democratic rights.[17]

If, on the other hand, the right man is "right" in the democratic sense of the word, he is prone to respond affirmatively to the dictates of public opinion. But public opinion may bid him on occasion do an undemocratic thing, in which case he must choose between conflicting policies. As a right man, he wants to give the people what they want; but as a right man, he is committed also to the preservation of democracy itself. To remain loyal to the latter obligation is to defy public opinion and thereby to risk dismissal from public office. To accede to the public will is to repudiate his greater allegiance and thereby to retain public office only at the cost of ceasing to be the right man. In the first case, he is right but he may also prove ineffective; in the second case, he is neither right nor effective. In both cases, therefore, the appeal to the right man, to the leadership of, say, the democratic personality, provides no sure solution to the abuse of power.

I do not mean to carry this self-defeating perplexity too far. The fact that too many men would rather have power than be right does not necessarily imply that all right men will seek at all costs to retain power. Not all power corrupts all men. Some power, in fact, is requisite to the making of a man. Without some autonomy of action, without some delegation of power and the responsibility to administer that power wisely, a man may never grow out of the mentality of a child; he may remain always a dependent animal. And if experience is any guide, the histories of the British and the American democracies make it abundantly clear that, within a respected tradition and an institutional framework that renders rule neither permanent nor absolute, power does not necessarily corrupt; by affording opportunities, it enables many to rule moderately, and some to achieve greatness.[18]

But the temptations of power, though resisted by some, envelop many more. The lure of glory, of pride, of material gain, no less than the conviction that given the power to implement his will one can achieve great things, the right things, for the whole of his people—all these combine to make the pursuit, and later the retention, of power a more than necessary thing. Good men may begin the quest reluctantly, but they rarely end that way. The game is too serious, the weapons too biting, the stakes too high, for them to remain in fact what they strive to appear to be—selfless and genteel servants or would-be servants of the body politic. Those who lack power yearn for what appears now to be well within their grasp, and the failure to achieve it but stimulates them to greater endeavors than before; while the actual conquest and enjoyment of power, despite its bitter fruits, is yet so sweet as to seduce those who possess it into thinking that they were destined for the offices they hold, or (what amounts to the same thing) that their achievements will be destroyed if they surrender their protective role. And always there are the courtiers—the flatterers and the sycophants, the profit-seeking groups and the glory-seeking adventurers—whose own possibilities of success are linked to that of the rulers and who are ready, therefore, always to praise their rulers' actions and to encourage their idolatry of themselves.

It is not, therefore, surprising that even good men should begin to think that their power should be commensurate with their goodness, and that this being (in their own eyes at least) unlimited, they should desire their power to be unlimited too. It is true that many have echoed D'Avenant's warning that "no one man ought to think of being omnipotent, unless he could be omniscient and omnipresent." [19] It is true also that in this respect the American political system has heeded only too well Montesquieu's warning "that every man invested with power is apt to abuse it, and to carry his authority as far as it will go. . . . To prevent this abuse, it is necessary from the very nature of things that power should be a check on power." [20] But those who look to the guardianship of a right man do so precisely because the power which was designed to check the abuses of a lesser power is seen to require a check on its own abuses in turn. And those who, while recognizing the impossible requirement of omniscience and omnipresence, insist nevertheless on omnipotence (or a near-omnipotence) in the hands of a right man do so precisely because they are confident that the right man, because he is a "democratic" man, will not abuse his power.

Yet surely it is here, at the level of such absolute or near-absolute power, that the greatest danger of tyranny lies. For while power in itself may have no more than a tendency to corrupt, absolute power, as Mill and Acton said, corrupts absolutely. It gives its holders a new importance, a new set of habits. Finding themselves worshiped by others, they soon come to worship themselves. Finding that they can do as they like, they indulge in actions that previously seemed so improbable of achievement as to be put beyond the realm of serious contemplation. This is why it is foolish to assume, as the theorists of "democratic" personality are too often inclined to do, that a man out of power will remain the same man when in power. We must never forget, after all, that temptations come more often to him who is in power, and who can by his indulgence advantage the tempter, than to one who is out of power, and who can therefore indulge but give nothing in return.[21] Or that the removal of restraints on the bad as well as the good parts of one's nature makes possible the release of inhibitions that may work to the detriment of the community.[22]

What requires emphasis here, however, is not the corrupting effects of absolute power; for absolute power, even in the hands of the best, the most "democratic" man, is incompatible with democracy. What must be noted is the more relevant fact that even a limited grant of power works somehow in invidious ways to corrupt many of those who exercise it. It is, therefore, a wise political system that looks not only to the beneficent uses that good men will make of power but also to the unhappy consequences that might flow from power in the hands of those who were the wrong men before they achieved power or who became the wrong men after they obtained it.

I have argued, to this point, two things: first, that those who appeal to the right man to control abuses of power have provided no satisfactory definition of that right man; and second, that even if that right man were adequately defined, he would not necessarily remain the right man or do the right things. I have suggested, conversely, that the idea of the wrong man, of, say, the authoritarian personality, is of no real value to a democratic society, and this for two reasons in turn: first, that the definition of the wrong man is hardly less ambiguous or more applicable than is that of the right man;[23] and second, that since oppressive policies are the product of other, and more important, factors than that of personality alone, the repudiation of the wrong man would not necessarily secure the democratic state from the excesses of arbitrary rule.

It remains now only to stress one further point—namely, that it is the very meaning of democracy to accommodate the different personality types (if there be such) on equal terms, and not to discriminate among them. Democracy as a method of resolving differences among equals does not guarantee that the best or the right or the so-called democratic man will be put into positions of power, though it should be added that it is preferable for that purpose to other methods of choice. It is no proper concern of a democratic state that one man resents criticism while another welcomes it, that one man lacks independent and critical judgment while another is a creative thinker, that one man seeks power while another shies away from it, that one man is seemingly "well adjusted" while another is a solitary and difficult or "ill-adjusted" man. Men with such personality traits are to be found in every society, democratic and oligarchic alike, for there is no demonstrable relation between a democratic man and a democratic society, or between an authoritarian man and an oligarchical society. What history teaches is always, of course, a matter of considerable controversy, but this much at least seems clear: that democratic societies have always produced some "authoritarian" men, and that authoritarian societies have been confronted in every age by men who have been "democrats" both in personality and belief.

Whatever the historical teaching, however, it is the logic of the democratic principle that all men,[24] and not just a particular few, be admitted on equal terms to the rights of citizenship, to the contest for political power. It is also a part of that logic to insist that even the best men, when in power, be held responsible for their actions; for in no other way can a people hope to correct the errors that even the best, because they are still fallible, men commit. And it is a part of the faith, if not the necessary logic, of democracy that improvement in human affairs is to be anticipated not when a society is made up of like men, for that is the way of stagnation; but when a society cultivates, perhaps to an even greater degree than we thus far have, those conflicts of values, those differences in personality traits, that give challenge and variety and zest to the otherwise drab and penurious existence that is the everyday lot of so many men.

XI

The Appeal to an
Alternative Mode
of Democracy

Like the appeals to principle and to personality, the appeal to an alternative mode or organization of democracy assumes that the problem of the abuse of power within the democratic state is a single problem, readily and even (in some doctrines) objectively identifiable, and consequently susceptible of a single solution. Unlike them, however, it accounts for the failure of the American system to have solved this problem not by the fact that it employs an institutional approach—for the institutional approach is still, in this view, the correct approach—but by the fact that it employs the wrong institutions.

Thus, there are some theorists who conceive the problem of the abuse of power to reside in what they like to call the tyranny of the majority, and who, to curb this tyranny, would introduce additional structural or constitutional checks into the American system. On the other hand, there are those who are primarily concerned with what they call the tyranny of the minority, and who, in the effort to free the majority of what they conceive to be unwarranted restraints imposed on that majority by the ruling minority (or by that minority which has an effective veto power over the proposed acts of the majority), would remove even those checks and other hindrances to majority rule that the American system presently provides. Still others look outside the majority-minority conflict, outside the consequences of the struggle for and the possession of political power, to the dangers of oppression that reside in economic and other forms of private power, and propose, in the effort to eliminate this oppression, to reorder the economic and other power systems so as to limit the degree of power in private hands. In these and other ways, men who tend to explain the problem of power in terms of a single-factor analysis seek to meet that problem by a single-factor solution.

But if the problem of the abuse of power is not one but many problems, then a single-factor solution, no matter what its effectiveness in dealing with a particular phase or aspect of that multifaceted problem, is incapable of eliminating or controlling oppression. At best, it may control a particular manifestation of the abuse of power, a particular oppressive action; it cannot control all abuses of power. At worst, it might not only fail to curb the particular abuse it is designed to suppress, but even give rise to a new abuse (or set of abuses) of its own. In the light of such considerations, let us examine the suggested ways of reorganizing the American democracy.

THE APPEAL TO A CONCURRENT OR PROLIFERATED MAJORITY

Take, first, that view of oppression which equates it with the tyranny of the majority. This builds on the age-old argument that where men act in terms of their self-interest rather than in terms of the common good, they are likely to injure those whose interests move them into an antagonistic camp. Since, in this view, men customarily act in terms of their self-interests—in the judgment of a thinker like Calhoun, they necessarily do so—either the minority will abuse the majority or the majority will abuse the minority. Plato and Aristotle contemptuously termed the first of these abuses oligarchy, and the second democracy, and would have neither of them. But in the city of man, where men and not angels rule, the one or the other is sometimes (perhaps always) the inevitable choice. Those who cast their lot with democracy, whether in qualified or in absolute degree, do so because they can see no

justice in a scheme of government which permits a few to dominate, and to enjoy the disproportionate fruits of that domination,
over the many. But not all who thus side with democracy are prepared to see the majority abuse the minority in turn. They cling
still to the principle of quality or, more strictly, to what they
conceive to be the principle of right; they reject the mere claim
of numbers.[1] Consequently, they have sought, like Madison, to
control in some way the vexatious effects of majority rule. But
unlike Madison, who seemed confident (at least in Number 10
of *The Federalist*) that federalism and the involved system of
checks and balances established by the American Constitution
would prevent governments from abusing their powers, they believe that experience has demonstrated the essential inadequacy
of that constitutional arrangement as an effective instrument of
control. They would not, to be sure, remove the division and
separation of powers; for the consequences of such removal would,
in their eyes, but increase the power of the majority and thereby
the evils of its impulsive and frequently despotic actions. What
they recommend instead is the adoption of *additional* checks and
balances; they seek further and more effective methods of imped-
ing or restraining simple majority rule.

Of the various formulae that have been suggested to effectuate
this end, none has enjoyed so long and so great an eminence as has
Calhoun's doctrine of the concurrent majority.[2] Calhoun did not,
of course, entertain the naïve hope that he, or any one else, could
construct a wholly foolproof system—"one that would completely
counteract the tendency of government to oppression and abuse."
Such perfection, he readily conceded, "has thus far exceeded human wisdom and possibly ever will." What he did believe, however, was that he had uncovered the *ideal* solution—one which, to
the extent that it might be properly applied (i.e., most closely
approximate the perfect organism), would exclude the possibility
of oppression. This *ideal* solution, he maintained, was the government of the concurrent majority.[3]

Rulers and ruled, Calhoun believed, stand always in antagonistic relation to each other: the one tends always to oppress and

abuse the other; the other seeks always an effective and peaceable means of resistance. Hence, it is never enough to rely merely on the numerical majority; for while the numerical majority can, through the right of suffrage, prevent the rulers from oppressing the ruled, what will prevent the numerical majority from becoming oppressive in turn? Surely not a greater power, Calhoun argued, for the majority, by asserting its control over those it has elected, has become the greatest power. Surely not a sense of common interest, for the community—whatever its bonds—is divided also into a multiplicity of conflicting interests. The oppression and abuse of the dominant majority, Calhoun concluded, can only be restrained in one way, namely, by giving "to each division or interest . . . either a concurrent voice in making and executing the laws, or a veto on their execution." In this way each interest or portion of the community would be afforded "the means of protecting itself, by its negative, against all measures calculated to advance the peculiar interests of others at its expense." [4]

Now where a community is a relatively small and homogeneous one, with its citizens (or the overwhelming bulk of them) fundamentally committed to the same hierarchy of values, Calhoun's solution is a plausible one. For then the differences among men and groups would revolve primarily about questions of means, not of ends; they would disagree as to the way in which something should be done, not as to whether it should be undertaken. This is why a society like the Quakers can prolong its discussions until it arrives at a sense of the meeting, why it can refuse to act simply at the behest of a majority will. Since its members share the same principles, respect each other's interests and judgments, and tend through repeated experiences to approach problems in like ways, they encounter no great difficulty in securing agreement on particular courses of action.

But where the community is rent by factions and a diversity of interests, where men and groups are profoundly disagreed not only as to how something should be done but also as to what it is that ought to be done, such unanimity cannot readily be obtained.

In such a society, Calhoun's solution would tend to exacerbate rather than to mediate controversies; for by insisting on a forced rather than a natural unanimity—or, more strictly, on the assent of a majority of each interest that is adversely affected in addition to that of the majority of the whole—it would give disproportionate power to a recalcitrant few. The difficulty with Calhoun's solution, that is to say, is not that it would fail to protect a minority interest from the iniquitous actions of a majority; for clearly if no majority could act a minority without that minority's consent, the minority would always be able to preclude hurtful measures. What is wrong with Calhoun's solution is that, among other things, its very success would put an end to government, to the principle of democracy itself; or, short of this, that it might enable a determined minority to precipitate such chaos as to achieve capitulation from the majority, thereby restoring the very tyranny of the minority that the principle of the numerical majority was supposed to foreclose.

It is surely the height of naïveté to assume, as Calhoun did, that the requirement of unanimity would compel diverse interests to compromise their differences and acquiesce, through necessity, in some one opinion or course of action. On the contrary, the compulsion to protect their interests might well lead a particular interest group to adopt an intransigent position, to stand forth as an insuperable barrier to change. For, from the standpoint of a minority about to suffer an indignity or a disadvantage or the deprivation of a cherished right, it may be better to suffer the displeasure of the rest of the community, it may be better even to force anarchy, than to acquiesce in its own destruction. From the standpoint of the majority, however, this recalcitrance may well appear to be no more than an arbitrary assertion of minority will, a stubborn insistence by a particular interest group that it will play the game only on condition that it always win.

What, then, a democrat may ask, is the point of having a state at all? Why seek even to discover the will of the numerical majority? Suppose, for example, a numerical majority favored a Wagner Act or a Taft-Hartley Law. If the consent of management in the first instance, and of labor in the second, were necessary before that majority will could be transformed into law, the probability is that there would be no national labor relations act at all. So, too, with other regulatory legislation. To expect each interest —rural and urban, commercial and industrial, producer and consumer, etc.—to consent to measures that would adversely affect it is to expect the impossible.[5]

There are, of course, very great difficulties involved even in the creation of the machinery necessary for a concurrent majority to function, not least the problem of determining which among the vast horde of competing interest groups merit representation: for if all interests are represented, the overlapping of some and the trivial size of others would soon render the effort to represent all of them futile or irksome; while if only some (the so-called major) interests are to be given representation, those interests excluded from a concurrent voice would have no effective way of blocking the despotic actions of others. But it is less the mechanical details of Calhoun's scheme than it is the failure to appreciate the need of government for some coercive power against inevitable opposition, that provides the major difficulty. For always, on Calhoun's own premises, there will be opposition; and as one of Calhoun's more perceptive commentators observed, "unless differences of interest are somehow compromised within the ordered framework of a legal system, irreconcilable minorities will be created which must in the end be coerced."[6] The alternative is to permit the minority, or a particular minority, to hamstring the majority; to deny not merely the right of the numerical majority to rule but to insist that, if the viewpoint of a concerned minority—and it ought never to be forgotten that there are always minorities within minorities—is not to prevail, there shall be no political rule at all.

This being so, the government of the concurrent majority, while it may prevent the so-called tyranny of a numerical majority, does so only at the twofold cost of reestablishing the tyranny of the minority and of sacrificing effective government itself. In this respect it gives rise to a greater set of abuses than the one it purports to remove; for in the absence of effective government, as Calhoun himself repeatedly argued, neither liberty nor security, neither the perfection nor the protection of society, can be achieved. And in the presence of the tyranny of a minority, the principle of democracy is outraged.

THE APPEAL TO BARE MAJORITY RULE

In contrast to those who, like Calhoun, concentrate on the dangers of majority rule and seek devices further to constrain the power of a numerical majority, a number of democratic theorists have been troubled by what they conceive to be the continuing absence of majority rule in America. In their view, the institutional devices established by the framers of the American Constitution to fragment and diffuse political powers have in fact prevented the majority from ruling, or, more strictly, from effectively controlling those who rule in its name. Consequently, what oppressive measures have been enacted in America are to be accounted for in terms of a dominant and abusive minority will, or the will of a minority that is itself a coalition of minorities, not in terms of a tyrannical majority will. For if the majority has not in fact ruled, it cannot be said to have ruled oppressively.[7] Nor, in the very nature of things, argue the proponents of this view, is it likely to do so; for then it would but tyrannize over itself, which is an absurdity. As a result, what is required is not a further proliferation of majorities, not additional restraints on the normal processes of majority rule, but rather a reordering of the American political system so as to give effective political power to the majority rather than, as they insist it has thus far been given, to the minority of the people.

Now to the extent that the advocates of majority rule assert no more than that a majority is entitled to have its way, they affirm a primary and indispensable principle of democracy. One may concede that it is ideally best for a community to act only after it has achieved unanimity of opinion—not only because a unanimous will is strongest and most binding, but because it includes the will of those who claim to be wise as well as that of "lesser" men. But in a complex and heterogeneous society the quest for unanimity is an impossible one; it is as vain as the quest for the Holy Grail. Men will always be divided on any question of policy. Always differences of knowledge, of character, of intelligence, of temperament, of interest, of circumstance, and the like will drive men to opposing positions. To insist on unanimity in the face of such differences is to insist either on inaction or, what is more likely, on domination by a minority sufficiently determined to frustrate the majority's preference, even to the point of making its own will prevail. This, at any rate, is the experience of all attempts to establish the principle of unanimity in government through the grant of an effective veto to any one of the members—whether we look at the Roman tribunate or the Polish Diet or the United Nations. The practical alternative to majority rule, therefore, is not unanimity but some form of minority rule. It is to substitute the less universal will for an impossible universal will. It is to enable the smaller rather than the greater part to carry the day. And this, from the standpoint of democratic principle, is intolerable.

In these terms, R. M. MacIver is surely right when he asserts that "decision by majority is in matters of policy a practical necessity." [8] And in these terms, those defenders of the principle of majority rule who urge the modification of the American political system so as to do away with such impediments to that rule as judicial review, the equal representation of the states in the Senate, and the system of staggered national elections have the logic of democracy—as well, it should be added, as the experience of Great Britain—on their side.[9]

It does not follow, however, that *what* the majority wills is necessarily right; that a majority unimpeded in exercising the powers it has acts wisely or properly in determining the ends or objects of public policy. It is one thing to argue for absolute or simple majority rule with respect to the way in which governments shall arrive at their decisions; it is a quite different thing to conclude from this that such decisions, because they are arrived at by the majority process, are wise or right. To affirm the latter involves an ethical judgment, and a corresponding criterion, that must be drawn from a source outside the majority process itself. If it is drawn—as I shall draw it here—from the principle of democracy or, more directly, from the principles of equality and liberty as I have earlier used these terms, then clearly a majority can, through the normal processes of democracy, violate those principles by enacting laws that deny to certain of its citizens a full measure of equality before the law, or the freedom to express certain disliked political opinions. A majority can, through the procedures of democracy, violate the principle of majority rule itself. If it does so, or to the extent that it may do so, it acts oppressively.

Now those who are the most vigorous adherents of a system of bare majority rule are the first to recognize the vital distinction between majority rule as the *method* by which a state (or, more broadly, a community) makes its decisions and majority rule as the *standard of legitimacy* by which the limits of the sovereign power of that state (or community) are determined.[10] And while the burden of their argument is generally addressed to the method rather than to the limits of decision making—sometimes (as with Willmoore Kendall) on the ground that this latter question is properly a question of ethics and thus outside the domain of political science or political theory—they nevertheless invariably conclude that majority rule is either itself the best means of determining what those limits are, whether they are being respected, and whether they require adaptation to changing circumstances, or that majority rule, while sometimes invidious, is, on the record, the best, the most judicious, calculated risk against the dangers of abusive power.[11]

I will bypass here the question whether or not political theory, properly understood, is, or can be, value-free; [12] for the answer to this question, whatever it may be, remains irrelevant to the more important issue here, which is whether majority rule, conceived as a standard of authority or of jurisdiction, really promises to preclude oppressive political behavior. And to this question, surely a negative is the only possible answer.

It is almost startling to read today, more than a century after it was written, the assured words with which Jared Sparks, a noted American historian and contemporary of Tocqueville, dismissed Tocqueville's fears of the tyranny of the majority as being "entirely mistaken." Sparks said:

His ideas are not verified by experience. The tyranny of the majority, if exercised at all, must be in the making of laws; and any evil arising from this source operates in precisely the same manner on the majority itself as on the minority. Besides, if the majority passes an oppressive law, or a law which the people generally disapprove, this majority will certainly be changed at the next election, and be composed of different elements. M. de Tocqueville's theory can only be true where the majority is an unchangeable body and where it acts exclusively on the minority, as distinct from itself,—a state of things which can never occur where the elections are frequent and every man has a voice in choosing the legislators.[13]

Even apart from the fact that this so-called tyranny of the majority may be exercised through other than legal means, Sparks's several statements—whether applied to the time in which he lived or to our own day—are little more than a tissue of errors. Laws do not operate on majorities or on minorities at all, but on *individuals,* and they do not affect all individuals alike; hence, a law which oppresses one man or a group of men may leave other men unaffected, or may operate on them with much less abusive effect. Consequently, a law which is oppressive to some men may not be disapproved by all; on the contrary, it may be precisely what a majority of men applaud. And because a majority may applaud it, the next election may see it reaffirmed rather than altered or removed. Even Sparks's stated conditions—frequent elections and universal suffrage—do not debar abuses of power; for in the American democracy, where both conditions are presently met (or, with respect to universal suffrage, are nearly met), the majority is almost unchangeable with respect to certain racial and national minority groups. As a result, that majority *can* act on the minority (i.e., on individuals who comprise a minority) as distinct from itself,[14] and it has in fact done so. It is not at all clear, to take a case in point, that a modern version of Tocqueville's *Democracy in America* would differ other than in detail and in severity of treatment from his account of the oppressive conditions under which the Negro and the Indian are compelled to live; certainly, such a modern version would have to conclude, as Tocqueville did, that both of these minority peoples "suffer from tyranny." [15]

It may, of course, be argued that these abuses are but exceptional instances, and that, taken as a whole, the case for bare majority rule, while not perfect, is so substantially superior to the case against it, or the case for any alternative mechanism, that it provides, if not "a *true* principle in the scientific sense or ethically ideal . . . the second strongest ethical claim on democrats." [16] But exceptions, of course, *disprove* rather than prove the rule; and while I am, with certain reservations,[17] partial to the argument for majority rule, I cannot set aside the fact that majorities are not always blessed with wisdom and compassion, with tolerance and an inflexible will to justice, or the fact that even if they were so endowed they would still (in all probability) differ in their interpretations as to what these terms mean in a particular situation. On the record, however powerful we may concede the institutional restraints on majority rule in America to have been, it is surely incorrect to say that none, or only a very few, of the abuses of power cited in Chapters IV and VI, for example, have had the support of a majority of the people. Consequently, majority rule, while preferable to any form of minority rule, cannot be said to provide a sure guarantee that oppressive actions will not occur.

In fact, the effort to establish a system of bare majority rule is likely—if pushed hard and far enough—to produce the very despotism that a majoritarian system is designed to preclude. For, in what must be accounted one of the great paradoxes of our time, the majority of the American people do not seem to want a system of majority rule.[18] They do not trust themselves to rule wisely. They welcome formal or institutional restraints on their own powers and desires. This, surely, is the unavoidable lesson to be drawn from President Roosevelt's unsuccessful attempt to alter the composition of the Supreme Court in 1937, and from the continuing attachment of the people to the Court, as well as to such other undemocratic institutions as the American Senate, the filibuster, and the electoral college. In this respect tradition plays an important and inhibiting role. The people are habituated to, and appear overwhelmingly to approve, the myriad of institutional restraints on the popular will. They do not want, on the contrary, they resent and violently resist, efforts to alter the system so as to increase their own powers, or to give to that government which has the support of a majority an absolute right to have its way. Consequently, the attempt to impose a system of majority rule, to transplant or import (as it were) the British political system or a modified version of that system, is bound to create fundamental antagonisms and divisions within the American commonwealth. It is bound to array majority against minority, but in that strange alignment of forces which will pit a minority urging majority rule against a majority stoutly opposing it. Thus, to secure majority rule, it may be necessary for the minority to impose it contrary to the will of the majority itself. And this, of course, is not majority rule but a form, however benevolent, of minority rule.

THE APPEAL TO AN ECONOMIC AND SOCIAL DEMOCRACY

The fact that majorities and minorities are both motivated by considerations of self-interest—and that, consequently, both the partisans of Calhoun and the advocates of bare majority rule are right in what they affirm to be the dangers of the other but wrong in what they deny to be the dangers of their own positions —suggests that very great, perhaps insuperable, difficulties beset those who seek a solution to the problem of abusive power simply within the majority-minority process, within the normal or accepted patterns of democratic procedures. It is possible, however, in the eyes of certain thinkers, for this troublesome question of internal political arrangements to be satisfactorily resolved, and still to find that the problem of oppression has been but partially met. For there is still a need to control the oppressive acts of private powers, to temper and (ideally) to remove the abuses that men suffer at the hands of those more powerful than themselves.

Political power, after all, is but one of many forms of social power. Always those who own or control access to the means of production, who have a primary say as to the allocation of a country's resources, who largely determine the distribution of income, possess a degree of power that enables them to affect—sometimes inescapably and always profoundly—the lives of others. Invariably the head of a family, or of an educational institution, or of a church, or of any other social or cultural organization exercises power over those subject to his jurisdiction. In a democratic society, such organizations are afforded a considerable degree of autonomy, so that those who exercise power within them are rarely rendered responsible to those over whom that power is exercised. In corporate economic organizations particularly, the lines of power take on definite oligarchical, sometimes even dynastic, overtones. How, then, are we to check the abuses of power to which such rulers, no less than their political counterparts, are prone?

In part, of course, the answer is that unless a society is to turn totalitarian, some abuses—which are the necessary consequences of some freedoms—cannot be controlled. It is difficult to see, for example, how the head of a family or of a church (if it is an orthodox church of a revealed religion) can be made responsible to his subordinates for all of his actions and teachings, or how he can be subjected to outside (e.g., political) controls, without destroying the very nature of the family and church as we know them. It is no less apparent that for a state completely to control all private economic power is not only to destroy that power, but, by the very fact that it thereby unites both political and economic power within a single orbit, to prepare the conditions for a monolithic empire; and when there is no longer any effective economic power outside of government, the probability is, in the modern world, that there will no longer be any effective way to check the abuses of government. The costs of controlling private economic power, that is to say, may be more dangerous than the arbitrary exercise of that power itself. For this reason, among others, democratic theorists have generally sought to restrain the state from undue encroachments on private activities in the economic and social realms.

It does not follow, however, that because the state should not do everything, it should do nothing. And despite such considerations as those just set forth, the modern democratic state has in fact embarked on a series of regulatory acts that do limit the powers of private rulers. Parents cannot send their children, at least in certain formative years, to the factory rather than to school. Ministers and priests cannot flog or otherwise corporally punish their parishioners, or through such procedures as an Inquisition condemn heretics to be burned at the stake. And through a vast network of labor and business law, the governments of economic organizations find themselves seriously circumscribed in what they may or may not do. In these and other ways, democratic states have employed their political powers to control what they have conceived to be intolerable excesses of private power.

Much, however, according to certain thinkers, remains to be done. Most commonly, it is argued that a democratic political system must, if it is to fulfill itself, so transform the capitalist foundations on which the society is built as to become a social and an economic democracy.

Now it is clearly beyond the scope of this work to evaluate the vast number of schemes that men have proposed to effectuate what they variously (and not always consistently) call an economic or a social democracy,[19] or to consider anew the age-old question of the primacy of economic as against political power.[20] But if we set aside those doctrines that have elicited but minor popular support—e.g., the idea of functional or economic representation advocated by syndicalists and guild socialists—and focus on that general and (in certain Western democracies such as Sweden and England) widely approved collectivist approach which would have the state embark on large-scale government ownership and operation of the basic industries, or assume what have come to be called welfare responsibilities, we can see that the problem of abusive power is by no means thereby overcome.

For one thing, to the extent that government ownership or nationalization concentrates attention on, and designs corrective measures for, the abuses of economic and social power, it leaves unaffected the vital question of oppression by political powers. In fact, by transferring to the state a number and range of problems heretofore outside its jurisdiction, both the gravity of political abuses of power and the opportunity for such abuses to occur may well be intensified. In the second place, a transfer of title is often no more than that; it need not involve a removal or a lessening of abuses. For then bureaucrats, or managers employed by the state, rather than owners, or managers employed by the owners, will make the immediate and most directly felt decisions; and in place of the distant stockholders there will be the distant executive and the legislature. This is not to say, as I sought to point out earlier, that controls exercised by such agencies are insignificant. It is rather to note that the managerial function, whatever the nature of the economic system, remains a technical one, and as such it is not readily susceptible to the sort of democratic responsibility that is commonly institutionalized in the political sphere. Managers cannot, if an economic system is to function effectively, be elected and removed at the will of the men who work under them, or at the pleasure of the consumers who ultimately buy their products. The controls, if any, must lie elsewhere —in the hands of the policy-determining agencies such as the President and the Congress. But since, in the modern democratic state, strikes against the government are disallowed, workers (and their unions) who would press for the redress of certain grievances might find that their chances of victory are less, not greater, than before. They may find, in fact, that while nationalization has removed them from the arbitrary controls of a private employer, it has done so (in effect) only to subject them instead to the controls of their government.[21] And the latter, it is hardly necessary to add, is a considerably more potent force than the former.

Nationalization of the basic industries, that is to say, affords no sure guarantee that abuses of power will be eliminated. At best, it eliminates one *source* of such abuses of power, namely, private rulers or private governments. But it can do this only by replacing those private rulers with public officials, who may themselves act oppressively—either on their own initiative or in accord with instructions given them by a superior official or agency —in turn. Consequently, the problem—to the extent that it may be considered "a" problem—is shifted to another battleground; it is not solved.

So, too, with the tendency of modern democratic governments to adopt some form of welfare economics. It is clear that the welfare state, by providing (or guaranteeing) certain minimum standards of health, education, and welfare, alters the bargaining position of some groups with respect to others. Those who are no longer threatened by starvation can more easily resist the impositions of better-circumstanced groups, and to that extent the welfare state limits the power of private governments to oppress weaker, because more dependent, men.

But the welfare state is still open to the same sort of dangers that attend a nationalized economy. For it transfers rather than eliminates the power of deprivation; it lodges that power in the hands of political officials, where before it had resided in the hands of private rulers. And such a transfer, it is plain, carries with it no assurance that this power will be more wisely, or less arbitrarily, used. In fact, by enabling administrative officials to withdraw benefits—e.g., social security and unemployment compensation payments, or access to state-owned or state-aided low-cost housing—from certain dissident individuals or groups, it gives those officials a degree of power, and therefore of potentially oppressive power, at least the equal of that of private governments. That such a grant of power can be, and on occasion has been, abused has been time and again clearly demonstrated during the past decade.

I conclude, therefore, that while both nationalization of the basic industries and the trend toward welfare economics promise to alleviate or to remove some abuses of power, or the sources of some abuses of power, they do not constitute a bar to all of them. In fact, where the abuse now occurs, it may well prove—because of the increased strength of the oppressive power—to be even more oppressive than before.

XII

The Quest for
a Solution

I have argued thus far that abuses of power, which are intrinsic to oligarchical forms of government, are not *necessarily* eliminated by the mere fact that a state is democratic. Actual states being always but approximations of an ideal, it follows that all democratic states—both through the laws (including the administration of the laws) and through the practices of private powers—fail in some measure to live up to the principles which are supposed fundamentally to distinguish them from nondemocratic systems. Democratic states always deny—or at least have denied—some democratic rights to some of their citizens. Some private powers always fail—or at least have failed—to respect the legitimate egalitarian claims of the less powerful. Such abuses cannot be, as they have not been, eliminated by an institutional approach that fragments and decentralizes power in the way that the American political system, for example, has diffused it. Nor are those abuses likely to be eliminated by an appeal to certain allegedly objective right principles, or by a trust in certain "well-adjusted" or "democratic" or other allegedly right men, or by a reordering of the political or economic system so as to achieve an alternative mode of democracy.

What, then, if we are not always to dwell under an oppressive government, is to be done?

THE PROBLEM REFORMULATED

I want to suggest here that, so long as the question is put in this way, it does not admit of an answer. All governments, including democratic governments, are in fact oppressive to some people with respect to some things; no governments, not even the most oligarchical of governments, are oppressive to all of their citizens with respect to all things. Consequently, the question is not: are we always to be either anvil or hammer? or, are we always to dwell under an oppressive government? or even, preferably, can we hope someday to have a nonoppressive government? It must rather be phrased in terms of specific acts of oppression, and in terms that relate to some people with respect to some things, and not to all people with respect to all things.

Thus, while it is true that an oligarchical government seeks to satisfy the interests of only some rather than of all of its citizens, for the favored few it is not necessarily oppressive. On the contrary, it may accurately reflect their notions as to who should rule, and for what purposes. Even with respect to those of its subjects who oppose it, an oligarchical government need not tyrannize over them in all the phases of their being. It may find it expedient to let even an antagonistic majority alone—at least with respect to certain things, e.g., religious worship. As a result, an oligarchical government can provide certain important liberties for some or all of its people without giving them what democrats would hold to be the vital liberties. It is only when we turn to the totalitarian dictatorships of our own day that we approach a degree of oppression and of control that affects nearly all of the citizens in nearly all of the important phases of life. But here too, even apart from those who may actively or passively support the regime, no totalitarian state has yet been able to destroy all liberties—to close, for example, and to keep closed the doors of the churches, to banish all untoward thoughts, to stifle the laughter and the ridicule and at times (as Hungary in 1956 made clear) even the violence that fragmentarily erupt against those who pose as secular gods.

If this is true of oligarchical states, the converse is no less true of democratic states. For while the democratic state should be rooted in the consent of its people, it cannot pretend to rest on the consent of *all* of them. Always some among the people withhold their consent—e.g., anarchists, monarchists, Fascists, Communists—and for such people the democratic state appears as an instrument of force, not as a vehicle of agreement. Even some of those who regard themselves as democrats and who therefore subscribe to the system as a whole do not always welcome or approve the acts of a particular government, for at most that government represents and rules in the name of a temporary—and perhaps antagonistic—majority; while the majority itself—or, more accurately, the members of the diverse groups that temporarily comprise that majority—may find, on occasion, that it opposes a particular act or proposed act of its own government. Consequently, a government produced by a democratic system may appear, not only to antidemocrats but also to many convinced democrats, to act oppressively some of the time.

This being so, the problem of power, to be adequately understood and dealt with, must be reduced at the outset to a series of problems involving specific oppressive acts that affect particular individuals or groups in a particular area of their civic life; it is not an act or a series of acts that necessarily (or even customarily) affects all of the people in all of the areas that have meaning and importance for them.

Judged from this standpoint, those who talk of and who attempt to build safeguards against the abuses of an oppressive government, or of a majority, or of a minority, are alike deficient in their analyses and in their proposed solutions. They all (by and large) fail to see that the problem of power is not a single problem, capable of being dealt with by a single solution, but that it is many problems, requiring a multiplicity and variety of solutions, each calculated to meet a particular difficulty in an appropriate way. In other words, the "problem" of abusive power (to the extent that we may still employ the word "problem") is the never-ending problem of isolating and controlling particular abusive acts. And as such, no single-factor analysis or solution can hope to carry us very far. It may well be that a particular method that allows for a diversity of solutions may be considered "the" solution to the problems of power, but—assuming that such a single method can be devised—it is still a means to a solution, not the solution itself. In this sense, democracy as a method of government can be defended as a better device than its alternative, oligarchy, to control the variety of oppressive acts that repeatedly appear in a society—not on the ground that it constitutes "the" solution but rather on the ground that it better guarantees the right of free, experimental choice among different "solutions."

The problem of power, then, like the problem of freedom, becomes (in part at least) the problem of choosing between restraints of different orders of severity, scope, and enforceability. Some restraints may, to be sure, restrain other restraints—e.g., where A (the government) restrains B (an employer) from interfering with C (the latter's employee)—and this may, in a particular situation, maximize the conditions of freedom (or of a particular freedom) for some men, e.g., C. But not all restraints operate to this effect. Some restraints, clearly, remain interferences with freedom. Hence, to choose between restraints is sometimes to choose the lesser of probable evils. And where the restraint is both inevitable and a marginal—i.e., oppressive—one, the act of choice may require acceptance of, or at least resignation to, some form of oppressive rule. It becomes not simply a choice between restraints but a choice between abuses—between the abuses, say, of government with respect to otherwise oppressive private powers or of private powers with respect to individuals. Since it is the oppressors rather than the oppressed who, in actual fact, commonly make that choice—who determine which abuses, not merely which alternative choices (as they must appear to their victims), shall be imposed—what is at stake is a determination between forms or grants of power that entail the possibility of certain abusive acts. Sometimes, to be sure, it is maintained that such grants of power—e.g., to government—are made in order that (other) abuses of power—e.g., by private associations—might be effectively curbed. But sometimes the effect, if not the calculated intent, of such grants is to exacerbate the oppression.

Thus, the question for the democratic (as for every) state is not whether or not there shall be restraints, whether or not there shall be abuses. The question is one of values, of the proper primacy or hierarchy of freedoms, and of the order or classes of men who shall enjoy or be denied those freedoms, or some of them. Conversely, it is a question of which restraints or oppressive measures men are willing to accept the better to eliminate or to avoid other, and more intolerable, restraints or oppressive measures.

This is a hard and perhaps paradoxical conclusion, but it is, I believe, the inescapable consequence of any attempt to apply the democratic principle in actual political practice. In all states men willingly, if unhappily, suffer some restraints, some deprivations of their esteemed liberties, if in their judgment such restraints or deprivations are the necessary price of securing other, and more highly esteemed, freedoms. They also, reluctantly or otherwise, impose some restraints or deprivations on other men, when in their judgment those restraints or deprivations are necessary or even (in some cases) merely convenient to their own advantage, or where they believe that the subjects of their oppressive actions merit them. What the principle of democracy does is to provide a criterion or set of criteria that enables us to discriminate certain politically vital from other (and therefore, in this context, subordinate if still precious) liberties, and thereby to determine which of the many restraints or deprivations of power we are prepared to tolerate. For while all restraints involve a limitation of some freedoms, the creation of means necessary to the elimination of some of those restraints may involve a restraint on other, and more important, freedoms. Thus, the paradox is affirmed that some restraints—even such as might otherwise be deemed an abuse of power—may, in an indirect fashion, further rather than restrict the preservation and enjoyment of the vital liberties. More directly, the cost of eliminating some restraints, even (it may be) of some abuses of power, may prove in its net effect to be more destructive of certain of the fundamental liberties than would be the cost of suffering them.

THE NEVER-ENDING QUEST FOR PIECEMEAL SOLUTIONS

The question of oppression, then, cannot properly be posed as a single problem to be solved; for it is not a single problem but a series of *problems*. Consequently, there is no one answer, no one solution; there are only approximate solutions, or (more accurately) there is only a never-ending quest for particular solutions, to the innumerable specific abuses of power that constantly occur under all forms of political organization. In this respect politics, like philosophy, is (at least in part) "a battle against the bewitchment of our intelligence by means of language." [1] Hence, if we are not to foreclose the possibility of obtaining significant or meaningful answers, we must take care not to ask the wrong question, however all-inclusive and therefore fascinating it may be to some minds.

In these terms, the problem of power in the democratic state must be reduced in the first instance to the problem (or problems) of controlling particular abuses of power, or, since such abuses are limitless in number and in some respects unforeseeable, to the problem (or problems) of meeting the various types or categories of abuses of power. I suggested earlier that these categories are essentially two: the first embracing those acts that are oppressive irrespective of the form of government; the second embracing those acts that are oppressive only with respect to the principles of a democratic state. In the first category, the preeminent problem is clearly that of authority—i.e., of discovering and maintaining a mode of government that respects the principle of consent as the legitimate source of power. In the second category, the primary problem is to maintain relatively inviolate certain rights which are indispensable to the very principle of democracy—namely, such freedoms as the freedoms of speech and of political association, and such equalities as equality of citizenship and equality of opportunity. These may not, of course, be the only rights intrinsic to democracy, but they are surely among those minimum rights without which no state can be termed democratic.

Now what democracy does is to provide an appropriate solution or remedy to the first of these categories of potentially abusive acts. It meets the problem of the usurpation of power by establishing a political structure that is rooted in consent—not, to be sure, a universal or unanimous consent (for such things are not of this world), but that general consent or consensus that derives from a broad agreement on the fundamentals of the political and social order. But this institutionalization of consent does not by itself provide a solution or set of solutions to the problems of oppression *within* the democratic state. Here, because the threats to fundamental rights are multiple—emerging both from governments and from private powers—the problems and (perhaps) the solutions cannot be circumscribed within a single principle.

It is easy enough to say, and to say with considerable justification, that the abuses of private powers can be controlled by governments. But apart from the fact that no democratic government has attempted to control all the potentially vexatious behavior of individuals or of groups, it is doubtful that it could do so even if the attempt were to be made; for if a government is truly representative of the popular will, if it is really rooted in consent, it may find, on the one hand, that it is carrying out oppressive policies that the people support, or, on the other hand, that it is unable—without extreme violence or the resort to such violence as might endanger the viability of the political system itself—to enforce such prohibitions on invidious conduct as it may enact and seek to enforce. The unprecedented action of the United States Supreme Court in holding segregation in education to be unlawful but in directing the Southern states to continue to practice this unlawful and even tyrannical conduct until such time as they (or public opinion in their states) can adjust to the required change is a remarkable instance in point. In any case, it is certain that no democratic government can hope to control the potentially oppressive conduct of all men without transforming itself, in turn, into the greatest of Leviathans—and therefore, in all probability, into the greatest of tyrants.

This is not to say, as I have previously sought to emphasize, that a government which abstains from imposing restraints on all phases of human activity must refuse to impose any restraints at all. To the degree that a government can use its powers to prevent individuals and groups from infringing on the fundamental rights of citizens—e.g., from discriminating in education and in employment for racial or religious reasons—it should do so; for here government would act in defense of democratic principles. And while it must be admitted that such governmental action constitutes a restraint on some liberties of some men to do some things, that very restraint frees other men from even more grievous (because antidemocratic) restraints that would otherwise be imposed on them. Once again, the question is one of values.

Thus, the problem of controlling the abuses of democratic governments still remains. And since a democratic government is not monolithic but distributes power among many individuals and agencies, the effort to curb (for it is impossible altogether to prevent) the arbitrary and oppressive actions of those individuals and agencies is a very involved affair. It requires, at the very least, both a determination of who the responsible—i.e., decision-making —individual or agency is, and a grant of sufficient power to some other individual or agency as to enable him or it to check the first power, or to remove it from office. To the extent that this second power does its job, the problem is solved—with respect, that is, to the particular act or intended act of the first power. But the second power may sometimes fail to do its job; or it may be oppressive in turn. Then we can either attempt further to proliferate the checking powers—which is an endless affair and which carries with it the danger that government will be so weakened in the process that it will be unable to carry on its elementary tasks—or look to public opinion to remove the oppressive powers and replace them with reasonable rulers.

The American democracy somewhat illogically unites both

alternatives. It appeals to public opinion to select good men, then establishes an elaborate system of checks and balances that makes it difficult for those men to perform what they were chosen to do. This is defended by the quite proper argument that even good and reasonable men are sometimes driven by their interests to practices that contravene democratic principles: they sometimes do what they should not do; they sometimes fail to do what it would seem they ought to do. Moreover, governments, like other organizations, are also inundated by incompetent as well as by unreasonable men, by men who greedily seize the opportunities that power gives them to exploit their prejudices as well as by men who love power and find a sort of ego-satisfaction in the use and even (if need be) the abuse of it. Hence, the argument for institutional restraints can hardly be said to be without warrant.

But if public opinion selects men to do a job that they cannot (because they are hampered by institutional restrictions) do, or can do only with great difficulty, why bother to select, or to try to select, good men? If the purpose of an election is to elicit the public will so as to translate this will into the law of the land, but this will is then frustrated and sometimes defeated by a horde of institutional restraints that impede the elected agents of that will from carrying out their assigned tasks, why hold elections? For this reason, some democratic theorists are as little impressed by the utility as they are by the logic of the American political system. Instead of the fragmentation and separation of powers as here institutionalized, they would prefer to approximate the British system of a more direct line of legislative and executive accountability. Their trust, in so far as the problem of controlling abuses of power is concerned, is in an educated and enlightened public opinion.[2] Is that trust, however, justified? Can we rely on an educated and enlightened people to ward off abuses of power in the democratic state?

When stated this way, however, the question is an ambiguous one; for oppression, as I have said, is not reducible to a single entity but must be understood and dealt with as a series of isolated or, at most, as a complex of particular oppressive acts; and words

like enlightenment and education carry peculiar difficulties of
their own. Those who use these terms in political debate generally
employ them interchangeably, or regard education as the path to
enlightenment. This latter is the correct formulation, provided we
do not identify education with formal schooling; for what passes
for schooling is not always education. Sometimes it is vocational
training, very often it is propaganda; sometimes it involves so
great a reduction of standards as to denude education—particularly at the higher levels—of its intellectual content; increasingly
it involves so great a concentration on specialization of learning
as to produce men who are well informed in some fields but
abysmally ignorant in others. Rarely does it produce a man im-
mune to irrational beliefs; rarely does it remove the prejudices
that are characteristic even of our so-called educated and professional classes.

But even if the goal of enlightenment were attained, it would
not follow that enlightened men would act rightly. For right
action involves more than a recognition of right principles; it is
more than merely intellectual. It derives most commonly from
the emotions or, if you will, from the character of a man; it is a
product of his opinions, of his attitudes, even more than of his
learning or intelligence. This is why prejudice is so largely im-
pervious to the appeal to the facts, why it is so little affected by
reason.[3] And because prejudice cannot easily be overcome by
education or enlightenment, as it certainly cannot be abolished
by law, the various discriminatory practices that flow out of
prejudice are bound to continue.[4] It is true that law can restrain
some discriminatory practices, *some* coercive restraints that limit
the rights—the democratic liberties and opportunities—of *some*
citizens. But it cannot restrain all of them. Nor does a public
opinion in which those prejudices abound seek to restrain all of
them. Hence, the appeal to an enlightened public opinion is in
large part either utopian or limited: it is utopian if it expects
either universal enlightenment or a consistently "right" application of enlightenment to conduct; it is limited if it recognizes
that reason and kindliness can lead only *some* men to abandon

some of their prejudices and therefore *some* of their discriminatory practices. This, of course, is no mean achievement; but it cannot be said to remove the possibility that a democratic state will still continue to abuse some of its citizens with respect to some things.

It is pertinent at this point to bear in mind that often, in a concrete case, there is a conflict of principles. We argue, for example, both for equality of opportunity and for the liberty of a parent to rear his child. To assure the former, democratic states have generally interfered with the latter—e.g., by requiring the compulsory attendance of the child in the schools. But it is surely an inadequate notion of equality of opportunity that looks only to formal schooling and not to such other things as the size and economic status of the family, the educational background of the parents, the racial and religious differences that carry (to some minds) imputations of superiority and of inferiority, and the like. To assure *real* equality of opportunity in the face of such barriers, a democratic state may find that it would have to move toward Plato's republic, and probably to cease being democratic in the process. To avoid this last contingency, as well as to provide a maximum degree of liberty for the parent with respect to his child, a democratic state may be forced to avoid pushing its insistence on equality of opportunity to its logical consequences. It may have to choose a particular liberty for some people rather than a particular equality for others. Where, in this and in other areas of human life, the principles of liberty and of equality thus come into conflict with each other, so that both cannot be satisfied at the same time, some such preference must be asserted. Whichever way that preference goes, the absolute inviolability of the corresponding right is abridged. This is why a democratic state can assert no more than the *relative* inviolability of such a right. And whatever the preference of a democratic state may be, its mere assertion always carries with it the possibility that the enforcing authority may abuse its power.

I conclude, then, that just as there is no one solution to *the* problem of power, so there is no solution or set of solutions that will effectively and permanently eliminate the innumerable oppressive acts of governments and of private powers. A free society is, among other things, a dangerous society. It opens the avenue to greatness but also the avenue to disaster. We can meet, or hope to meet, some disasters (or potential disasters) by creating certain institutional arrangements that, on the basis of experience, seem most likely to curb them. But it is still the case that the people who actually rule are not the same as those over whom their power is exercised. Consequently, while a system of majority rule, for example, has the inestimable value of preventing a minority from oppressing the majority, it carries no assurance that the majority will not act oppressively over that minority, or a portion of that minority, in turn. In the same way, while a democratic state saves us from the despotic acts of kings and of self-styled aristocrats, it does not necessarily save us from the abuses of democratic governments or of private powers within the democratic state.

For the control of private powers, we can look to governments and to a sense of self-restraint. Both are effective where they are applied, but in many cases they are not applied; and it is often thought desirable that intrusion by governments should not (in the specific instance) be applied. For the control of governments, we can look to internal institutional restraints such as the fragmentation and separation of powers, to a sense of responsibility and therefore of self-restraint on the part of those who temporarily reside in the seats of political power, and to external controls such as popular elections. All of these are in some measure effective, the last especially so since it enables a people (or, more properly, a majority of the voters among them) to dismiss those who neglect or who injure their interests. For whatever else may be said of the competence of public opinion, this much at least is clear: that with respect to the general purposes or public policies of government, a people can and on the whole do judge wisely of the satisfaction of their own interests; they can tell when the shoe pinches.[5] But it remains true that with respect to a particular situation, the majority may judge incorrectly; it may support rather than reject the oppressive measures of its government. And it is always true—in democracy no less than in oligarchy—that a minority may also feel the pinch yet lack the power to dismiss the government that pinches it.

Consequently, the final (because ultimate and inescapable) trust remains a trust in the wisdom—which is not, let it be emphasized, to be equated with schooled "enlightenment"—and in the intrinsic sense of decency of a people. If they are motivated by good will and are guided by reason, they can, perhaps, work out piecemeal solutions to each of the problems of oppressive power as these manifest themselves. They can enforce desegregation in one town, if not in another; eventually, if they retain both courage and a respect for democratic rights, they can enforce desegregation everywhere. They need look for no patented solution to all the injustices that some men are prone to impose on other men. They can seek instead to effect running adjustments, to work out tentative and even imperfect (because experimental) solutions. And for this task the principle of democracy particularly commends itself: for it enables men freely to ventilate their grievances, and it provides a political mechanism whereby those grievances can be constitutionally—and therefore peacefully—corrected.

This is at once the genius and the tragic paradox of democracy. It gives its citizens the opportunity to combat injustice, but that opportunity is dependent for its fulfillment on the will of those who impose the injustice. We must appeal to the conformists to respect the right of nonconformity, to the intolerant to act tolerantly, to the prejudiced to deal with others in an unbiased way. Such an appeal is perhaps the strongest, as it is the most legitimate, of democratic weapons, but it is not guaranteed to carry the day. For, on the one hand, the court in which reason must battle today is not the same court in which it once appeared. The participants are different: they are men deprived (in part at least) by the media of mass communications and other modern "conveniences" of that autonomy and leisure time that are requisite for reflective and independent judgment. And the relevance (and impact) of their judgments is not the same; for the elongation of our social and political structure is such as to place a vast distance between the electorate and the actual decision makers, as also between the decision makers and their policy advisers and administrative officials. On the other hand, men who have learned to enjoy the pleasures that their oppressive behavior seems to bring them are not quick to relinquish those pleasures merely in order to observe a principle. It is true that in the name of this principle men have fought long and nobly—but generally, it must be added, because they deemed it to be in their interests to do so. If reason can make plain to those whose sense of justice does not already reveal it to them, that it is in the interests of all men for abuses of power to be combated wherever they may appear, the terrors of oppression, though they can never be eliminated, may yet be lessened.

Whether reason, so feeble in its persuasive power in the past, can yet prove equal to the task is still an enigma of the future.

Notes

CHAPTER I: THE PROBLEM OF POWER STATED

1. See Rousseau, *The Social Contract,* Book III, chap. 10. For the Greek view, see Xenophon, *Hiero,* whose work Rousseau follows here. See further Andrewes, *The Greek Tyrants,* especially chap. 2; Monnerot, *Sociology of Communism,* chaps. 11 and 12; and Strauss, *On Tyranny,* especially p. 107, note 7.

2. Aristotle, *Ethics,* 1160*b; Politics,* 1279*b;* and cf. Monnerot, *Sociology of Communism,* p. 179.

3. See J. S. Mill, *Dissertations and Discussions,* II, 158.

CHAPTER II: CONSENT AS A LEGITIMATE SOURCE OF POWER

1. It can, of course, be argued that such an appeal is only an expedient device to sustain more easily those who would defend their power on other grounds. But the mere fact that such an appeal is made is a sufficient indication that without such consent the foundations of government are precarious indeed; and if government is, as I later argue, a practical rather than an ideal activity, then what is necessary is as important to a valid political theory as that which is held to be desirable.

2. For Niebuhr, see particularly *The Children of Light and the Children of Darkness.* For Maritain, see *Man and the State,* especially pp. 126 *et seq.* For an analysis of Niebuhr's and Maritain's ideas of democracy, see S. D. Cook, "An Inquiry into the Ethical Foundations of Democracy," chaps. 3 and 4; and cf. further Frankel, *The Case for Modern Man,* chaps. 4–6.

3. See the classic argument in Rousseau, *The Social Contract,* Book I, chap. 3.

4. To deny the paradox by contending that those who appeal to might to overthrow a democratic state are in fact appealing to those who have the force but do not use it—e.g., because of psychological

inhibitions—is to assume, quite erroneously, that might is a matter of physical force alone, and not a matter of intelligence and will as well. See on this point my *Patterns of Anti-Democratic Thought,* pp. 81–88.

5. Cf. Strauss, *Natural Right and History,* pp. 138–43.

6. It is true that some writers have sought in experience or in intuition or in natural law a criterion in terms of which they could show that democracy (and the principle of consent) is intrinsically and absolutely best, but all such efforts rest ultimately on certain indemonstrable assumptions. See further my "Power, Law, and Freedom of Inquiry," in Hullfish, ed., *Educational Freedom in an Age of Anxiety,* pp. 59–65, and the discussion in chap. 9 in the text.

7. Colonel Thomas Rainborough was a spokesman for the Levelers in the famed Putney Debates of 1647. The quotation is from the Clarke Manuscripts, in Woodhouse, ed., *Puritanism and Liberty,* pp. 53, 56.

8. I have sought to develop this argument elsewhere. See my paper, "Democracy and the Problem of Civil Disobedience," *American Political Science Review,* XLVIII (1954), especially pp. 393–95.

9. For the doctrine of consent, see Bassett, *The Essentials of Parliamentary Democracy,* especially pp. 112–18, 123–30; Lindsay, *The Essentials of Democracy* and *The Modern Democratic State,* chap. 10; and MacIver, *The Modern State,* pp. 9–16, 193–201, 442–46, and *The Web of Government,* chaps. 5 and 8.

CHAPTER III: THE ABUSES OF POWER IN DEMOCRACY

1. I except here, of course, those emissaries who create or who inherit and maintain the modern totalitarian state, which lives on terror.

2. Tocqueville, *Democracy in America,* II, 337–38 and *passim.* See further the comment on this point by Bryce, *Studies in History and Jurisprudence,* pp. 338–39.

3. Bryce, *The American Commonwealth,* Vol. II, chap. 84.

CHAPTER IV: DEMOCRATIC GOVERNMENTS AS OPPRESSIVE POWERS

1. Of the considerable body of literature on the American Indian, see especially Meriam and Associates, *The Problem of Indian Administration,* and F. S. Cohen, *Handbook of Federal Indian Law.* See further Blumenthal, *American Indians Dispossessed;* F. S. Cohen, "Ameri-

canizing the White Man," *The American Scholar*, XXI (1952), 177–91, and "The Erosion of Indian Rights, 1950–1953: A Case Study in Bureaucracy," *Yale Law Journal*, LXII (1953), 348–90; Debo, *And Still the Waters Run;* Embry, *America's Concentration Camps;* Fey, *Indian Rights and American Justice;* and the several works of Oliver LaFarge, for example, *As Long as the Grass Shall Grow.* For the contempt with which various state courts continue to view the "inferior" Indian, see State v. Rorvick, 76 Idaho 58 (1954), upholding an Idaho law prohibiting the sale of intoxicating liquors to Indians; note especially the doctrine of "racial" inferiority expressed in the several judicial opinions quoted therein.

2. 347 U.S. 483 (1954), reversing the "separate but equal" doctrine of Plessy v. Ferguson, 163 U.S. 537 (1896).

3. See the monumental study by Myrdal, *An American Dilemma,* and the Report of the President's Committee on Civil Rights, *To Secure These Rights.* Cf. further Davie, *Negroes in American Society;* Frazier, *The Negro in the United States,* especially Part V; Johnson, *Patterns of Negro Segregation,* Part I; Will Maslow and J. B. Robison, "Civil Rights Legislation and the Fight for Equality, 1862–1952," *University of Chicago Law Review*, XX (1953), 363–413; Weaver, *The Negro Ghetto;* Walter White, *How Far the Promised Land?;* the Report of the National Committee on Segregation in the Nation's Capital, *Segregation in Washington;* and the issue of the *Annals* devoted to "Racial Desegregation and Integration." The annual reports of the American Civil Liberties Union are, of course, a veritable mine of information.

4. For the treatment of Chinese, Japanese, and other Asiatic peoples, see Konvitz, *The Alien and the Asiatic in American Law,* and McWilliams, *Brothers under the Skin,* chaps. 2, 4, 5, and 7. For the Mexicans and other Latin American peoples, see Bogardus, *The Mexican in the United States;* Kibbe, *Latin Americans in Texas;* Sanchez, *Forgotten People;* and McWilliams, *North from Mexico* and *Brothers under the Skin,* chap. 3. For the story of the evacuation of the Japanese-Americans, see Grodzins, *Americans Betrayed;* McWilliams, *Prejudice;* and Rostow, "The Japanese American Cases—a Disaster," *Yale Law Journal*, LIV (1945), 489–533.

5. West Virginia State Board of Education v. Barnette, 319 U.S. 624 (1943), reversing Minersville School District v. Gobitis, 310 U.S. 586 (1940).

6. See the annual reports of the Anti-Defamation League of B'nai

B'rith, especially those prepared by Weintraub, *How Secure These Rights?*, chaps. 1–3, and Forster, *A Measure of Freedom*, chaps. 7 and 10.

7. See the account in Murray, *Red Scare*, pp. 226–29, 235–38.

8. See her autobiography, *Living My Life*, Vol. II, chaps. 45–51. In one instance, Emma Goldman's traveling companion was, with police collusion, kidnaped and not only beaten and tarred but, feathers not being at hand, subjected to sagebrush being rubbed into his body and the letters IWW burned into his flesh. The self-appointed defenders of America then forced him to kiss the flag and to sing the national anthem, gestures which (one must assume) were calculated to produce not simply outward compliance but inner belief. See the account in *ibid.*, I, 494–501.

9. The problem of making comparisons between different historical periods is a notoriously treacherous one, and I am quite aware that the American past does not disclose an uninterrupted record of progress. Nevertheless, it is well to note that despite the instances of violence against dissenters in American history, the problem today is a more formidable one—not least because of the growing centralized power of the national government and the presence of new media of mass communication, elements which afford less play in, and fewer opportunities of escape from, the system of controls. The difference, that is to say, is a qualitative rather than—or, if one were to speak in terms of *potential* power, in addition to—a quantitative one, a fact seemingly ignored by those who take a more optimistic view of the situation. See, for example, Roche, "We've Never Had More Freedom," *New Republic*, CXXXIV (January 23, 1956), 12–15; *ibid.* (January 30, 1956), 13–16; *ibid.* (February 6, 1956), 13–15; and *contra* Harrington, "Coué and the Liberals," *Dissent*, III (1956), 214–15.

10. Schenck v. United States, 249 U.S. 47 (1919); Abrams v. United States, 250 U.S. 616 (1919); Gitlow v. New York, 268 U.S. 652 (1925); Whitney v. California, 274 U.S. 357 (1927).

11. It is to be noted that Henry, who elsewhere condemned slavery and expressed the thought that emancipation "would rejoice my very soul," at the same time opposed the ratification of the Constitution on the ground that sooner or later the central government would insist on the abolition of slavery, a consequence that, Henry believed, would jeopardize the property of the people of Virginia and disrupt their peace and tranquillity. "As much as I deplore slavery," Henry argued,

Errata

The title of the book by Sidney Hook that is cited on pages 185, 186, and 215 is in error. The correct title should be *Heresy, Yes — Conspiracy, No.*

"I see that prudence forbids its abolition." For this convenient invocation of prudence, see his speech of June 24, 1788, in W. W. Henry, *Patrick Henry,* III, 576–77.

12. Mill, *On Liberty,* in *Utilitarianism, Liberty and Representative Government,* chap. 2, pp. 111–12.

13. For a forceful statement of this position, see Hook, *Conspiracy, Yes—Heresy, No,* especially Part I; also T. I. Cook, *Democratic Rights versus Communist Activity.*

14. By "Communists" I mean here not those who subscribe to any of the various doctrines, including Marxism, that have at one time or another been termed Communist, but those who adhere to the Soviet idea of Communism, who accept and consistently follow the policies and tactics set forth by the rulers of the Soviet Union. See my article, "Why Communists Are Not of the Left," *Antioch Review,* IX (1949–50), especially pp. 496–99.

15. For the nonconspiratorial nature of the Communist appeal, see for example Watnick, "The Appeal of Communism to the Underdeveloped Peoples," in Hoselitz, ed., *The Progress of Underdeveloped Areas,* pp. 152–72.

16. The Supreme Court recognized this rather elementary but now seemingly forgotten point in Schneiderman v. United States, 320 U.S. 118 (1943), where it said (p. 136) "that under our traditions beliefs are personal and not a matter of mere association, and that men in adhering to a political party or other organization notoriously do not subscribe unqualifiedly to all of its platforms or asserted principles." See further Hartman, "Group Membership and Class Membership," *Philosophy and Phenomenological Research,* XIII (1953), 353–69.

17. For the Smith Act, see note 18 below. For the McCarran Act, see Sutherland, "Freedom and Internal Security," *Harvard Law Review,* LXIV (1951), 383–416; and Chafee, *The Blessings of Liberty,* chap. 5 and *passim.* For the Humphrey Act, see "The Communist Control Act of 1954," *Yale Law Journal,* LXIV (1955), 712–65.

18. For the argument that the ancient law of conspiracy cannot constitutionally be used to turn speech into seditious *conduct,* see the dissenting opinion of Justice Douglas in Dennis v. United States, 341 U.S. 494, 581 (1951). For Vinson's opinion, see *ibid.,* p. 495. For Hand's opinion, see United States v. Dennis, 183 F.2d 201 (1950)—so strikingly at variance, it ought to be noted, with his test (enunciated more than a quarter of a century ago) of "direct incitement to violent resistance."

Masses Publishing Co. v. Patten, 244 Fed. 535, 540 (S.D.N.Y., 1917). For a reasoned defense of the Smith Act, see Hook, *Conspiracy, Yes—Heresy, No,* chap. 5. For a criticism, see the analysis by the American Civil Liberties Union, *The Smith Act and the Supreme Court,* and the brilliant dissection of Judge Hand's opinion by Wormuth, "Learned Legerdemain: A Grave but Implausible Hand," *Western Political Quarterly,* VI (1953), 543–58. See further the recent holding by the Supreme Court in Yates v. United States, 354 U.S. 298, 320 (1957), that the Smith Act does not enjoin "advocacy of forcible overthrow as an abstract doctrine" but only "advocacy of action to that end."

19. Cf. Wormuth, "On Bills of Attainder: A Non-Communist Manifesto," *Western Political Quarterly,* III (1950), 52–65, and "Legislative Disqualifications as Bills of Attainder," *Vanderbilt Law Review,* IV (1951), 603–19; also Chafee, *The Blessings of Liberty,* p. 32.

20. "We do not claim," said Marx, "that the means necessary for bringing about this aim [the emancipation of labor] will be the same everywhere. We know that we must take account of the institutions, customs and traditions of the various countries, and we do not deny that there are countries, such as the United States and Great Britain . . . where the workers will be able to achieve their aims by peaceful means. But this is not the case in all countries." Speech at Amsterdam at the conclusion of The Hague Congress of the First International in 1872; quoted in Laurat, *Marxism and Democracy,* p. 36. For other versions of this statement, see Fr. de J., "Amsterdam Meetings of the First International in 1872," *Bulletin of the International Institute of Social History,* No. 1, pp. 1–15.

Engels repeatedly emphasized this point. See, for example, his preface (written in 1886) to the first English translation of Marx's *Capital,* p. 32; his statement in 1891 that "in democratic republics such as the United States and France, and in monarchies such as Great Britain, . . . it is conceivable that the old society may be peaceably transformed into the new . . . in a constitutional manner as soon as a majority of the people is behind it" (quoted in Laurat, *Marxism and Democracy,* p. 36); and his introduction (written in 1895) to Marx's *The Class Struggles in France,* reprinted in Marx and Engels, *Selected Works,* I, 109–27.

See further Bober, *Karl Marx's Interpretation of History,* pp. 262–67, and Laurat, *Marxism and Democracy,* pp. 31–47.

21. See Lenin, *State and Revolution,* chap. 3, § 1; reprinted in his *Selected Works,* Vol. II, Part 1, pp. 235–39.

22. Lenin, letter on "Marxism and Insurrection," in *Selected Works,* Vol. II, Part 1, pp. 167–73; italics in the original. See also Lenin's pamphlet in 1920 entitled *"Left-Wing" Communism, an Infantile Disorder,* § ix, in *ibid.,* Vol. II, Part 2, p. 412, where he said: "The fundamental law of revolution . . . is as follows: it is not enough for revolution that the exploited and oppressed masses should understand the impossibility of living in the old way and demand changes; it is essential for revolution that the exploiters should not be able to live and rule in the old way. Only when the *'lower classes' do not want* the old way, and when the 'upper classes' *cannot carry on in the old way—* only then can revolution triumph. This truth may be expressed in other words: revolution is impossible without a nation-wide crisis (affecting both the exploited and the exploiters). It follows that for revolution it is essential, first, that a majority of the workers (or at least a majority of the class-conscious, thinking, politically active workers) should fully understand that revolution is necessary and be ready to sacrifice their lives for it; secondly, that the ruling classes should be passing through a governmental crisis, which draws even the most backward masses into politics . . . , weakens the government and makes it possible for the revolutionaries to overthrow it rapidly." Italics in the original. See also *ibid.,* § vii.

If Lenin's views can be rejected as those of a moderate Communist, then it is well to observe that conspiratorial activities and an undiscriminating reliance on violence are also rejected not only by Engels, to whom Lenin paid regular obeisance, but also by Georg Lukács, a noted Communist theorist who belonged to the very "leftist" group against which Lenin's pamphlet, *"Left-Wing" Communism,* was directed. Thus Engels, in his draft of what was later to become the Communist Manifesto, declared: "Communists [i.e., Marxists] know only too well that all conspiracies are not only useless but even harmful. They know all too well that revolutions are not made intentionally and arbitrarily, but that everywhere and always they have been the necessary consequence of conditions which were wholly independent of the will and direction of individual parties and entire classes." Engels, *Principles of Communism,* Question 16, p. 13. See also Engels's preface to the 1888 English edition of *The Communist Manifesto,* in

Marx and Engels, *Selected Works,* I, 28. And thus Lukács: "As with every question that concerns forms of action, so as regards an inquiry into [the problem of] legality and illegality in the class struggle of the proletariat, the motives and the tendencies arising therefrom are often more important and more illuminating than the bare facts. For the mere fact of legality or illegality of a section of the labor movement is so very much dependent on historical "accidents" that its analysis is not always capable of yielding guiding principles. There is no party, be it ever so opportunistic, indeed even treacherous [to its social class], that cannot through circumstances be forced into illegality. Conversely, circumstances are entirely conceivable in which the most revolutionary Communist party, least given to compromise, may function temporarily in almost complete legality." *Geschichte und Klassenbewusstsein,* p. 261. (I owe this reference and translation to Morris Watnick.) I would note, to obviate criticism, that Lukács's book was all but suppressed—though not for ideas like this one.

For a non-Communist interpretation of the relation between legality and revolution, see F. S. Cohen, "Socialism and the Myth of Legality," *American Socialist Quarterly,* IV (November, 1935), 3–33.

23. See the analyses in Kecskemeti, "Totalitarianism and the Future," in Friedrich, ed., *Totalitarianism,* pp. 354–57, and Morris, "Some Perspectives on the Nature and Role of the Western European Communist Parties," *Review of Politics,* XVIII (1956), 157–69.

24. See especially the speeches of Khrushchev and Mikoyan, reprinted in the Cominform journal, *For a Lasting Peace, for a People's Democracy!,* February 17, 1956, and March 2, 1956.

25. For a detailed account of the proceedings and documents relating to the inclusion of the Independent Socialist League (formerly the Workers Party) on the Attorney General's list, see *Labor Action,* September 28, 1953. For the Court's ruling on the passport issue, see Schachtman v. Dulles, 225 F.2d 938 (1955).

26. The Independent Socialist League was the first of the organizations cited on the list of subversive organizations to be accorded a hearing. This came about only after seven years and some fifteen separate but unsuccessful requests for such a hearing since its initial listing in 1948. The hearing, which began in July, 1955, and was concluded in July, 1956, has not yet (January, 1958) brought forth a final judgment. See the New York *Times* and the Washington *Post and Times-Herald* of July 26, 1955; *Labor Action,* August 1 and 8, 1955, May 28–July 23,

September 10, and October 15, 1956; and the Proposed Findings of Fact submitted on December 17, 1956, by Joseph L. Rauh, Jr., and Isaac H. Groner, attorneys for the Independent Socialist League.

27. From the wealth of literature dealing with infringements of procedural rights by congressional investigating committees, governmental agencies, and administrative officials, see Barth, *The Loyalty of Free Men*, especially chaps. 3–6, and *Government by Investigation;* Biddle, *The Fear of Freedom;* Bontecou, *The Federal Loyalty-Security Program;* Carr, *The House Committee on Un-American Activities* and *The Constitution and Congressional Investigating Committees;* Chafee, *The Blessings of Liberty*, especially chaps. 1 and 7 and pp. 80–100; Commager, *Freedom, Loyalty, Dissent* and "The Perilous Delusion of Security," *The Reporter*, XIII (November 3, 1955), 32–35; Emerson and Helfeld, "Loyalty among Government Employees," *Yale Law Journal*, LVIII (1948), 1–143, and the exchange between these authors and J. Edgar Hoover in *ibid.*, LVIII (1949), 401–25; Fellman, "The Loyalty Defendants," *Wisconsin Law Review* (January, 1957), 4–39; Gellhorn, *The States and Subversion;* Griswold, *The Fifth Amendment Today;* O'Brian, *National Security and Individual Freedom;* Schaar, *Loyalty in America*, especially chaps. 5 and 6; Taylor, *Grand Inquest;* Westin, *The Constitution and Loyalty Programs;* and the Report of the Special Committee of the Association of the Bar of the City of New York, *The Federal Loyalty-Security Program*.

28. The bizarre consequences to which this may lead are well illustrated by the remarkable memorandum submitted to the Secretary of War by General John L. DeWitt, commanding general of the Western Defense Command and Fourth Army, explaining why he deemed it necessary to evacuate the Japanese-Americans from the West Coast. After stating that "the Japanese *race* is an enemy race," and that, therefore, "over 112,000 *potential enemies*, of Japanese extraction, are at large today," he concluded: "The very fact that no sabotage has taken place to date is a disturbing *and confirming* indication that such action will be taken." *Final Report, Japanese Evacuation from the West Coast, 1942*, p. 34. My italics.

29. These points are admirably treated in O'Brian, *National Security and Individual Freedom*, especially pp. 22–42.

30. This can no longer be done without regard to the "sensitivity" (in security terms) of the particular appointment. See Cole v. Young, 351 U.S. 536 (1956). It ought not to follow, in any case, that one should

be judged ineligible illegally. The fact that government employment is held to be a privilege rather than a right is no warrant for giving administrators the power to deny such employment on arbitrary or discriminatory grounds.

31. See Kecskemeti, "The Psychological Theory of Prejudice," *Commentary*, XVIII (1954), 359–66; Allport, *The Nature of Prejudice*, especially chap. 13; and Saenger, *The Social Psychology of Prejudice*, Part II.

32. See Russell, "The Harm That Good Men Do," in his *Sceptical Essays*, pp. 111–33, and J. L. Adams, "The Evil That Good Men Do," in *Voices of Liberalism*, II, 53–64. I return to this point in chap. 10, pp. 143–47.

CHAPTER V: THE "TYRANNY" OF PUBLIC SENTIMENT

1. For Mill's indebtedness to Tocqueville, see his review of Tocqueville's *Democracy in America*, reprinted in his *Dissertations and Discussions*, II, 79–161; the opening pages of the essay *On Liberty;* and *Representative Government*, especially chaps. 6 and 7.

2. Tocqueville, *Democracy in America*, II, 276, 275.

3. *Ibid.*, I, 273.

4. *Ibid.*, I, 274–75; and see further pp. 265, 409.

5. One has only to compare the complex idea of loyalty in a democracy, dependent as this is on a multiplicity of nonnational loyalties, with the rigid simplicity of the exclusive national loyalty demanded by the modern totalitarian state to perceive that the loyalty oath is not merely futile but contrary to the very principle of democracy that it purports to secure. See, for various aspects of the problem, Grodzins, *The Loyal and the Disloyal*, especially chaps. 3–6, 13–14; H. B. White, "The Problem of Loyalty in American Political Thought," *Social Research*, XXI (1954), 314–38, and "The Loyalty Oath," *ibid.*, XXII (1955), 77–109; and MacIver, *Academic Freedom in Our Time*, pp. 41–42, 174–77, 194–98, and *passim*. See further the works of Barth, Biddle, Commager, and Schaar cited in chap. 4, note 27 above.

6. Tocqueville, *Democracy in America*, II, 275.

7. Hartz, *The Liberal Tradition in America*, p. 285. See, in the same vein, Commager, *Freedom, Loyalty, Dissent*, p. 15.

8. Bryce, *The American Commonwealth*, II, 331.

CHAPTER VI: THE ABUSES OF PRIVATE POWERS

1. Cf. my article, "Power, Law, and Freedom of Inquiry," in Hull-fish, ed., *Educational Freedom in an Age of Anxiety*, pp. 55–59.

2. Rev. George W. Lee was killed by a series of shotgun blasts fired from a passing automobile in Belzoni, Mississippi, on May 7, 1955. The fourteen-year-old Emmett Louis Till was kidnaped at pistol point from his uncle's home in Money, Mississippi, on August 28, 1955; his mutilated, shot, and water-swollen body was found three days later in the Tallachatchie River some miles away. The figure for Mississippi's lynching record is reported in Davie, *Negroes in American Society*, p. 343, as 574 for the period 1882–1947.

Evidences for these and other illustrations used in this chapter can be found in the recent annual reports of the American Civil Liberties Union, the Anti-Defamation League of B'nai B'rith, and the National Association for the Advancement of Colored People. Further evidences and illustrations are available in Myrdal, *An American Dilemma*, especially chaps. 9, 13, 14, 27–31; Davie, *Negroes in American Society*, especially chap. 16; MacIver, *The More Perfect Union*, especially chap. 3; Arnold and Caroline Rose, *America Divided*, especially chaps. 3 and 6; Walter White, *How Far the Promised Land?;* the various writings of Carey McWilliams on minority groups in America, especially his *Brothers under the Skin;* the Report of the President's Committee on Civil Rights, *To Secure These Rights;* and the issue of the *Annals* devoted to "Racial Desegregation and Integration." The notes that follow refer only to additional materials.

3. The conviction of Carl Braden was set aside by the Kentucky Court of Appeals on June 22, 1956, not on the merits of the case, but in compliance with the decision of the United States Supreme Court in Pennsylvania v. Nelson, 350 U.S. 497 (1956), holding that only the Federal government has the power to prosecute sedition cases. For the facts in the case, see Appellant's Brief to the Kentucky Court of Appeals, Braden v. Commonwealth, submitted November 15, 1955.

4. It is to be noted, however, that while Miss Lucy was admitted to the classrooms, she was denied access to the dormitories and dining halls of the University.

5. See the accounts in the New York *Times* and the Washington *Post and Times-Herald*, February 7–9, 1956. In all fairness to the South, it must be noted that while Alabama, Florida, Georgia, Missis-

sippi, and South Carolina still enforce complete segregation in state-supported colleges, some 95 privately and publicly supported institutions of higher learning in Southern and border states and the District of Columbia have desegregated at some level in the two-year period since the historic Supreme Court decision of May 17, 1954. In the case of the University of Louisville, such desegregation was even extended to dormitories. And in every instance the adjustment was made smoothly and quietly. Hence, what is most noteworthy about the Autherine Lucy case is that, at the college and university level though not at the elementary and secondary school levels, it is a unique rather than a typical reaction. (See, for a generally optimistic progress report, Loth and Fleming, *Integration North and South*, especially pp. 62 ff.) In all fairness to the governor and to the University of Alabama, too, it ought to be registered that one white student was subsequently dismissed from the University, though for statements and actions on his part *after* the violent outbreak against Miss Lucy; and that Governor Folsom's conduct, while hardly comparable to that of his counterparts in, say, Kentucky and Tennessee when confronted with related situations in the towns of Sturgis and Clinton, respectively, contrasts quite favorably with that of some other Southern governors—e.g., Governor Shivers in connection with the outbreak in Mansfield, Texas.

6. Though the Communist, Frank Hashmall, was away from his home when a mob broke into it, while a larger mob outside watched and cheered the criminals on, the sheriff put the blame for this incident on the victim himself. Said the sheriff: "He [Hashmall] has incited the public." Not untypically, the county chapter of the American Legion promptly commended the police for their alertness. For an account of this incident, and for the quotations given here, see the Columbus *Citizen*, March 19–April 12, 1948.

7. On the use of violence in labor relations, see especially the Report of the La Follette Committee, *Violations of Free Speech and the Rights of Labor;* also Yellen, *American Labor Struggles;* Seidman, *Labor Czars;* and Barbash, *Labor Unions in Action*, chap. 7, and *The Practice of Unionism*, pp. 227–30. There have, of course, been any number of cases before the National Labor Relations Board in recent years involving violence in labor-management relations.

8. See, for example, the New York *Times*, November 21, 1955, and September 30, 1956.

9. For the exclusionist and discriminatory practices of unions, see

Barbash, *Labor Unions in Action,* pp. 61–62, 89, 127, and *The Practice of Unionism,* pp. 72–76; also, more exhaustively, Northrup, *Organized Labor and the Negro.* For the item on the strike to secure the dismissal of a worker who had invoked the Fifth Amendment, see the New York *Times,* May 15, 1954.

10. The moral irresponsibility of such dismissals is heightened when such enforcing authorities move precipitously to condemn a man before any allegation is made that he has acted unlawfully, or before it has been determined that he was asked to submit to a legitimate rather than to an *illegitimate* demand by a governmental power. Thus, a group of employees was dismissed by the General Electric Company in 1954 even though the congressional committee before which those employees had pled the Fifth Amendment did not cite them for contempt or for any other crime; a professor was dismissed from Temple University in 1953 even though a Federal court was later (in 1955) to acquit him of the charge of contempt of Congress, the court declaring that the professor had been within his rights in invoking the Fifth Amendment privilege against self-incrimination; and courts have since, in dismissing other contempt citations, castigated the congressional committees involved for improper conduct in asking unwarranted and therefore illegitimate questions—i.e., questions which, as the Supreme Court said in Quinn v. United States, 349 U.S. 155, 161 (1955), "inquire into private affairs unrelated to a valid legislative purpose," or extend the power to investigate into "an area in which Congress is forbidden to legislate," or confuse the power to investigate with "any of the powers of law enforcement." See also United States v. Lamont, 236 F.2d 312 (1956); Sweezy v. New Hampshire, 354 U.S. 234 (1957); and especially Watkins v. United States, 233 F.2d 681 (1956). The reversal of this last decision by the full bench of the same Court of Appeals on April 23, 1956, was itself reversed by the Supreme Court on June 17, 1957, when the Court, in striking language, affirmed that "there is no congressional power to expose for the sake of exposure." Watkins v. United States, 354 U.S. 178, 200.

It should, perhaps, be added that the position argued in the text is in substantial accord with the dissenting opinion of Justice Douglas in Black v. Cutter Laboratories, 351 U.S. 292 (1956), where the majority of the Court in effect upheld the right of an employer to dismiss (or, as Justice Douglas put it, "to discriminate against") an employee by reason of his political ideology.

11. See, for example, Cogley, *Report on Blacklisting.*

12. Cf. McWilliams, *A Mask for Privilege,* pp. 229–36, and Hale, *Freedom through Law.*

CHAPTER VII: THE LIMITATIONS OF THE AMERICAN DEMOCRACY

1. I do not, of course, imply by this that all of the changes effected during the Jackson era were, properly speaking, democratic reforms. The introduction of the presidential nominating convention is a case in point.

2. For Madison's views and the quotations given in the text, see *The Federalist,* especially Nos. 10 and 51. See further Riemer, "James Madison's Theory of the Self-Destructive Features of Republican Government," *Ethics,* LXV (1954), 34–43.

3. I cannot take seriously the contention that, in the light of new technological developments such as the television set and electronic devices that might enable citizens to register an affirmative or negative vote on every issue simply by pressing an appropriate button in their living rooms, voters both can and should determine the details of government. Clearly, this sort of "direct democracy" not only negates the idea of representative government but, by removing all discretion from governing officials, imposes a rigidity that renders responsible (as well as wise) government impossible. If the representative is not to act on his own initiative, he need not think, nor need he be held responsible for acts that are not of his own making. Conversely, if the citizen is to judge not only the general direction of public policy but also its legislative and administrative details, he requires a kind of technical competence, not to speak of a degree of leisure time, that he does not and is not likely to command. For these and other reasons, when I speak of responsibility in the democratic state, I apply it to "representatives" (i.e., men entrusted with discretion to act for those who have chosen them) and not to "delegates" (i.e., men authorized to act only in accordance with definite instructions).

4. See, for example, Kendall, "The Majority Principle and the Scientific Elite," *Southern Review,* IV (1939), 465. For later and more elaborate statements of Kendall's position, see his "Prolegomena to Any Future Work on Majority Rule," *Journal of Politics,* XII (1950), 694–713, and (with Austin Ranney) his *Democracy and the American Party System,* chaps. 1–3 and 22.

It ought, perhaps, to be noted that Kendall rejects majority rule *of the limited type* only in the sense that he does not approve of *institutional* restraints imposed on the majority to safeguard the democratic rights of a minority. What he does endorse is a principle of *self-restraint* by that majority as indispensable to the functioning of a democratic state. He goes on to argue, however, that a majority which is checked only by its self-imposed restraints exercises power which is in fact identical with the *absolute* power of a majority. (*Democracy and the American Party System*, pp. 29–37, especially pp. 31 and 36 f.) "Some writers who advocate 'limited' majority rule," he says, "do not propose any *formal* limitations upon the power of popular majorities. They hold, instead, that in a true democracy majorities will not *be* restrained but rather will *restrain themselves* from violating human rights. Now if 'limited' majority rule means nothing more than this, then the authors of this book have no quarrel with it; for such a 'limitation' is no limitation at all upon the *power* of the majority, and therefore cannot become, strictly speaking, minority *rule*. At most it is no more than a way of saying that if the majority chooses to destroy any of the elements of democracy, then democracy will no longer exist —that democracies which have committed suicide are democracies no longer. Since the propositions just stated are undeniable, there are no significant logical differences between this third version of the 'limited' majority rule position and the 'absolute' majority position outlined previously." (*Ibid.*, pp. 36–37; italics in the original.) In effect, then, Kendall would have it that any majority which knows only those restraints that are self-imposed *can* in fact abridge fundamental democratic rights, though it *ought not* to do so. (*Ibid.*, pp. 49–51, 519–32.)

Kendall's position on this matter clearly confuses his own definitions. If a system of limited majority rule is defined, as it is by Kendall, as one in which a majority enjoys unlimited power in a limited sphere of governmental action, it is a confusion of terms to identify it with the altogether different system of absolute majority rule identified by Kendall himself (*ibid.*, p. 31) as one in which such a majority has absolute power in *all* spheres of possible governmental action. Nor, for that matter, does it follow from Kendall's own definitions that a system of limited majority rule is, in effect, a system of minority rule.

For the rest, Kendall's disparaging judgment of the restraining power of self-control is purely a matter of his own formal definition, hardly a conclusion supported by the experience of modern times. It is difficult to see, for example, how the most formidable system of institutional controls could debar a Fascist or Communist movement from power if a majority of the population were to repudiate the democratic tradition, including its own sense of self-restraint.

5. See, for example, McClosky, "The Fallacy of Absolute Majority Rule," *Journal of Politics*, XI (1949), 637–54; Pennock, "Responsiveness, Responsibility, and Majority Rule," *American Political Science Review*, XLVI (1952), 790–807; and my *Patterns of Anti-Democratic Thought*, pp. 4–5, 51–52, 107–8. See further the references cited in *ibid.*, p. 271, note 56, and, more generally, Heinberg, "Theories of Majority Rule," *American Political Science Review*, XXVI (1932), 452–69, and "History of the Majority Principle," *ibid.*, XX (1926), 52–68; also Baty, "The History of Majority Rule," *Quarterly Review*, CCXVI (1912), 1–28.

6. It would seem hardly necessary to add that I speak here only of that organization of the political power apparatus that is designed to facilitate the formulation, and not the administration, of public policy. It is the business of administration to apply power in an interest-neutral way, and for this purpose the power apparatus must be so organized as to set limits to the coercive powers of administrative officials; it must compel them—e.g., by the need to coordinate the component parts—to work within the limits of the law. This distinction between "policy" (or content) and "administration" cannot, of course, be pushed too far, but in its broad outlines it remains a real and vital one. For a recent perceptive statement of its significance, see Kecskemeti, "Why Freedom Needs Authority," *The New Leader*, XXXVI (March 9, 1953), 15–17. But cf. Waldo, "Development of Theory of Democratic Administration," *American Political Science Review*, XLVI (1952), 81–103.

7. But see *contra* A. B. Hall, *Popular Government*, chap. 7, and Lewis, *An Essay on the Influence of Authority in Matters of Opinion*, pp. 162–65 and chap. 8.

8. To state this in somewhat different terms, the nine largest states, with slightly over 50 percent of the national population (as of 1950), have only about one-sixth of the total representation in the Senate (i.e., 18 Senators), while the nine smallest states, with 2.3 percent of the population, also have a sixth of the representation. The twelve largest states, with almost 60 percent of the population, have 24 Senators, or

25 percent of the total number; the twelve smallest states, with 4.1 percent of the population, also have 24 Senators, or 25 percent of their number. Thus, almost 60 percent of the American people have the same representation in the Senate as do 4.1 percent of the people. For a detailed analysis, see the speeches of Senator Paul H. Douglas on March 26 and 29, 1956 (*Congressional Record*, 84th Congress, 2d session).

9. Thus, Wilson in 1912 and Truman in 1948 were elected by but a plurality of the national popular vote, and Cleveland in 1888 and (probably) Tilden in 1876 were defeated even though each had received a majority of the national popular vote.

10. Dicey, *Introduction to the Study of the Law of the Constitution,* p. lxxv.

11. For an effective statement of this position, see MacIver, *Community,* pp. 264–66, and *The Modern State,* pp. 378–81.

12. I have dealt more fully with this problem in my paper, "Robert M. MacIver's Contributions to Political Theory," in Berger, Abel, and Page, eds., *Freedom and Control in Modern Society,* pp. 301–2, 306–8. For a more general assessment, see Macmahon, ed., *Federalism Mature and Emergent.*

13. This is denied, for example, by B. F. Wright, Jr., who argues that the separation of powers in America was derived from the institutional history of the colonies, and not from Montesquieu or any of the other exponents of the doctrine. See his "The Origin of the Separation of Powers in America," *Economica,* XIII (1933), 169–85. Cf. more generally Wormuth, *The Origins of Modern Constitutionalism,* especially chaps. 8 and 20.

14. See my paper, "Some Animadversions on Montesquieu's Theory of Freedom," *Ethics,* LXIII (1953), 210, and p. 213, note 31.

15. I am aware that at the present time this may well be an impolitic argument, for the Supreme Court by its recent decisions invalidating segregation in education and certain infringements on the rights of political nonconformists has taken a stand that cannot but commend itself to those of us who both believe in democracy and take it seriously. But the fortuitous role of a particular Court should not blind us to the broader issue that I have tried to state here. It was the Supreme Court, after all, that first established the noxious "separate but equal" doctrine in our constitutional law and that (by its decision

in Plessy v. Ferguson, as well as in the Civil Rights Cases, 109 U.S. 3 [1883], that preceded it) helped to produce the evil discrimination it has only now—more than a half-century later—seen fit to retract.

For the broad question of the compatibility of judicial review with democracy, see Boudin, *Government by Judiciary;* M. R. Cohen, *Law and the Social Order,* especially Parts II and III; Corwin, *The Twilight of the Supreme Court* and *Court over Constitution;* and Commager, *Majority Rule and Minority Rights.*

16. Cf. Montesquieu, *Spirit of the Laws,* Book XI, chap. 6, Book XII, chap. 1; also note 6 above.

17. Cf. my discussion of this problem in my paper on Montesquieu, "Some Animadversions on Montesquieu's Theory of Freedom," *Ethics,* LXIII (1953), especially pp. 210–13.

18. The historical situation in Madison's day was, of course, more congenial to his theory than is the case today: the country was smaller and more homogeneous; the conflicts of interest were simpler; and the fragmentation of power did not, consequently, involve as ready a paralysis of political authority.

19. Mill, *Representative Government,* chap. 6, pp. 250–51.

20. If we accept, not the bizarre statistics that modern totalitarian despots have cited as proof that they command unanimous or near-unanimous support, but the more plausible claim that in a free election they—say Hitler and Mussolini and Stalin in the mid-thirties—would in all likelihood have received at least the endorsement of the majority, it becomes clear that oppression is not uniquely an attribute of minority-supported governments.

21. Tocqueville, *Democracy in America,* II, 344.

22. Cf. MacIver, *Academic Freedom in Our Time,* chap. 1; also Kendall, "On the Preservation of Democracy for America," *Southern Review,* V (1939), 53–68.

23. See the discussion in chap. 11, pp. 160–65.

24. Though I think one must be cautious not to exaggerate this sense of responsibility, as Norton Long does when he argues that the bureaucracy is in fact the more representative, the more responsive, and therefore the more responsible of our organs of government. See his "Bureaucracy and Constitutionalism," *American Political Science Review,* XLVI (1952), 808–18, especially p. 815; and cf. note 6 above.

25. See, for example, Selznick, "An Approach to a Theory of Bureaucracy," *American Sociological Review,* VIII (1943), 47–54.

26. See Gerth and Mills, eds., *From Max Weber: Essays in Sociology,* pp. 232–35, and Weber, *The Theory of Social and Economic Organization,* pp. 337 ff.

27. It is strange that men have forgotten so soon that we revere Justices Holmes, Brandeis, and Cardozo less for their concurring than for their dissenting opinions.

CHAPTER VIII: THE FUTILITY OF WITHDRAWAL

1. Dewey, *Freedom and Culture,* p. 54.

2. I set aside too—as extraneous here—the question of moral cowardice: whether one who thus deserts his fellows in order to save himself does not commit an ignoble deed.

3. It seems hardly necessary to add that not all acts of selective withdrawal are taken in response to oppressive treatment. The necessities of modern civilization—with its innumerable specializations in the midst of complexity—compel all men to withdraw from some areas of activity in order to carry on effectively their work in others. I restrict my remarks in the text, accordingly, only to those acts of selective withdrawal that are produced by abuses of power.

4. Wolff, ed., *The Sociology of Georg Simmel,* p. 284; and see further Kahler, *The Tower and the Abyss,* chap. 4. Regrettably, Kahler's remarkable book came to my attention too late for me to discuss it in the context of this study; but the evidences marshaled in that book richly sustain many of the findings here.

5. Plato, *Republic,* 347; and cf. Bryce, *The Hindrances to Good Citizenship,* pp. 31–32.

6. If it is said that the individual who abstains, say, from political life may yet, by moral precept and example, influence other men and thereby help to achieve a more rational and just society, or that a group which withdraws from a particular activity and by that act of withdrawal exerts a moral or economic pressure which may force the correction of an existing iniquity, the answer is that such individual abstention or group passivity is not withdrawal but a form of resistance. Moral influence and passive resistance are both appeals to power; they interpose one form of power against another. Consequently, whatever their relative merits or defects, they are not, properly speaking, forms of withdrawal at all.

CHAPTER IX: THE APPEAL TO RIGHT PRINCIPLES

1. For a perceptive analysis of this problem, see MacIver, *The More Perfect Union*, pp. 87–90, 220–24.

2. Hillenbrand, *Power and Morals*, especially pp. 5–7, 192–93.

3. But see *contra* Taubes, "The Issue between Judaism and Christianity," *Commentary*, XVI (1953), 525–33.

4. Hallowell, *The Moral Foundation of Democracy*, p. 100.

5. Voegelin, *The New Science of Politics*, p. 69.

6. Hallowell, *The Moral Foundation of Democracy*, pp. 113, 112; and see further pp. 79, 87, 129–32. See also Hillenbrand, *Power and Morals*, chap. 7; Maritain, *The Rights of Man and Natural Law*, especially pp. 27, 44–50, 57, 60; and Heimann, *Freedom and Order*, especially chaps. 1 and 8.

7. Cf. Hallowell, *The Moral Foundation of Democracy*, p. 128.

8. *Ibid.*, pp. 58, 122. This is why Yves Simon, for example, insists that in the democratic state "deliberation is about means and presupposes that the problem of ends has been settled." See his *Philosophy of Democratic Government*, p. 123.

9. Cf. Hillenbrand, *Power and Morals*, pp. 101–2. The same point holds true, of course, for secular natural law or natural right theories. See, for example, Strauss, *Natural Right and History*, pp. 162–63.

10. See, for example, Voegelin, *The New Science of Politics*, especially p. 144. Despite Maritain's professions to the contrary, this is held by some writers to be the necessary consequence of Maritain's own teachings; see, for example, Knight, "The Rights of Man and Natural Law," in his *Freedom and Reform*, especially pp. 276–81.

11. *Summa Theologica*, II, ii, Q. 11, A. 3.

12. Eliot, *The Idea of a Christian Society*. See also his *Notes towards the Definition of Culture*.

13. For perceptive discussions of some of these and other religious thinkers, see Kelsen, "Foundations of Democracy," *Ethics*, Vol. LXVI (1955), No. 1, Part II, §§ 1 and 2; Coker, "Some Present-Day Critics of Liberalism," *American Political Science Review*, XLVII (1953), especially pp. 12–25; and the review of Hallowell's book by Wormuth in the *Indiana Law Journal*, XXX (1955), 374–81.

14. Hillenbrand, *Power and Morals*, p. 77.

15. Kirk, *A Program for Conservatives*, p. 302. Indeed, continues

this writer, it is only through the veneration of our sacred institutions and of the wisdom of our ancestors that we can hope to achieve that piety that can raise us above the brutes. "Traditions are the wisdom of the race; they are the only sure instruments of moral instruction; they have about them a solemnity and a mystery that . . . [science] . . . never can compensate for; and they teach us the solemn veneration of the eternal contract which cannot be imparted by pure reason." *Ibid.*, pp. 296, 305. See also the same author's *The Conservative Mind,* and Rossiter, *Conservatism in America,* especially pp. 48, 71 ff., 201. Both Kirk and Rossiter, to be sure, look to the truth that allegedly lies in tradition rather than to tradition as the *sole* repository of truth; and Kirk in particular returns always, in the ultimate analysis, to the source of the eternal order, which is (in his view) God. But to the extent that they appeal to tradition at all—and they do so to a very considerable degree—they are properly subsumed under the traditionalist school. For a more exclusive reliance on tradition, see the writings of Michael Oakeshott, especially his "Rationalism in Politics," *Cambridge Journal,* I (1947), 81–98, 145–57, and *Political Education;* and cf. the commentaries on these works by Postan and Krook in the *Cambridge Journal* and by Rees in *Mind.*

16. Unless, of course, we retreat into that tradition of despair which holds, with Oakeshott (who I think here quotes Bradley), that "the world is the best of all possible worlds, and *everything* in it is a necessary evil." *Political Education,* p. 28; italics in the original.

17. See, for example, Wright, *American Interpretations of Natural Law,* pp. 331–41, and Neumann, "Types of Natural Law," *Studies in Philosophy and Social Science,* VIII (1939), 338–61.

18. In this sense it can easily be shown that many of those who explicitly repudiate the natural law doctrine readmit it in different guise. Cf. M. R. Cohen, "Jus Naturale Redivivum," *Philosophical Review,* XXV (1916), 761–77.

19. The argument is elaborated in Lippmann, *Essays in the Public Philosophy,* especially pp. 100–115, 123, 132–35, 160–66, 174–75. And compare the classic statement in Cicero, *On the Commonwealth,* Book III, § 22: "There is in fact a true law—namely, right reason—which is in accordance with nature, applies to all men, and is unchangeable and eternal. By its commands this law summons men to the performance of their duties; by its prohibitions it restrains them from doing

wrong. . . . To invalidate this law by human legislation is never morally right, nor is it permissible ever to restrict its operation, and to annul it wholly is impossible."

20. Strauss, *Natural Right and History*, p. 7.

21. Lippmann, *Essays in the Public Philosophy*, pp. 106, 107.

22. Santayana, *Dominations and Powers*, p. 297. "What mind sees in nature," Santayana adds, "is always but a garment." *Ibid.*, p. 62.

23. Lippmann, *Essays in the Public Philosophy*, pp. 165, 115; and see further pp. 161–66, 175–76, 180. And cf. Strauss, "On Classical Political Philosophy," *Social Research*, XII (1945), 98–117, especially pp. 111–12, where the appeal is addressed to those men who take these principles for granted, who are "decent" rather than "intelligent" men.

24. Lippmann, *Essays in the Public Philosophy*, pp. 115, 135.

25. *Ibid.*, pp. 123, 160. My italics.

26. Lippmann explicitly accepts this conclusion in *ibid.*, p. 114.

27. M. R. Cohen, "Jus Naturale Redivivum," *Philosophical Review*, XXV (1916), 772–73.

28. On this score the words of Carlos Cardinal Vasconcelos, Archbishop of São Paulo, Brazil, are eloquent and clear. According to a report in the New York *Times* of August 18, 1953, he said: "Should any Brazilian Government dare to institute divorce in Brazil, the people would have the right to oppose by armed resistance this attempt to undermine the foundation of Christian family life in this country." This, to be sure, is the statement of a theological rather than a secular adherent of natural law, but in this respect the consequences of the two positions are identical.

29. It would take us too far afield to consider here whether there is a *necessary* relationship between one's moral philosophy or epistemology and his politics. For the view that philosophy and politics stand in a direct relationship, and that philosophic absolutism (e.g., natural law) and political autocracy, for example, logically go together, see Russell, "Philosophy and Politics," in his *Unpopular Essays*, chap. 1, and various writings by Hans Kelsen, for example his "Absolutism and Relativism in Philosophy and Politics," *American Political Science Review*, XLII (1948), 906–14; "Foundations of Democracy," *Ethics*, LXVI (1955), especially pp. 14–39; and "Natural Law Doctrine and Legal Positivism," reprinted as an appendix to his *General Theory of Law and State*. A similar correspondence between philosophy and

politics, now, however, affirming a contrary view that philosophical absolutism (e.g., natural law) is the necessary foundation of democracy, is argued in Williamson, "The Challenge of Political Relativism," *Journal of Politics*, IX (1947), 147–77, and Hallowell, *The Moral Foundation of Democracy*. A still different conclusion is drawn by some of those who accept this alleged necessary correspondence of philosophy and politics, but who hold that philosophical relativism (e.g., pragmatism or positivism) and political absolutism (i.e., totalitarianism) go together; see, for example, Strauss, *Natural Right and History*, introduction and chap. 2. For the argument (to which I am sympathetic) that there is no *necessary* connection between one's philosophy and his political theory, see Oppenheim, "Relativism, Absolutism, and Democracy," *American Political Science Review*, XLIV (1950), 951–60 (also his later articles, "In Defense of Relativism," *Western Political Quarterly*, VIII [1955], 411–17, and "The Natural Law Thesis: Affirmation or Denial?" *American Political Science Review*, LI [1957], 41–53), and Ginsberg, "Ethical Relativity and Political Theory," *British Journal of Sociology*, II (1951), 1–11.

30. I do not, of course, imply by this that a democrat cannot properly oppose the will of the majority where that will violates *democratic*, as distinct from natural law, standards. See my article, "Democracy and the Problem of Civil Disobedience," *American Political Science Review*, XLVIII (1954), 386–403.

31. It is curious to note that while Lippmann, for example, recognizes this difficulty (*Essays in the Public Philosophy*, pp. 147 ff.), he does not seem to perceive its necessary consequences.

32. Consider, for example, President Truman's reply, in his address of January 15, 1953, to the American Congress, to the question: Why doesn't the United States drop the atomic bomb in Korea? He said: "For most Americans, the answer is quite simple: We are not made that way. We are a moral people. . . . We cannot, of our own free will, violate the very principles that we are striving to defend." How, then, could that same President have previously ordered the atomic bomb dropped on Hiroshima and Nagasaki?

33. This is treated in chap. 10, pp. 132–33, 143–47.

34. English, "Conservatism and the State," *Virginia Quarterly Review*, XXXII (1956), 58. My italics.

35. Heckscher, *A Pattern of Politics*, pp. 198–99. My italics.

36. One democratic writer, in fact, goes so far as to argue that "the *objective* validity of moral judgments is known intuitively." Jerome Hall, *Living Law of Democratic Society*, pp. 80–81. My italics.

37. Cf. Vivas, *The Moral Life and the Ethical Life*, especially pp. 250–54.

CHAPTER X: THE APPEAL TO THE RIGHT MAN

1. For an analysis and criticism of the various forms of this aristocratic appeal, see my *Patterns of Anti-Democratic Thought*, chaps. 4–9, and MacIver, *The Ramparts We Guard*, chap. 5 and pp. 130–33.

2. Eccles. 7:20.

3. Santayana, *Dominations and Powers*, p. 413.

4. Mannheim, *Freedom, Power, and Democratic Planning*, especially chaps. 7–9. The quotation is on p. 231.

5. Lasswell, *Power and Personality*, pp. 110, 108, 115–18, 146, 187, 108.

6. As Else Frenkel-Brunswik, one of the authors of *The Authoritarian Personality* (see note 8 below), elsewhere put it: "Since every individual possesses features of the authoritarian as well as of the democratic personality, though in varying proportions, such objective factors as economic conditions and such psychological factors as feelings of dissatisfaction, helplessness, and isolation may decide the issue in a particular overall situation." "Interaction of Psychological and Sociological Factors in Political Behavior," *American Political Science Review*, XLVI (1952), 63. See further her paper, "Further Explorations by a Contributor to 'The Authoritarian Personality,'" in Christie and Jahoda, eds., *Studies in the Scope and Method of "The Authoritarian Personality,"* especially pp. 227 ff.

It ought to be observed in passing that what is true of personality is true also—in this respect at least—of society: for no society completely fits into one or the other of these rigid categories of the psychologist; every society contains both "democratic" and "authoritarian" elements. Mannheim occasionally pauses to recognize this point, both in relation to personality and to society (see, for example, *Freedom, Power, and Democratic Planning*, p. 208), but his argument generally ignores or minimizes the importance of this consideration.

7. Fromm, *Escape from Freedom*, pp. 163–64, 168, 236.

8. Adorno *et al*, *The Authoritarian Personality*, p. 228 and *passim*.

See also Frenkel-Brunswik, "Environmental Controls and the Impover-ishment of Thought," in Friedrich, ed., *Totalitarianism,* pp. 171–202, and her papers cited in note 6 above. Cf. further A. H. Maslow, "The Authoritarian Character Structure," *Journal of Social Psychology,* XVIII (1943), 401–11; Allport, *The Nature of Prejudice,* chap. 25; and Saenger, *The Social Psychology of Prejudice,* chap. 9.

9. Mannheim, *Freedom, Power, and Democratic Planning,* pp. 173–80.

10. For some of these and other criticisms as applied to *The Au-thoritarian Personality,* see Kecskemeti, "Prejudice in the Catastrophic Perspective," *Commentary,* XI (1951), 286–92, and Christie and Jahoda, eds., *Studies in the Scope and Method of "The Authoritarian Person-ality."* These findings are summarized in Glazer, "New Light on 'The Authoritarian Personality,' " *Commentary,* XVII (1954), 289–97.

11. Lasswell, "The Selective Effect of Personality on Political Par-ticipation," in Christie and Jahoda, eds., *Studies in the Scope and Method of "The Authoritarian Personality,"* especially pp. 220–24.

12. Thus A. H. Maslow, who finds it impossible to avoid using the term, admits that "the concept 'democratic personality' is simply not a scientific concept; there is no agreement whatsoever on its meaning." "Power Relationships and Patterns of Personal Development," in Kornhauser, ed., *Problems of Power in American Democracy,* p. 94. Other recent attempts to describe these traits—e.g., by Lasswell in his *Democratic Character* (published in *The Political Writings of Harold D. Lasswell,* pp. 465–525) and by Allport, *The Nature of Prejudice,* chap. 27—are quite unconvincing when read in the light of such strictures as those by Kecskemeti and Glazer (works cited above, note 10) and by E. A. Shils ("Authoritarianism: 'Right' and 'Left,' " in Christie and Jahoda, eds., *Studies in the Scope and Method of "The Authoritarian Personality,"* pp. 24–49) on the definition of the demo-cratic personality employed in *The Authoritarian Personality.*

13. Cf. Bendix, "Compliant Behavior and Individual Personality," *American Journal of Sociology,* LVIII (1952), 292–303; Riesman, *The Lonely Crowd,* pp. 172, 178, and *passim;* and Wrong, "Riesman and the Age of Sociology," *Commentary,* XXI (1956), 331–38.

14. Cf. Shils, "Authoritarianism: 'Right' and 'Left,' " in Christie and Jahoda, eds., *Studies in the Scope and Method of "The Authoritarian Personality,"* pp. 42–49.

15. Mill, *Representative Government,* chap. 8, p. 291.

16. Quoted in Wittke, *The Utopian Communist,* p. 234.

17. In this respect Santayana does no more than barely overstate a basic truth when he argues that "all living creatures become wicked under pressure. Absolute singleness of purpose cannot but be ruthless; it is ruthless initially, because it has no eye for any contrary interest; and it becomes ruthless again deliberately in the end, because all contrary interests seem odious and sinful to its fanaticism." *Dominations and Powers,* p. 436.

18. Cf., for example, Radcliffe, *The Problem of Power,* Lecture V.

19. D'Avenant, *An Essay upon the Probable Methods of Making a People Gainers in the Balance of Trade,* p. 270. And compare Tocqueville, *Democracy in America,* I, 270: "Unlimited power is in itself a bad and dangerous thing. Human beings are not competent to exercise it with discretion. God alone can be omnipotent, because his wisdom and his justice are always equal to his power. There is no power on earth so worthy of honor in itself or clothed with rights so sacred that I would admit its uncontrolled and all-predominant authority. When I see that the right and the means of absolute command are conferred on any power whatever, be it called a people or a king, an aristocracy or a democracy, a monarchy or a republic, I say there is the germ of tyranny, and I seek to live elsewhere, under other laws."

20. Montesquieu, *The Spirit of the Laws,* Book XI, chap. 4.

21. This is one of the reasons why extreme radicals and reactionaries, when out of power and with relatively little chance of getting into power, are so often men of inflexible principle. They are incorruptible because, in part, no one seeks to corrupt them. They are inflexible because, in part, no one seeks to compromise their differences in order to enlist their support.

22. Cf. Mill, *Representative Government,* chap. 6, pp. 252–53.

23. It ought perhaps to be added that if by an authoritarian personality is meant one who is congenial to totalitarianism, a distinction must be drawn between the kind of personality that seeks totalitarianism (e.g., a rebel or nonconformist) and that which remains under it (e.g., a conformist). Cf. Lauterbach, "Totalitarian Appeal and Economic Reform," in Friedrich, ed., *Totalitarianism,* p. 288. Unfortunately, those who most vigorously press the notion of the authoritarian personality rarely pause to note this distinction, much less to consider what it means.

24. I except, of course, children and the insane.

CHAPTER XI: THE APPEAL TO AN ALTERNATIVE MODE OF DEMOCRACY

1. For a recent effective statement, see Rotenstreich, "Rule by Majority or by Principles," *Social Research*, XXXI (1954), 411–27.

2. For the continuing interest in Calhoun, see (from among the many biographies) the sympathetic though critical work by Wiltse, *John C. Calhoun,* especially Vol. III, chap. 28; also the same writer's articles, "Calhoun and the Modern State," *Virginia Quarterly Review,* XIII (1937), 398–408, and "Calhoun's Democracy," *Journal of Politics,* III (1941), 210–23. See further Agar, *Pursuit of Happiness,* pp. 190–200 and *passim;* Bell, ed., *The New American Right,* p. 29, where Calhoun's doctrine is held to be "the solid basis for providing a check on the tyrannical 'popular' majority"; and especially Spain, *The Political Theory of John C. Calhoun,* where Calhoun's body of doctrine is said to remain, on the whole, as "unanswerable today" as it was to his contemporary antagonists (p. 256; and see, for the doctrine of the concurrent majority, chap. 5). Caustic appraisals are numerous: see in particular Hartz, *The Liberal Tradition in America,* pp. 158–67, 173, and Hofstadter, *The American Political Tradition,* chap. 4. See further Current, "John C. Calhoun, Philosopher of Reaction," *Antioch Review,* III (1943), 223–34.

3. *A Disquisition on Government,* in Crallé, ed., *The Works of John C. Calhoun,* I, 8, 38.

4. *Ibid.,* I, 25, 38.

5. It has nevertheless been argued—for example by Drucker, "A Key to American Politics: Calhoun's Pluralism," *Review of Politics,* X (1948), 412–26—that some form of the concurrent majority principle remains in fact the organizing principle of American political life. Drucker reaches this conclusion by substituting for the constitutional veto power that Calhoun would give to the states to enable them to block national legislation, the extraconstitutional and extralegal "veto power" actually possessed by major sectional and interest groups in Congress and within the political parties to *influence* political decisions affecting them. But in this form the power (and the doctrine) is a vastly different one from that conceived by Calhoun; for by abjuring *legal* restraints on the majority it enables some, though not all, minority interests to water down but not necessarily to block the majority's will. (The role of such veto groups is treated in a more general context in Riesman, *The Lonely Crowd,* chap. 11.)

6. Wiltse, "Calhoun's Democracy," *Journal of Politics*, III (1941), 223. I am heavily indebted to this superb article for my critical remarks here.

7. Cf. Dahl, *A Preface to Democratic Theory*, p. 133: "If majority rule is mostly a myth, then majority tyranny is mostly a myth too. For if the majority cannot rule, surely it cannot be tyrannical."

8. MacIver, *Community*, pp. 139–43; and cf. Lewis, *An Essay on the Influence of Authority in Matters of Opinion*, chap. 7.

9. See, for various degrees of commitment to this view, the following: Allen, *Democracy and the Individual*, pp. 42–59; Commager, *Majority Rule and Minority Rights;* Elliott, *American Government and Majority Rule;* Kendall, *John Locke and the Doctrine of Majority-Rule*, and his writings cited in chap. 7, note 4 above; Lerner, *It Is Later Than You Think*, chap. 5 and pp. 98–99, also his article, "Minority Rule and the Constitutional Tradition," in his *Ideas Are Weapons*, pp. 461–77; Mims, *The Majority of the People;* Riemer, "The Case for Bare Majority Rule," *Ethics*, LXII (1951), 16–32; and Smith, *The Spirit of American Government*. See further the references in chap. 7, note 5 above.

10. See, for example, Commager, *Majority Rule and Minority Rights*, p. 7, and Kendall, "Prolegomena to Any Future Work on Majority Rule," *Journal of Politics*, XII (1950), 706–10.

11. See works by Commager and Kendall cited in note 10 above; also Riemer, "The Case for Bare Majority Rule," *Ethics*, LXII (1951), 19–23, 26–27, 29.

12. Kendall follows here, of course, the work of Max Weber, for whom see especially his *The Methodology of the Social Sciences*. Kendall's view on this point is challenged by Coker, "Some Present-Day Critics of Liberalism," *American Political Science Review*, XLVII (1953), 8–9, 11–12; Weber's by, among others, Strauss, *Natural Right and History*, chap. 2.

13. Letter to Major Poussin, February 1, 1841, in H. B. Adams, *Jared Sparks and Alexis de Tocqueville*, pp. 43–44. See also Sparks's letter to Professor William Smyth later that year, in *ibid.*, p. 44.

14. I am not unmindful of the fact that discrimination and other acts of oppression have, in any ultimate sense, a deleterious effect on the majority which imposes them—e.g., in the corrosion of the majority's morals, in the intellectual and economic loss suffered by the majority (and the nation as a whole) through the deprivation of a

minority's skills and potential talents, in the fears, hatreds, and tensions bred among both majority and minority, and so on. (See, for example, F. S. Cohen, "The People vs. Discrimination," *Commentary*, I [March, 1946], 17–22; MacIver, ed., *Discrimination and National Welfare;* Moon, *The High Cost of Prejudice;* Saenger, *The Social Psychology of Prejudice,* chap. 2; and the works cited in chap. 4 above, notes 1, 3, 4, and 6.) But the majority does not always guide itself by the long- as against the short-term effects of its policies. Consequently, from a subjective point of view, it *can* act on the minority without feeling that it is thereby also acting on itself.

15. Tocqueville, *Democracy in America,* I, 344. It is puzzling to note, despite this, that so astute a student of Tocqueville as Professor Commager should criticize Tocqueville for not having cited any convincing examples of the tyranny of the majority (see his introduction to the World's Classics edition of Tocqueville's *Democracy in America* [London, 1946], p. xvi, and, more broadly, the argument in his *Majority Rule and Minority Rights,* chap. 3); and that, in the face of these and more recent examples, Professor Hartz, in an otherwise highly suggestive work, should term the American majority "an amiable shepherd dog . . . one of the tamest, mildest, and most unimaginative majorities in modern political history," and dissolve its despotic treatment of minority peoples in what he calls "America's liberal unity," even "virtual unanimity." *The Liberal Tradition in America,* especially pp. 129, 110, 141.

16. Riemer, "The Case for Bare Majority Rule," *Ethics,* LXII (1951), 29.

17. Most notably, of course, the reservation that whatever else the majority may do, or be empowered to do, it should not abrogate those basic liberties and equalities essential to democracy itself; it should not, among other things, destroy the majority *principle* through which majorities and minorities alike are formed, through which all factions or interests are free to plead their particular cause, to organize into political parties, and otherwise to enjoy an unfettered opportunity to submit their claims to the suffrage of the citizens. But here, to my knowledge, none of the majoritarians outside of totalitarian circles registers a thoroughgoing dissent.

18. Cf. Ranney and Kendall, *Democracy and the American Party System,* pp. 486–87, 502–4.

19. Some of the different meanings of the phrase are discussed in

MacIver, *Leviathan and the People,* pp. 79–86, 157–63, 168, and *The Ramparts We Guard,* chap. 4. See further Laidler, *Social-Economic Movements,* and the discussion in the text, chap. 7, pp. 90–92.

20. I have dealt with this problem in another connection. See my *Patterns of Anti-Democratic Thought,* chap. 2.

21. A consideration largely ignored even by so sensitive an observer as Harold J. Laski. See his *Trade Unions in the New Society* and my comment on this problem in my paper, "Labor and Liberty," *Antioch Review,* X (1950), 304.

CHAPTER XII: THE QUEST FOR A SOLUTION

1. Wittgenstein, *Philosophical Investigations,* § 109.

2. See, for example, Commager, *Majority Rule and Minority Rights,* especially pp. 75–78. Even those democratic theorists who see no necessary incompatibility between a system of checks and balances and a reliance on public opinion look also to the good sense of the latter. See, for example, Coker, "Some Present-Day Critics of Liberalism," *American Political Science Review,* XLVII (1953), 8–12; and more generally MacIver, *Community,* pp. 142–43; and Russell, *Power,* especially pp. 294–305.

3. Cf. MacIver, *The More Perfect Union,* chap. 9 and pp. 288 ff.; Allport, *The Nature of Prejudice,* pp. 483–86, 508–9; Russell, *Power,* pp. 300–301; and the last author's preface to his *Human Society in Ethics and Politics.*

4. For a somewhat less pessimistic outlook, see the various proposals considered in Allport, *The Nature of Prejudice,* chaps. 29–31; MacIver, *The More Perfect Union,* chaps. 5–10; and Saenger, *The Social Psychology of Prejudice,* chaps. 11–17.

5. Cf. my *Patterns of Anti-Democratic Thought,* chap. 4.

Bibliography of

Works Cited

Adams, Herbert B. Jared Sparks and Alexis de Tocqueville. Baltimore, 1898.

Adams, James Luther. "The Evil That Good Men Do," in Voices of Liberalism, Vol. II. Boston, 1948, pp. 53–64.

Adorno, T. W., Else Frenkel-Brunswik, D. J. Levinson, and R. N. Sanford. The Authoritarian Personality. New York, 1950.

Agar, Herbert. Pursuit of Happiness. Boston, 1938.

Allen, C. K. Democracy and the Individual. London, 1943.

Allport, G. W. The Nature of Prejudice. Cambridge, Mass., 1954.

American Civil Liberties Union. The Smith Act and the Supreme Court. New York, 1952.

Andrewes, A. The Greek Tyrants. London, 1956.

Aquinas, Thomas. Summa Theologica. 3 vols. Translated by the Fathers of the English Dominican Province. New York, 1947–48.

Aristotle. Ethics. Translated by D. P. Chase. Everyman's ed., New York, 1911.

—— Politics. Translated by William Ellis. Everyman's ed., New York, 1912.

Barbash, Jack. Labor Unions in Action. New York, 1948.

—— The Practice of Unionism. New York, 1956.

Barth, Alan. Government by Investigation. New York, 1955.

—— The Loyalty of Free Men. New York, 1951.

Bassett, Reginald. The Essentials of Parliamentary Democracy. London, 1935.

Baty, Thomas. "The History of Majority Rule," Quarterly Review, CCXVI (1912), 1–28.

Bell, Daniel, ed. The New American Right. New York, 1955.

Bendix, Reinhard. "Compliant Behavior and Individual Personality," *American Journal of Sociology,* LVIII (1952), 292–303.

Biddle, Francis. The Fear of Freedom. New York, 1951.

Blumenthal, W. H. American Indians Dispossessed. Philadelphia, 1955.

Bober, M. M. Karl Marx's Interpretation of History. 2d ed., Cambridge, Mass., 1948.

Bogardus, E. S. The Mexican in the United States. Los Angeles, 1934.

Bontecou, Eleanor. The Federal Loyalty-Security Program. Ithaca, 1953.

Boudin, L. B. Government by Judiciary. 2 vols. New York, 1932.

Bryce, James. The American Commonwealth. 2 vols. 2d ed., London, 1891.

—— The Hindrances to Good Citizenship. New Haven, 1909.

—— Studies in History and Jurisprudence. New York, 1901.

Calhoun, John C. Works. 6 vols. Edited by Richard K. Crallé. Columbia, S.C., 1851–56.

Carr, Robert K. The Constitution and Congressional Investigating Committees. Freedom Agenda Pamphlet, New York, 1954.

—— The House Committee on Un-American Activities. Ithaca, 1952.

Chafee, Zechariah, Jr. The Blessings of Liberty. Philadelphia, 1956.

Christie, Richard, and Marie Jahoda, eds. Studies in the Scope and Method of "The Authoritarian Personality." Glencoe, Ill., 1954.

Cicero. On the Commonwealth. Translated by George H. Sabine and Stanley Barney Smith. Columbus, Ohio, 1929.

Cogley, John. Report on Blacklisting. 2 vols. The Fund for the Republic, New York, 1956.

Cohen, Felix S. "Americanizing the White Man," *The American Scholar,* XXI (1952), 177–91.

—— "The Erosion of Indian Rights, 1950–1953: A Case Study in Bureaucracy," *Yale Law Journal,* LXII (1953), 348–90.

—— Handbook of Federal Indian Law. Washington, 1941.

—— "The People vs. Discrimination," *Commentary,* I (1946), 17–22.

—— "Socialism and the Myth of Legality," *American Socialist Quarterly,* IV (November, 1935), 3–33.

Cohen, Morris R. "Jus Naturale Redivivum," *Philosophical Review,* XXV (1916), 761–77.

—— Law and the Social Order. New York, 1933.

Coker, F. W. "Some Present-Day Critics of Liberalism," *American Political Science Review,* XLVII (1953), 1–27.

Commager, Henry Steele. Freedom, Loyalty, Dissent. New York, 1954.

—— Majority Rule and Minority Rights. New York, 1943.

—— "The Perilous Delusion of Security," The Reporter, XIII (November 3, 1955), 32–35.

"The Communist Control Act of 1954," Yale Law Journal, LXIV (1955), 712–65.

Cook, Samuel D. "An Inquiry into the Ethical Foundations of Democracy." Unpublished doctoral dissertation, Ohio State University, 1954.

Cook, Thomas I. Democratic Rights versus Communist Activity. Garden City, N.Y., 1954.

Corwin, E. S. Court over Constitution. Princeton, 1938.

—— The Twilight of the Supreme Court. New Haven, 1934.

Current, R. N. "John C. Calhoun, Philosopher of Reaction," Antioch Review, III (1943), 223–34.

Dahl, R. A. A Preface to Democratic Theory. Chicago, 1956.

D'Avenant, Charles. An Essay upon the Probable Methods of Making a People Gainers in the Balance of Trade. London, 1699.

Davie, M. R. Negroes in American Society. New York, 1949.

Debo, Angie. And Still the Waters Run. Princeton, 1940.

Dewey, John. Freedom and Culture. New York, 1939.

Dicey, A. V. Introduction to the Study of the Law of the Constitution. 8th ed., London, 1915.

Drucker, Peter F. "A Key to American Politics: Calhoun's Pluralism," Review of Politics, X (1948), 412–26.

Eliot, T. S. The Idea of a Christian Society. New York, 1940.

—— Notes towards the Definition of Culture. London, 1948.

Elliott, Edward. American Government and Majority Rule. Princeton, 1916.

Embry, C. B. America's Concentration Camps. New York, 1956.

Emerson, T. I., and D. M. Helfeld. "Loyalty among Government Employees," Yale Law Journal, LVIII (1948), 1–143.

Emerson, T. I., D. M. Helfeld, and J. Edgar Hoover. Exchange in Yale Law Journal, LVIII (1949), 401–25.

Engels, Frederick. Principles of Communism. Translated by Paul M. Sweezy. New York, 1952.

English, Raymond. "Conservatism and the State," Virginia Quarterly Review, XXXII (1956), 50–65.

The Federalist. By Hamilton, Jay, and Madison. Various editions.

Fellman, David. "The Loyalty Defendants," *Wisconsin Law Review* (January, 1957), 4–39.

Fey, H. E. Indian Rights and American Justice. Christian Century Foundation, Chicago, 1955.

Final Report, Japanese Evacuation from the West Coast, 1942. Washington, 1943.

Forster, Arnold. A Measure of Freedom. Garden City, N.Y., 1950.

Frankel, Charles. The Case for Modern Man. New York, 1956.

Frazier, E. F. The Negro in the United States. New York, 1949.

Frenkel-Brunswik, Else. "Environmental Controls and the Impoverishment of Thought," in Carl J. Friedrich, ed., Totalitarianism. Cambridge, Mass., 1954, pp. 171–202.

—— "Further Explorations by a Contributor to 'The Authoritarian Personality,'" in Richard Christie and Marie Jahoda, eds., Studies in the Scope and Method of "The Authoritarian Personality." Glencoe, Ill., 1954, pp. 226–75.

—— "Interaction of Psychological and Sociological Factors in Political Behavior," *American Political Science Review*, XLVI (1952), 44–65.

Friedrich, Carl J., ed. Totalitarianism. Cambridge, Mass., 1954.

Fromm, Erich. Escape from Freedom. New York, 1941.

Gellhorn, Walter, ed. The States and Subversion. Ithaca, 1952.

Gerth, H. H., and C. W. Mills, eds. From Max Weber: Essays in Sociology. New York, 1946.

Ginsberg, Morris. "Ethical Relativity and Political Theory," *British Journal of Sociology*, II (1951), 1–11.

Glazer, Nathan. "New Light on 'The Authoritarian Personality,'" *Commentary*, XVII (1954), 289–97.

Goldman, Emma. Living My Life. 2 vols. New York, 1931.

Griswold, E. N. The Fifth Amendment Today. Cambridge, Mass., 1955.

Grodzins, Morton. Americans Betrayed. Chicago, 1949.

—— The Loyal and the Disloyal. Chicago, 1956.

Hale, R. L. Freedom through Law. New York, 1952.

Hall, A. B. Popular Government. New York, 1921.

Hall, Jerome. Living Law of Democratic Society. Indianapolis, 1949.

Hallowell, John H. The Moral Foundation of Democracy. Chicago, 1954.

Harrington, Michael. "Coué and the Liberals," *Dissent*, III (1956), 214–15.

Hartman, R. S. "Group Membership and Class Membership," *Philosophy and Phenomenological Research,* XIII (1953), 353–69.

Hartz, Louis. The Liberal Tradition in America. New York, 1955.

Heckscher, August. A Pattern of Politics. New York, 1947.

Heimann, Eduard. Freedom and Order. New York, 1947.

Heinberg, J. G. "History of the Majority Principle," *American Political Science Review,* XX (1926), 52–68.

—— "Theories of Majority Rule," *American Political Science Review,* XXVI (1932), 452–69.

Henry, William W. Patrick Henry: Life, Correspondence, and Speeches. 3 vols. New York, 1891.

Hillenbrand, M. J. Power and Morals. New York, 1949.

Hofstadter, Richard. The American Political Tradition. New York, 1948.

Hook, Sidney. Conspiracy, Yes—Heresy, No. New York, 1953.

J., Fr. de. "Amsterdam Meetings of the First International in 1872," *Bulletin of the International Institute of Social History* (Amsterdam, 1951), No. 1, pp. 1–15.

Johnson, C. F. Patterns of Negro Segregation. New York, 1943.

Kahler, Erich. The Tower and the Abyss. New York, 1957.

Kecskemeti, Paul. "Prejudice in the Catastrophic Perspective," *Commentary,* XI (1951), 286–92.

—— "The Psychological Theory of Prejudice," *Commentary,* XVIII (1954), 359–66.

—— "Totalitarianism and the Future," in Carl J. Friedrich, ed., Totalitarianism. Cambridge, Mass., 1954, pp. 345–60.

—— "Why Freedom Needs Authority," *The New Leader,* XXXVI (March 9, 1953), 15–17.

Kelsen, Hans. "Absolutism and Relativism in Philosophy and Politics," *American Political Science Review,* XLII (1948), 906–14.

—— "Foundations of Democracy," *Ethics,* Vol. LXVI (1955), No. 1, Part II.

—— General Theory of Law and State. Translated by Anders Wedberg; appendix translated by Wolfgang Herbert Kraus. Cambridge, Mass., 1945.

Kendall, Willmoore. John Locke and the Doctrine of Majority-Rule. Urbana, Ill., 1941.

—— "The Majority Principle and the Scientific Elite," *Southern Review,* IV (1939), 463–73.

Kendall, Willmoore (*Continued*)
—— "On the Preservation of Democracy for America," *Southern Review*, V (1939), 53–68.
—— "Prolegomena to Any Future Work on Majority Rule," *Journal of Politics,* XII (1950), 694–713.
Kendall, Willmoore, and Austin Ranney. *See under* Ranney, Austin.
Kibbe, P. R. Latin Americans in Texas. Albuquerque, N. Mex., 1946.
Kirk, Russell. The Conservative Mind. Chicago, 1953.
—— A Program for Conservatives. Chicago, 1954.
Knight, F. H. Freedom and Reform. New York, 1947.
Konvitz, M. R. The Alien and the Asiatic in American Law. Ithaca, 1946.
Krook, D. "Rationalism in Politics: A Comment," *Cambridge Journal,* I (1948), 439–47.
LaFarge, Oliver. As Long as the Grass Shall Grow. New York, 1940.
Laidler, H. W. Social-Economic Movements. New York, 1944.
Laski, Harold J. Trade Unions in the New Society. New York, 1949.
Lasswell, H. D. The Political Writings of Harold D. Lasswell. Glencoe, Ill., 1951.
—— Power and Personality. New York, 1948.
—— "The Selective Effect of Personality on Political Participation," in Richard Christie and Marie Jahoda, eds., Studies in the Scope and Method of "The Authoritarian Personality." Glencoe, Ill., 1954, pp. 197–225.
Laurat, Lucien. Marxism and Democracy. Translated by Edward Fitzgerald. London, 1940.
Lauterbach, Albert. "Totalitarian Appeal and Economic Reform," in Carl J. Friedrich, ed., Totalitarianism. Cambridge, Mass., 1954, pp. 281–96.
Lenin, V. I. Selected Works. 2 vols. Moscow, 1952.
Lerner, Max. Ideas Are Weapons. New York, 1939.
—— It Is Later Than You Think. New York, 1938.
Lewis, George Cornewall. An Essay on the Influence of Authority in Matters of Opinion. 2d ed., London, 1875.
Lindsay, A. D. The Essentials of Democracy. 2d ed., London, 1935.
—— The Modern Democratic State. New York, 1947.
Lippmann, Walter. Essays in the Public Philosophy. Boston, 1955.
Long, Norton. "Bureaucracy and Constitutionalism," *American Political Science Review,* XLVI (1952), 808–18.

Loth, David, and Harold Fleming. Integration North and South. The Fund for the Republic, New York, 1956.

Lukács, Georg. Geschichte und Klassenbewusstsein. Berlin, 1923.

McClosky, Herbert. "The Fallacy of Absolute Majority Rule," *Journal of Politics*, XI (1949), 637–54.

MacIver, R. M. Academic Freedom in Our Time. New York, 1955.

—— Community. 3d ed., London, 1924.

—— Leviathan and the People. Baton Rouge, La., 1939.

—— The Modern State. London, 1926.

—— The More Perfect Union. New York, 1948.

—— The Ramparts We Guard. New York, 1950.

—— The Web of Government. New York, 1947.

MacIver, R. M., ed. Discrimination and National Welfare. New York, 1949.

Macmahon, A. W., ed. Federalism Mature and Emergent. Garden City, N.Y., 1955.

McWilliams, Carey. Brothers under the Skin. Rev. ed., Boston, 1951.

—— A Mask for Privilege. Boston, 1948.

—— North from Mexico. Philadelphia, 1949.

—— Prejudice: Japanese-Americans—Symbol of Racial Intolerance. Boston, 1944.

Mannheim, Karl. Freedom, Power, and Democratic Planning. New York, 1950.

Maritain, Jacques. Man and the State. Chicago, 1951.

—— The Rights of Man and Natural Law. London, 1944.

Marx, Karl. Capital. Vol. I. Translated by Samuel Moore and Edward Aveling, edited by Frederick Engels. Modern Library ed., New York, 1936.

Marx, Karl, and Frederick Engels. Selected Works. 2 vols. Moscow, 1950.

Maslow, A. H. "The Authoritarian Character Structure," *Journal of Social Psychology*, XVIII (1943), 401–11.

—— "Power Relationships and Patterns of Personal Development," in Arthur Kornhauser, ed., Problems of Power in American Democracy. Detroit, 1957, pp. 92–131.

Maslow, Will, and J. B. Robison. "Civil Rights Legislation and the Fight for Equality, 1862–1952," *University of Chicago Law Review*, XX (1953), 363–413.

Meriam, Lewis, and Associates. The Problem of Indian Administration. Baltimore, 1928.

Mill, John Stuart. Dissertations and Discussions. 3 vols. Boston, 1864.

—— Utilitarianism, Liberty and Representative Government. Everyman's ed., New York, 1910.

Mims, Edwin, Jr. The Majority of the People. New York, 1941.

Monnerot, Jules. Sociology of Communism. Translated by Jane Degras and Richard Rees. London, 1953.

Montesquieu, Charles de Secondat. The Spirit of the Laws (1748). 2 vols. Translated by Thomas Nugent. Hafner ed., New York, 1949.

Moon, Bucklin. The High Cost of Prejudice. New York, 1947.

Morris, Bernard S. "Some Perspectives on the Nature and Role of the Western European Communist Parties," Review of Politics, XVIII (1956), 157–69.

Murray, R. K. Red Scare: A Study in National Hysteria, 1919–1920. Minneapolis, 1955.

Myrdal, Gunnar. An American Dilemma. 2 vols. New York, 1944.

Neumann, F. L. "Types of Natural Law," Studies in Philosophy and Social Science, VIII (1939), 338–61.

Niebuhr, Reinhold. The Children of Light and the Children of Darkness. New York, 1945.

Northrup, H. R. Organized Labor and the Negro. New York, 1944.

Oakeshott, Michael. Political Education. London, 1951.

—— "Rationalism in Politics," Cambridge Journal, I (1947), 81–98, 145–57.

O'Brian, John Lord. National Security and Individual Freedom. Cambridge, Mass., 1955.

Oppenheim, Felix. "In Defense of Relativism," Western Political Quarterly, VIII (1955), 411–17.

—— "The Natural Law Thesis: Affirmation or Denial?" American Political Science Review, LI (1957), 41–53.

—— "Relativism, Absolutism, and Democracy," American Political Science Review, XLIV (1950), 951–60.

Pennock, J. R. "Responsiveness, Responsibility, and Majority Rule," American Political Science Review, XLVI (1952), 790–807.

Plato. Republic. Various translations and editions.

Postan, M. "The Revulsion from Thought," Cambridge Journal, I (1948), 395–408.

"Racial Desegregation and Integration," *Annals of the American Academy of Political and Social Science,* Vol. CCCIV (March, 1956).

Radcliffe, C. J. The Problem of Power. London, 1952.

Ranney, Austin, and Willmoore Kendall. Democracy and the American Party System. New York, 1956.

Rees, John C. "Professor Oakeshott on Political Education," *Mind,* LXII (1953), 68–74.

Report of the La Follette Committee (Committee on Education and Labor, Pursuant to Senate Resolution 266, 74th Congress). Violations of Free Speech and the Rights of Labor. Washington, 1939–41.

Report of the National Committee on Segregation in the Nation's Capital. Segregation in Washington. Chicago, 1948.

Report of the President's Committee on Civil Rights. To Secure These Rights. Washington, 1947.

Report of the Special Committee of the Association of the Bar of the City of New York. The Federal Loyalty-Security Program. New York, 1956.

Riemer, Neal. "The Case for Bare Majority Rule," *Ethics,* LXII (1951), 16–32.

—— "James Madison's Theory of the Self-Destructive Features of Republican Government," *Ethics,* LXV (1954), 34–43.

Riesman, David. The Lonely Crowd. New Haven, 1950.

Roche, John P. "We've Never Had More Freedom," *New Republic,* CXXXIV (January 23, 1956), 12–15; (January 30, 1956), 13–16; (February 6, 1956), 13–15.

Rose, Arnold, and Caroline Rose. America Divided. New York, 1948.

Rossiter, Clinton. Conservatism in America. New York, 1955.

Rostow, E. V. "The Japanese American Cases—A Disaster," *Yale Law Journal,* LIV (1945), 489–533.

Rotenstreich, Nathan. "Rule by Majority or by Principles," *Social Research,* XXXI (1954), 411–27.

Rousseau, Jean Jacques. The Social Contract. Translated by G. H. D. Cole. Everyman's ed., New York, 1913.

Russell, Bertrand. Human Society in Ethics and Politics. New York, 1955.

—— Power: A New Social Analysis. New York, 1938.

—— Sceptical Essays. New York, 1928.

—— Unpopular Essays. New York, 1947.

Saenger, Gerhart. The Social Psychology of Prejudice. New York, 1953.

Sanchez, G. I. Forgotten People. Albuquerque, N. Mex., 1940.

Santayana, George. Dominations and Powers. New York, 1951.

Schaar, John H. Loyalty in America. Berkeley, 1957.

Seidman, Harold. Labor Czars. New York, 1938.

Selznick, Philip. "An Approach to a Theory of Bureaucracy," *American Sociological Review*, VIII (1943), 47–54

Shils, E. A. "Authoritarianism: 'Right' and 'Left,' " in Richard Christie and Marie Jahoda, eds., Studies in the Scope and Method of "The Authoritarian Personality." Glencoe, Ill., 1954, pp. 24–49.

Simon, Yves. Philosophy of Democratic Government. Chicago, 1951.

Smith, J. Allen. The Spirit of American Government. New York, 1907.

Spain, A. O. The Political Theory of John C. Calhoun. New York, 1951.

Spitz, David. "Democracy and the Problem of Civil Disobedience," *American Political Science Review*, XLVIII (1954), 386–403.

—— "Labor and Liberty: A Note on Mr. Laski's Discourses," *Antioch Review*, X (1950), 301–4.

—— Patterns of Anti-Democratic Thought. New York, 1949.

—— "Power, Law, and Freedom of Inquiry," in H. Gordon Hullfish, ed., Educational Freedom in an Age of Anxiety. New York, 1953, pp. 52–69.

—— "Robert M. MacIver's Contributions to Political Theory," in M. Berger, T. Abel, and C. H. Page, eds., Freedom and Control in Modern Society. New York, 1954, pp. 293–312.

—— "Some Animadversions on Montesquieu's Theory of Freedom," *Ethics*, LXIII (1953), 207–13.

—— "Why Communists Are Not of the Left," *Antioch Review*, IX (1949–50), 495–508.

Strauss, Leo. Natural Right and History. Chicago, 1953.

—— "On Classical Political Philosophy," *Social Research*, XII (1945), 98–117.

—— On Tyranny: An Interpretation of Xenophon's *Hiero*. New York, 1948.

Sutherland, A. E., Jr. "Freedom and Internal Security," *Harvard Law Review*, LXIV (1951), 383–416.

Taubes, Jacob. "The Issue between Judaism and Christianity," *Commentary*, XVI (1953), 525–33.

Taylor, Telford. Grand Inquest: The Story of Congressional Investigations. New York, 1955.

Tocqueville, Alexis de. Democracy in America. 2 vols. Phillips Bradley ed., Vintage Books, 1954.

Vivas, Eliseo. The Moral Life and the Ethical Life. Chicago, 1950.

Voegelin, Eric. The New Science of Politics. Chicago, 1952.

Waldo, Dwight. "Development of Theory of Democratic Administration," *American Political Science Review*, XLVI (1952), 81–103.

Watnick, Morris. "The Appeal of Communism to the Underdeveloped Peoples," in B. F. Hoselitz, ed., The Progress of Underdeveloped Areas. Chicago, 1952, pp. 152–72.

Weaver, R. C. The Negro Ghetto. New York, 1948.

Weber, Max. The Methodology of the Social Sciences. Translated and edited by Edward A. Shils and Henry A. Finch. Glencoe, Ill., 1949.

—— The Theory of Social and Economic Organization. Translated by A. M. Henderson and Talcott Parsons, edited by Talcott Parsons, New York, 1947.

Weintraub, Ruth G. How Secure These Rights? Garden City, N.Y., 1949.

Westin, Alan. The Constitution and Loyalty Programs. Freedom Agenda Pamphlet, New York, 1954.

White, Howard B. "The Loyalty Oath," *Social Research,* XXII (1955), 77–109.

—— "The Problem of Loyalty in American Political Thought," *Social Research,* XXI (1954), 314–38.

White, Walter. How Far the Promised Land? New York, 1955.

Williamson, R. de V. "The Challenge of Political Relativism," *Journal of Politics,* IX (1947), 147–77.

Wiltse, Charles M. "Calhoun and the Modern State," *Virginia Quarterly Review,* XIII (1937), 398–408.

—— "Calhoun's Democracy," *Journal of Politics,* III (1941), 210–23.

—— John C. Calhoun. 3 vols. Indianapolis, 1944–51.

Wittgenstein, Ludwig. Philosophical Investigations. Translated by G. E. M. Anscombe. Oxford, 1953.

Wittke, Carl. The Utopian Communist: A Biography of Wilhelm Weitling. Baton Rouge, La., 1950.

Wolff, Kurt H., trans. and ed. The Sociology of Georg Simmel. Glencoe, Ill., 1950.

Woodhouse, A. S. P., ed. Puritanism and Liberty. 2d ed., London, 1951.

Wormuth, F. D. "Learned Legerdemain: A Grave but Implausible Hand," *Western Political Quarterly*, VI (1953), 543–58.

—— "Legislative Disqualifications as Bills of Attainder," *Vanderbilt Law Review*, IV (1951), 603–19.

—— "On Bills of Attainder: A Non-Communist Manifesto," *Western Political Quarterly*, III (1950), 52–65.

—— The Origins of Modern Constitutionalism. New York, 1939.

—— Review of John H. Hallowell's *The Moral Foundation of Democracy, Indiana Law Journal*, XXX (1955), 374–81.

Wright, B. F., Jr. American Interpretations of Natural Law. Cambridge, Mass., 1931.

—— "The Origin of the Separation of Powers in America," *Economica*, XIII (1933), 169–85.

Wrong, D. H. "Riesman and the Age of Sociology," *Commentary*, XXI (1956), 331–38.

Xenophon. Hiero. In his Scripta Minora. Translated by E. C. Marchant. Loeb Classical Library ed., New York, 1925.

Yellen, Samuel. American Labor Struggles. New York, 1936.

Index